AMERICAN STUDIES – A MONOGRAPH SERIES
Volume 153

Edited on behalf
of the German Association
for American Studies by
REINHARD R. DOERRIES
GERHARD HOFFMANN
ALFRED HORNUNG

MARTIN BUTLER

Voices of the Down and Out

The Dust Bowl Migration and the Great Depression in the Songs of Woody Guthrie

Universitätsverlag
WINTER
Heidelberg

Bibliografische Information der Deutschen Nationalbibliothek
Die Deutsche Nationalbibliothek verzeichnet diese Publikation in der Deutschen Nationalbibliografie; detaillierte bibliografische Daten sind im Internet über *http://dnb.d-nb.de* abrufbar.

Umschlagfoto / Cover Photograph:
Communist Party of the United States of America Photographs collection
Tamiment Library & Robert F. Wagner Labor Archives, New York University

ISBN 978-3-8253-5367-4

Imprimé en Allemagne · Printed in Germany
Druck: Memminger MedienCentrum, 87700 Memmingen

Gedruckt auf umweltfreundlichem, chlorfrei gebleichtem und alterungsbeständigem Papier

Den Verlag erreichen Sie im Internet unter:
www.winter-verlag-hd.de

For my parents

Table of Contents

Acknowledgements

Voices of the Down and Out is my doctoral thesis submitted to the Faculty of Arts of the University of Duisburg-Essen in October 2006. Writing this book was hard travelin' and there are a number of people to whom I am grateful for having kept me on the right track. First and foremost, I would like to thank HD Dr. Frank Erik Pointner, who helped start me off on this road and whose inspiring, respectful, but never confining advice as a colleague and friend has been a constant companion during my research and writing. I am also indebted to Prof. Dr. Michael Gassenmeier, whose scrutinizing readings, critical comments and valuable suggestions contributed to shaping this book and its author. For her meticulous feedback on the various chapters and for the time she spent helping me weave the central thread of my study, I owe many thanks to Prof. Dr. Marion Gymnich. During my research at the Woody Guthrie Archives in New York City, I was offered kind assistance by a number of people: For warmly welcoming me to the Archives, for including me in one or the other thoughtful conversation and for their generous support, I am grateful to Nora Guthrie and Michael Kleff. I would like to thank Felicia Katz and Hillel Arnold for helping me find my way through the archival material, as well as Michael Smith for his splendid support concerning the copyright credits. In Washington, D.C. it was Dr. Todd Harvey who patiently guided me through the massive collection of the American Folklife Center at the Library of Congress; Jeff Place and Dr. Stephanie Smith facilitated my research at the Smithsonian Center for Folklife and Cultural Heritage and kindly offered their expertise in (folk) song. In March 2005, I had the great opportunity to talk to Maxine Dempsey, whom I owe special thanks for sharing some personal reminiscences of Woody, her singing colleague at KFVD radio in Los Angeles in 1937/38. Furthermore, I would like to thank Adam von Wald who did a great job proofreading the manuscript. I am also grateful to the International PhD Program (IPP) "Literary and Cultural Studies" at the University of Giessen, which provided an excellent platform to discuss chapters of my thesis – particular thanks go to Prof. Dr. Ansgar Nünning and Prof. Dr. Wolfgang Hallet for their constructive advice during their colloquia. Moreover, various research trips to the United States would not have been possible without the IPP's generous funding. Finally, I am indebted to Ariane Gehl de Romero for believing in me and my endeavor, for never losing her patience and for continually encouraging me to 'take it easy, but take it.'

Songs are the statement of a people. You can learn more about people by listening to their songs than any other way, for into the songs go all the hopes and hurts, the angers, fears, the wants and aspirations.

(John Steinbeck)

1 Introduction: Woody Guthrie and his Sung Legacy

In September 1996, the Rock and Roll Hall of Fame and Museum, in collaboration with the Woody Guthrie Foundation and Archives and Case Western Reserve University in Cleveland, Ohio, held a ten day celebration of the life and legacy of Woody Guthrie, which included a conference, a photo exhibition, films, and two concerts.[1] Music experts, fans and artists such as actor and director Tim Robbins, rock legend Bruce Springsteen and Grammy Award winner Dave Pirner of Soul Asylum were among those who contributed songs, readings and other such offerings to the event. The celebration thus, on an unprecedented scale, underlined the cultural significance of Guthrie, who, as one of the "transitional agents carrying the folk song from the parochial to the popular sphere of song,"[2] has strongly influenced and shaped the evolution of folk and rock music.

Woodrow Wilson Guthrie was born in Okemah, Oklahoma, on July 14th, 1912,[3] as the son of the local politician and real estate agent Charles Guthrie and his wife Nora Belle Guthrie. Already in his early childhood, Guthrie enjoyed listening to his parents singing traditional blues or parlor ballads at home and soon became captivated by the power of music. He started his first band, the Corncob Trio, in Pampa, Texas, after the folk revival of the early 1920s had brought fiddle and guitar music back to the rural areas of the American Southwest.[4] In 1935, while working odd jobs painting signs for drugstores and groceries and by occasionally performing with his band at Saturday-Night-dances or on local radio stations, Guthrie compiled his first collection of songs in a typewritten songbook.[5] Although

1 The Clevelend event was officially called "Hard Travelin': The Life and Legacy of Woody Guthrie." For further details, cf. the liner notes to *'Til We Outnumber 'Em: Live from Cleveland*, (Buffalo, NY: Righteous Babe Records, 2001), n. pag.

2 Edwin Cohen, "Neither Hero nor Myth: Woody Guthrie's Contribution to Folk Art," *Folklore* (1980): 11.

3 Guthrie died on October 3rd, 1967, after he had spent more than thirteen years in state mental hospitals suffering from Huntington's chorea, the symptoms of which he had already begun experiencing in his late thirties.

4 The short sketch of Guthrie's biography and the respective cultural contexts is mainly based on Ed Cray's illuminating study *Ramblin' Man: The Life and Times of Woody Guthrie* (New York/London: W.W. Norton, 2004).

5 This songbook was called *Alonzo M. Zilch's Own Collection of Original Songs and Ballads* and consisted of fourteen songs (cf. Cray 86.).

he was not very interested in politics at that time, some of the songs in this first songbook reveal his awareness of the increasing social inequalities, the imbalanced distribution of power and wealth and the need for economic and political change in the middle of the decade.[6] Two years later, Guthrie, who was then married with one child and a second one due the following summer, decided to leave Pampa, where he had spent much of his youth, in order to travel the country.

By then, America was stuck in the grips of the Great Depression, which radically put its laisser-faire capitalism to the test. The American Southwest, Guthrie's home territory, was not only affected by the general economic recession, but also stricken by a terrible drought – a drought which caused a series of devastating dust storms that, in turn, forced thousands of Southwestern families to migrate to California, as their fields had been turned into a barren wasteland. Hoping for a second chance in the 'Golden State,' the migrants' 'Californian Dream' of prosperity and abundance soon turned into a horrible nightmare. They were discriminated against by the Californian landowners, who exploited them as a cheap labor force in the fields on the American west coast. Woody Guthrie internalized the people's hardships on the road and in the 'Golden State.' He, alongside others, such as photographer Dorothea Lange or writer John Steinbeck, raised his voice for their cause and rendered the experience of dislocation and migration in his songs. The human catastrophe of the Dust Bowl migration[7] soon became a political issue and stirred drives for unionization at the end of the 1930s and the beginning of the 1940s, a movement that Guthrie supported by bluntly pronouncing the discontent of the oppressed in his songs and by heralding the eventual triumph of the working people.

6 One of these more political songs is "If I Was Everything On Earth," in which the speaker of the song imagines himself to be the President and, in a utopian vision, describes the things he would do then: "If I was President Roosevelt / I'd make the groceries free – / I'd give away new Stetson hats, / And let the whiskey be / I'd pass out suits of clothing / At least three times a week – / And shoot the first big oil man / That killed the fishing creek" (quoted in Cray 86).

7 Actually, the large-scale migration to the American west coast in the second half of the 1930s, which became known as the Dust Bowl migration, included more migrants from the states of Oklahoma, Texas, Arkansas and Missouri than from the Dust Bowl proper. Moreover, the dust storms were only one reason why people moved westwards (cf. also 119n9). However, despite the somewhat misleading character of the term 'Dust Bowl Migration,' and due to the fact that, in the 1930s, it was a widespread belief that the majority of the migrants indeed came from the Dust Bowl, I consider it legitimate to use this term in the context of this study.

Guthrie's songs about the Great Depression, particularly those about the Dust Bowl and the migration of Southwestern farmers to California, are still in vogue today and have not lost their appeal. It may thus not be by chance that Ani DiFranco's performance of "Do Re Mi," a song about the discriminatory Californian immigration policy during the Dust Bowl migration written by Guthrie in 1937, attracted major attention and strongly affected the audience during the above mentioned tribute to Guthrie's influence on the development of (political) folk and rock music. His daughter Nora remembers: "Me, I started crying at the git go when Ani sang the first verse of 'Do Re Me' […]."[8] It seems reasonable to suppose that the appeal of the song is, at least to a certain extent, due to its subject matter, which tackles an event still present in the American collective memory.

It is surprising that, in spite of the lasting success of Woody Guthrie's songs and their strong impact on the development of the (political) folk song, his sung legacy has received only little scholarly attention. "We often become embroiled in Woody's politics, his Union activities, and make moral judgements of his life, losing sight of the real issue in evaluating the artist: the contribution of his works," Edwin Cohen complains in his account of Guthrie's role in the folk movement.[9] With my study, I propose to address and, to a certain extent, fill this gap in examining the contribution of Guthrie's works by contextualizing his songs about the Great Depression, and about the Dust Bowl migration in particular, correlating his lyrics with the socioeconomic, political and cultural environment in which they were composed and sung. In so doing, this study not only attempts to revive the cultural and political significance the songs once possessed; it also tries to reconstruct the various cultural and political discourses[10] which were both rendered in and shaped by Guthrie's

8 Nora Guthrie, liner notes, *'Til We Outnumber 'Em: Live from Cleveland*, (Buffalo, NY: Righteous Babe Records, 2001), n. pag.

9 Cohen 11.

10 I will follow the concept of 'discourse' as outlined in Michael Titzmann, "Kulturelles Wissen – Diskurs – Denksystem: Zu einigen Begriffen der Literaturgeschichtsschreibung," *Zeitschrift für französische Sprache und Literatur* 94 (1989): 47–61; for Titzmann, a discourse is defined by a shared topic ("durch einen der Textklasse gemeinsamen *Redegegenstand*" [51]), a set of rules of speech, which have to be adhered to while talking about this topic ("durch die *Regularitäten der Rede über diesen Gegenstand*" [52]) and by the relation of the discourse at stake to other discourses ["durch seine *Relationen zu anderen Diskursen*" [53]). Titzmann also points out that discourses are (only) accessible through and reconstructable by the analysis of texts and, at the same time, hints at the interdiscursive function of literature ("Ein Diskurs kann sich in verschiedenen Texttypen manifestieren.[…] In einem Text oder Texttyp wiederum können

songs, thereby shedding light on aspects of the decade's cultural knowledge,[11] some of which have not been thoroughly investigated yet.

1.1 Guthrie's Songs about Dust and Depression: Culturally Produced and Culturally Productive[12]

In one of his numerous unpublished manuscripts, Woody Guthrie once claimed that "songs don't make history," but that "history makes up songs."[13] Had Guthrie known that he was to become one of the most influential folksingers and songwriters in the western world, whose impact is still felt today, he would probably have thought twice about the first part of his statement. Guthrie's songs, most of them written in the late 1930s and 1940s and rediscovered during the folk revival of the 1960s, influenced a whole generation of songwriters in their themes, forms, and rhetorical strategies, including heavyweights like Joan Baez, Bruce Springsteen, and the uncrowned poet laureate among political protest singers, Bob Dylan, who once proclaimed that "[Woody Guthrie] just car-

verschiedene Diskurse koexistieren. Insbesondere die Literatur kann im Prinzip verschiedenste Diskurse in sich aufnehmen." [54-55]). For the textuality of discourses cf. also Moritz Baßler, *Die kulturpoetische Funktion und das Archiv: Eine literaturwissenschaftliche Text-Kontext Theorie* (Tübingen: Francke, 2005).

11 According to Titzmann 'cultural knowledge' may be defined as the sum of those propositions which are considered to be true by the members of a particular culture or group, or by a sufficient number of texts of that particular culture or group respectively. Here the term 'knowledge' will be used in a wide sense, also including common beliefs, attitudes and mental dispositions. Titzmann further argues that elements and patterns of 'cultural knowledge' can be made accessible through texts: "Wir erschließen also das kulturelle Wissen aus den Texten einer Kultur. [...] Texte [...] sind zum einen in unterschiedlichem Ausmaß Quellen kulturellen Wissens, zum anderen Quellen unterschiedlichen kulturellen Wissens" (50). For a more detailed conceptualization of 'cultural knowledge' cf. Birgit Neumann, "Kulturelles Wissen und Literatur," *Kulturelles Wissen und Intertextualität: Theoriekonzeptionen und Fallstudien zur Kontextualisierung von Literatur*, ed. Marion Gymnich, Birgit Neumann and Ansgar Nünning. (Trier: WVT, 2006) 29-51.

12 The chapter headline refers to one of the central dicta of New Historicism, coined by Louis A. Montrose, who pointed out that (literary) texts are not only "socially produced" but also "socially productive" (Louis A. Montrose, "Professing the Renaissance: The Poetics and Politics of Culture," *The New Historicism*, ed. H. Aram Veeser [New York: Routledge, 1989] 23). By replacing the attribute "social" with "cultural," I propose to extend this notion, assuming that the term "cultural" covers the complexity of the relationship between a text and its various context(s) more appropriately.

13 Woody Guthrie Archives (WGA), New York City, Songs I, Box 1, Folder 1.

ried a book of Man an' gave it t' me t' read a while an' from it I learned my greatest lesson."[14] Of course, one must not forget that the rediscovery of Guthrie's songs during the folk revival was politically motivated, which, in turn, meant that only a small selection of his songs was revived by the singers and songwriters of the 1960s. This selection was far from being representative of Guthrie's entire oeuvre, which contains – apart from a distinguishable number of political songs – numerous love songs, religious songs as well as songs for children.[15] Thus, though there is no doubt that Guthrie *also* wrote and sang political lyrics, it would be hazardous to label Guthrie exclusively as a protest singer.

However, despite the fact that his political songs only made up a relatively small share of his sung legacy, it was these songs that made him famous posthumously, and which, starting with the folk revival in the 1960s, would influence entire generations of singers and songwriters to come. Some of Guthrie's political songs even became part of the standard repertoire of American folksongs. Probably his most famous one, "This Land is Your Land," eventually made it to the status of an unofficial national anthem with which every American is familiar. To date, many of Guthrie's political songs have been and continue to be covered and reappropriated in new contexts by musicians of various cultures and styles – be it the Mexican folklorist Lila Downs or the Bostonian punk-rock Band Dropkick Murphys, the English musician and political activist Billy Bragg or the German singer and songwriter Wenzel, all of whom seem to have been attracted by the almost timeless appeal of Guthrie's tunes and lyrics.

Thus, taking his enormous influence on following generations of singers and songwriters into account, one might be tempted to state that Guthrie's songs did indeed 'make history' in that they heavily contributed to the heritage of American folk music. Yet the potential of Guthrie's songs to 'make history' must not be limited to his impact on subsequent musical styles and traditions. This study aims to further the argument that the songs' potential already unfolded in the time of their composition and performance, that Guthrie's songs were not only 'made up by history,' that is, shaped by the contemporary socioeconomic and political discourses, but took an active part in the very creation and formation of these discourses.

14 Bob Dylan. *Eleven Outlined Epitaphs/Elf Entwürfe für meinen Grabspruch: Englisch/Deutsch mit Übersetzungen von Wolf Biermann* (Köln: Kiepenheuer & Witsch, 2003) 80-81.

15 Cf. Jeff Morgan, "Hard Travelin': The Construction of Woody Guthrie's legacy," unpublished article, 2004.

In order to show that Guthrie's songs were 'made' by history and, at the same time, 'made' history, I will take recourse to central ideas of New Historicism as a framework for the contextualizing analysis of the songs, which seems to be, due to its strong focus on the mutual correspondence between a text and its contexts, the most appropriate theoretical concept for such an analysis (chapter II.2). In contrast to traditional, text-centered approaches to literary analysis, which "had once the text as their home for studying it as a hermetically sealed entity,"[16] the New Historicist approach highlights the historicity of texts and aims at re-activating the political potential they once possessed in a particular context. In a contextualizing analysis of Guthrie's songs, it thus becomes necessary to correlate his songs with the socioeconomic, political and cultural contexts of the 1930s and early 1940s.

Starting from the semiotic notion (also highlighted by New Historicism) that these contexts are only accessible via texts, I will further apply concepts of intertextuality in order to make the New Historicist ideas applicable to my project (chapter 2.3.1). Regarding Guthrie's songs as an interdiscursive framework in which elements of the economic, political and cultural discourses of the time are combined, configured, simplified and thus communicated to their audience, a correlation of the songs to other contemporary literary and non-literary texts such as John Steinbeck's novel *The Grapes of Wrath*, newspaper articles or political pamphlets will help to fathom the social energy the songs once possessed.

In order to embed the songs into a synchronic network of other cultural manifestations of the contemporary archive,[17] I am going to make use of close readings of the relevant songs, which will predominantly center on the interfaces between the texts and their context rather than on the texts as autonomous literary artifacts, or, as Laurenz Volkmann put it, "hermetically sealed entit[ies]."[18] This synchronic contextualization of Guthrie's songs will demonstrate that his oeuvre is both culturally produced, as it draws from and renders elements of contemporary discourses, and culturally productive, for it actively took part in shaping, maintaining and changing these discourses.

Since the songs' cultural productivity is partly derived from their references to both musical traditions and traditional poems and song lyrics,

16 Laurenz Volkmann, "Reconstructing a Useable Past: The New Historicism and History," *Why Literature Matters: Theories and Functions of Literature*, ed. Rüdiger Ahrens and Laurenz Volkmann (Heidelberg: Winter, 1996) 328.

17 I employ the concept of the archive as outlined by Moritz Baßler, who defines it as the sum of all available texts of a particular cultural paradigm.

18 Volkmann 328.

I will also analyze their diachronic intertextual potential. Though the examination of synchronic intertextual relations will certainly be foregrounded in this study, it may indeed be worthwhile to examine the songs' references to traditional tunes, well-established topoi or rhetorical strategies, which, particularly for the genre of the (political) folk song, certainly contributed to the songs' semantic surplus value and thus enhanced their potential to configure and shape cultural knowledge.

Moreover, a contextualization of Guthrie's songs, which aims at the revival of their social energy, must not neglect to consider aspects of music and performance. Therefore, it seems worthwhile to both consider the role of the audience as an active participant in a performance (chapter 2.3.2) and reflect on the relationship between lyrics and music (chapter 2.3.3), as particular rhythmical, melodic and vocal patterns emphasize the lyrical content of songs and thus carry meaning as well, enhancing the potential of the sung word to configure and disseminate cultural knowledge and, in so doing, to shape (collective) identities.

After outlining the aforementioned theoretical framework and developing an analytical toolkit to contextualize Guthrie's songs, I will provide contextualizing readings of a selection of his songs on the Great Depression, particularly focusing on those songs that render the Dust Bowl migration (chapters 3.1-3.7). In order to maintain narrative stringency, these analytical chapters are predominantly structured along chronological lines.[19] Starting with a discussion of the songs dealing with the dust storm disaster of the mid-1930s, I will then analyze songs that render the subsequent migration of the Southwestern farmers to California, before I consider the songs that configure their resettlement in California.[20] Furthermore, I will also provide a contextualizing analysis of some of Guthrie's songs that are not directly concerned with the Dust

19 The chronological order does not refer to the dates of the songs' composition or performance, but to the historical events rendered in the songs. Sometimes, to be sure, it is indeed necessary to leave this chronological track, as a number of songs which will be discussed are not concerned with particular historical events in the first place. Though their reference to the Dust Bowl migration and the Great Depression is obvious, it is thus hard to put them into a chronological order. Moreover, the New Historicist approach of this study sometimes makes back- or crossreferences inevitable. Thus, it lies in the nature of things that a strictly chronological structure is not possible anyway.

20 As far as the chronological order is concerned, I am essentially referring to the suggestion outlined by James R. Curtis in "Woody Guthrie and the Dust Bowl," *The Sounds of People and Places: A Geography of American Folk and Popular Music*, ed. George O. Carney (Lanham: Rowman & Littlefield, 1994) 12-38.

Bowl migration, but with the problems and politics of the Great Depression in general.

As hinted at earlier, all analytical chapters aim to explore the manifold synchronic (and diachronic) intertextual references in a selection of Guthrie's songs in order to illustrate and examine both their cultural embeddedness and their cultural productivity. The correlation of Guthrie's songs with various synchronic (and diachronic) inter- or pretexts will essentially be grounded on the analysis of (1) rhetorical correspondences, i.e., correspondences in stylistic devices, such as metaphors or imagery, (2) linguistic correspondences, i.e., correspondences in the choice of words or the lexicon used in texts, and (3) structural (or generic) correspondences, i.e., correspondences between the overall form or structure of texts, also including, for the case of musical intertexts, compositional features. Applying these criteria, which might provide at least a heuristic frame for the investigation into the songs' negotiations with their contexts, the various contextualizing analyses are supposed to reveal the different strategies and (possible) functions of rewriting or refashioning which are employed in Guthrie's songs, and by which the songs distinctly take a stand on contemporary discourses, thereby actively participating in and contributing to them.

The analysis of Guthrie's ballad on the Oklahoman outlaw Charles Arthur Floyd (chapter 3.2), to give an example, is concerned with Guthrie's fashioning of the outlaw as a modern Robin Hood. Emplotted along the lines of a traditional Robin Hood ballad, the song fashions Floyd as a modern underdog, taking from the rich in order to give to the poor. The criminal is depicted as a gallant, lawless ally of the Oklahoman farmers, who, at that time, had to cope with enormous financial problems, as the prices for agricultural products dramatically decreased in the first years of the Great Depression. When we relate Guthrie's song to various (inter)texts of the cultural archive, it becomes evident that Guthrie's rendering of the deeds of the Depression gangster is not only an articulation of the dramatically worsening economic situation in the 1930s; by taking up, perpetuating and enhancing images and rhetorical strategies deriving from the contemporary media discourse on Floyd, the song also contributed to the media creation of the Floyd legend and thus actively took part in the contemporary discourse on moral integrity.

Another example of the cultural embeddedness of Guthrie's songs, manifesting itself in the manifold intertextual references, will be provided in the analysis of his (re)fashioning of Jesus Christ in a ballad (chapter 3.7). The song fashions the Savior as the first union organizer and thus combines the religious with the political. In Guthrie's song, it is the police and the bankers, representing the capitalist system, who are held responsible for the death of Jesus Christ, who is portrayed as a hard-working man trying to earn his living. Retelling the life of the carpenter's son as a poor member of the working class victimized by capitalists, the song strips off any spiritual implication and propagates what one might well call an idea of socialist salvation.

A close analysis of the textual archive of the Great Depression reveals that the fashioning of Jesus as a carpenter's son, or, better, only as the carpenter's son, was certainly not Guthrie's original idea. Rather did it correspond with the rhetorics of the political left, which fused elements of socialist ideology with the Christian idea of charity. This integration of political and Christian ideas, which found expression in an abundance of left-wing pamphlets and propaganda material of the time, was typical of the so-called 'social gospel movement' – a movement that emerged at the end of the nineteenth century, lost its general appeal in the 'Roaring Twenties,' and was eventually revived during the social and economic plight of the 1930s. The Great Depression, as one might argue, thus worked as a catalyst of a radical turn towards a 'new' or 'second' social gospel, whose ideas and ideals manifested themselves in a variety of texts of the contemporary cultural archive, one of them being Guthrie's song about Jesus Christ, which was shaped by, and, at the same time, contributed to the revival and the distribution of the social gospel. Moreover, the song's social energy was enhanced by Guthrie's use of the tune of a ballad about Jesse James, assumedly the most prominent outlaw in the American Southwest. This tune, which the majority of Guthrie's listeners were certainly familiar with, added – as a musical intertext – a semantic surplus to the lyrical rendering of Jesus Christ as an ally of the poor and an opponent of the rich.

1.2 Selection of Texts and Intertexts: Addressing the Problems of Representativity and Connection

Probably one of the most outstanding of Woody Guthrie's qualities was his extraordinary productivity, as far as his songwriting is concerned. Therefore, a contextualizing analysis can only treat a very small part of his oeuvre. I opted for his songs about the Dust Bowl and the Great Depression, not only because they are Guthrie's most popular musical pieces, but also as they render the significant social, economic and cultural transitions of one of the most turbulent decades in American history in an unparalleled manner.

Consequently, there are two essential criteria for the selection of songs. Firstly, the songs contextualized in this study all deal with the Dust Bowl migration and, in order not to limit the corpus of texts too much, some other facets and problems of the Great Depression, particularly with regard to its effects on California. This means, secondly, that the songs which I am concerned with were written between 1936, the time of Guthrie's first trip to California and the dawn of his political awareness which found its expression in song, and 1940/1, when Guthrie moved to New York and his songs became strongly affected by the socialist ideology of the union movement. Of course, this study will not and cannot provide a contextualization of all of Guthrie's songs about the Dust Bowl migration and the Great Depression. What it will and can provide, however, are exemplary contextualizations of selected songs, which will, in turn, allow me to draw some general conclusions regarding the ways in which Guthrie's songs corresponded with and reacted to their cultural contexts.

Following a New Historicist approach, contextualizing Woody Guthrie's songs means, first and foremost, correlating them with other, contemporary texts in order to reconstruct the negotiations between the songs and their cultural environment.[21] Therefore, apart from the selection of songs which are going to be situated into their socioeconomic, political and cultural contexts, the present analysis will have to resort to a variety of (inter)texts, the choice of which is, to be sure, not unproblematic. There are, to be more specific, *two* major problems as far as the selection of intertexts is concerned, which have been formulated as a general critique of New Historicism, and which will have to be reflected upon in the present study as well.

The first problem to be addressed is the problem of representativity. In an analysis that seeks to explore a text's references to other contemporary literary and non-literary texts, the number of texts that might be taken into consideration is virtually unlimited. The New Historicist notion of the 'textuality of history,' which "unsettl[es] [...] the relation between [literary] background and foreground, [...] gives rise to a sense of archival and interpretive inexhaustibility," as Stephen Greenblatt

21 Of course, a contextualizing analysis must not forget to explore the diachronic references in Guthrie's songs, which will also be examined, always in regard to the question in how far these references to pretexts contribute to the songs' social energy in their synchronic contexts. Yet, what will be focussed on in the first place is a synchronic contextualization of Guthrie's songs.

critically remarks about his poetics of culture.[22] The seamy side of New Historicism then, which has always regarded itself as a 'science of the particular,' is its alleged arbitrariness in the selection of textual 'material.' Following from this, choosing the 'right' intertexts in a contextualizing analysis of Guthrie's songs seems to be a highly problematic endeavor, which will, to a certain extent, remain contingent. The second problem which has to be reflected upon while selecting suitable intertexts for such an analysis is how to link or connect the chosen texts with the songs. What is it, one may well ask, that ties some texts together and not others? Alan Liu hints at this problem in a more critical way, pointing out that "[a] New Historicist paradigm holds up to view a historical context on one side, a literary text on the other, and, in between, a connection of pure nothing."[23]

In order to tackle these problems and to establish a general set of criteria for the selection of intertexts in spite of the "archival and interpretive inexhaustibility" proclaimed by Greenblatt, I suggest resorting to the concept of the cultural archive as outlined by Moritz Baßler. According to Baßler, the archive is defined as the sum of all (accessible) texts of a particular culture. Within this synchronic textual corpus, there are texts or parts of texts which can be characterized as 'equivalent,' or, to put it differently, which form an intertextual structure of equivalence.[24] Following Baßler's notion that discourses are (analyzable as) intertextual relations, all these equivalent texts or parts of texts, which belong to the

22 Katherine Gallagher and Stephen Greenblatt, *Practising New Historicism* (Chicago: U of Chicago P, 2000) 15.

23 Liu, Alan, "The Power of Formalism: The New Historicism," In: *ELH* 56, 1989: 743. For a more detailed account of these major problems of the New Historicist approach, cf. Baßler.

24 Cf. Baßler 196: "Als Archiv bezeichnen wir [...] die Summe aller Texte einer Kultur, die einer Untersuchung zu Verfügung stehen. Im Archiv sind die Texte einander gleich- und nebengeordnet zugänglich. Das Archiv ist ein Textkorpus. Innerhalb dieses Korpus können, sozusagen per Suchbefehl, Stellen markiert werden, die untereinander äquivalent sind [...] Diese Stellen ergeben eine intertextuelle *Äquivalenzstruktur*." Titzmann comes up with a similar concept of the archive the examination of which is necessary in order to reconstruct what he calls the 'cultural knowledge' of a particular epoch: "Gegeben sei also eine Kultur und die Menge ihrer Texte; vorausgesetzt sei unsere Kenntnis der Sprache dieser Kultur. Ein aus diesem Textkorpus erschließbares Wissen muß notwendig eine Teilmenge der Bedeutungen der Texte sein, die ihrerseits zunächst interpretatorisch rekonstruiert werden müssen" (48).

archive, can be regarded as representing a particular discourse.[25] By conceptualizing a discourse as an intertextual relationship and by, in turn, defining an intertextual relationship as equivalent occurrences in a particular cultural paradigm, Baßler, at least theoretically, manages to solve the above mentioned problems of representativity and connection. Not only does he put an end to the archival inexhaustibility by providing a clear-cut definition of the cultural archive, he also, at least to a certain extent, limits the interpretative inexhaustibility feared by Greenblatt in that he recommends searching for textual paradigmatic equivalences which, as intertextual structure, constitute a discourse.

The present study will follow Baßler's suggestion in that it takes his notion of the paradigmatic equivalence between texts of the cultural archive as an essential criterion for the selection of intertexts. Thus, in the contextualization of Woody Guthrie's songs, those texts or parts of texts will be considered that are, either in form or content, comparable, or, to use Baßler's term again, equivalent to Guthrie's songs or parts of his songs. Only if we relate these texts of the cultural archive to Guthrie's songs will we be able to both examine the songs' historicity and to gauge their potential cultural productivity in the contexts of the Great Depression.[26] The intertexts considered in the present study are both fictional and non-fictional texts of various genres, ranging from John Steinbeck's novel *The Grapes of Wrath* (1939) to contemporary poetry, to newspaper articles, sermons and political pamphlets of the time.[27] Moreover, I will also consider the manuscripts, diaries and prose writings of Guthrie, which (as co-texts) also help to contextualize his songs. Sometimes, the references to one or the other of these (inter)texts of the cultural archive

25 Cf. Baßler 197: "Ein Diskurs ist (oder ist analysierbar nur als) ein intertextueller Zusammenhang." Likewise Titzmann: "Ein Diskurs kann sich in verschiedenen Texttypen manifestieren" (55).

26 Cf. Baßler 68: "Ein Text wird erst lesbar in seinem Verhältnis zu einem Korpus von Texten; 'die Geschichte und die Gesellschaft' gelangen nur in textueller Form in den Text."

27 The reference to *The Grapes of Wrath* as one prominent intertext for my contextualizations of Guthrie's songs is based on two considerations. First, Steinbeck's novel, which rendered the Dust Bowl experience and the subsequent migration of thousands of Southwestern farmers in a meticulous, albeit ideologically biased manner, drew public attention to this political and human disaster. Due to its strong public appeal, it must have been a source of inspiration for Woody Guthrie as well, who, in a number of songs, such as "Tom Joad" or "Vigilante Man," directly referred to Steinbeck's story. Second, taking a piece of canonized literature as well as popular texts into account, it might be possible to gauge the actual scope of the dissemination of particular elements of cultural knowledge in the American collective memory in the second half of the 1930s.

of the Great Depression are marked, e.g. the reference to John Steinbeck's novel. Yet, more often, the cultural connotations of Guthrie's songs can only be traced by comparing them to texts of the same cultural paradigm, the reference to which is only noticeable by the texts' formation of a structure of equivalence.

After all these reflections considering the selection of intertexts, it seems worthwhile to once again ponder the two problems addressed earlier, which have been dealt with theoretically, but which are still not solved entirely. In spite of all the considerations made to deal with the virtually limitless textual corpus of the cultural archive, it remains impossible to come up with a representative cross-section of texts and intertexts. Self-critically as ever, Greenblatt points out that "from the thousands, we seize upon a handful of arresting figures who seem to contain within themselves much of what we need, who both reward intense, individual attention and promise access to larger cultural patterns."[28] However, though the choice of texts may indeed remain arbitrary to a certain extent, it is still possible to establish plausible and informative readings which do the 'science of the particular' justice.[29] Following from that, the readings of Guthrie's songs provided in this study cannot, of course, be completely exonerated from being based on a somewhat arbitrary selection of (texts and) intertexts. Still, with an awareness of the problems of representativity and connection, the selection will certainly be made more carefully. After all, one should feel consoled by Greenblatt pointing out that "after a thousand [of other texts], there would be another thousand, then another, and it is not at all clear that we would be closer to the understanding we seek."[30]

Yet, before I will come to terms with a more detailed outline of the theoretical framework for the contextualizing readings of Guthrie's sung legacy, I will scrutinize the approaches and the results of past examinations of Guthrie and his songs with respect to their relevance to the endeavor of the present project.

28 Stephen Greenblatt, *Renaissance Self-Fashioning: From More to Shakespeare.* (Chicago: U of Chicago P, 1980) 6.

29 After all his theoretical considerations about how to make New Historicism work, Baßler points out: "Nicht nur der historische Text ist 'ein Gewebe von Zitaten, die den unzähligen Bereichen der Kultur entstammen', auch der Forschungstext muss solche Zitate auswählen und in geeigneter, Evidenz erzeugender und Erkenntnis fördernder Weise zusammenstellen, und das wird immer ein willkürlicher Akt bleiben" (339).

30 Greenblatt, *Renaissance Self-Fashioning* 6.

1.3 Contextualizing Woody Guthrie's Songs: Critical History and the Present Study

Despite the fact that there are numerous publications on Woody Guthrie, surprisingly few of them are concerned with his songs. It seems that the *person* Woody Guthrie has always been felt to be more fascinating than the musical and lyrical legacy he has left behind. Already in 1967, David A. DeTurk and A. Poulin, Jr. stated in their study on American folk culture that "[e]veryone is eager to talk about Guthrie the man, the son, the father, the rambler; almost no one discusses Guthrie the artist, which obviously, will be the basis for determining Guthrie's essential contribution to folk music."[31] Forty years after DeTurk and Poulin's assessment, there is still an abundance of Woody Guthrie biographies, but only a scant number of studies that are (predominantly) concerned with his "contribution to folk music," i.e., his songs. The following examination of the history of critical scholarship on both Guthrie and his songs shall show (1) that, among those contributions that deal with his songs, there is hardly any profound (synchronic) contextualization of Guthrie's songs about the Great Depression, or particularly about the Dust Bowl migration; (2) that the various existing approaches to Guthrie and/or his songs provide a number of fruitful theoretical and analytical insights which will be reexamined and extended in the present study. In order to examine these scholarly contributions systematically, it seems worthwhile to categorize them into (1) biographies which correlate Guthrie's songs with his life, (2) studies that are predominantly concerned with diachronic contextualization, and (3) contributions that investigate the correlation between Guthrie's songs and their cultural contexts of the 1930s and early 1940s and/or address, albeit on a very general level, aspects of their social and cultural productivity.[32]

Biographical Contextualizations of Guthrie's Songs

As already pointed out above, biographies probably constitute the largest group of contributions to Guthrie research. Though these might seem irrelevant to a close analysis of his songs at first sight, biographies do time and again provide fruitful starting points for a contextualizing anal-

31 David A. DeTurk and A. Poulin, eds., *The American Folk Scene: Dimensions of the Folksong Revival* (New York: Dell Laurel, 1967) 19.

32 Both the selection of scholarly contributions and the subdivision into biographies, diachronic and synchronic studies are, of course, not exhaustive. Yet, such a systematic overview might make it easier to position the present study within the critical debate and to define it in demarcation to past approaches.

ysis of Guthrie's songs. Instead of discussing the long list of Guthrie biographies in detail,[33] I will only look at two of them, which, besides their detailed depictions of the life of the Depression balladeer, also elaborate on his songs and their respective cultural contexts.

Soon after its publication in 1980, the biography that was to become the main reference work on Guthrie's life for more than twenty years was Joe Klein's *Woody Guthrie: A Life*.[34] This biography is illuminating in that it meticulously investigates each and every detail of Guthrie's life, the disintegration of his family and his career as a political songwriter. Moreover, while providing insight into Guthrie's lifelong political commitment as an advocate of the working people, it does not neglect to point out Guthrie's personal flaws and his failures as a father and husband. In his book, Klein mentions a number of Guthrie's songs and, at least in some cases, quotes and interprets them. However, his readings of Guthrie's songs are far from being comprehensive and are only integrated into the book in order to establish a coherent and plausible, albeit sometimes fictitious narrative of Guthrie's life. Still, they tackle links between the songs and their contexts, which might well be taken as starting points for closer analyses of Guthrie's songs in the present study.

After the Woody Guthrie Archives in New York City opened its doors for scholars in 1996, further Guthrie biographies appeared on the market, the majority of which were based on Klein's research and some new data that Klein could not have been aware of and that an analysis of the material in the Archives had shed light on. The most outstanding of these new biographies is Ed Cray's *Ramblin Man: The Life and Times of Woody Guthrie*, which was published in 2004. Due to his access to thousands of pages from the Woody Guthrie Archives, which contain previously unpublished letters, diaries, and journals, one may well say that Cray succeeded Klein as the definitive Guthrie biographer. In his book, Cray also attempts to contextualize Guthrie's songs by reconstructing the cultural contexts of the Depression era in a very illuminating manner, which makes his biography resemble a cultural history. Just like in Klein's book, though in a more detailed fashion, the contextualization serves the overall narrative of the biography and is not based on a close examination of his lyrics and music.

33 The list of Guthrie biographies includes: Elizabeth Partridge, *This Land Was Made For You And Me: The Life And Legacy of Woody Guthrie* (New York: Viking, 2002); Janelle Yates, *Woody Guthrie: American Balladeer* (Staten Island, New York: Ward Hill Press, 1995).

34 Joe Klein, *Woody Guthrie: A Life* (New York: Delta, 1980).

Diachronic Contextualizations of Guthrie's Songs

Besides numerous biographies there are a number of monographs and articles dealing with Guthrie and/or his songs which take a diachronic perspective, attempting to position Guthrie and his songs in the tradition of the protest song. Wayne Hampton's *Guerilla Minstrels* deals with the protest song culture in America and focuses on the role of hero-worship in this tradition over time. Starting with a chapter on John Lennon, Hampton goes on to then trace the roots of the protest tradition in subsequent chapters on Joe Hill, Guthrie and, last but not least, Bob Dylan.[35] It is his chapter on Hill which is of particular relevance for the present study, as it points, though indirectly, to the diachronic intertextual references in a number of Guthrie's songs, some of which follow a rhetorical strategy clearly reminiscent of that in the majority of Hill's songs. This diachronic intertextual potential of Guthrie's songs still needs to be explored in detail.

In his analysis of Woody Guthrie's contribution to this tradition, Hampton categorizes the songs of the "working-class mind guerilla"[36] into documentary and organizational songs. Whereas the former "dwell mostly on what is wrong and are vividly descriptive ballads of disasters and tragedies, tributes to the suffering of the people, but without providing solutions to the problems they portray,"[37] the latter category subsumes his union songs and labor hymns. Interestingly enough, Hampton chooses Guthrie's *Dust Bowl Ballads* as examples of the category of documentary songs and claims that "their authenticity and conviction are attributable to their emergence from his own personal experiences trying to survive the devastation of the dust bowl."[38] Though such an autobiographical approach to Guthrie's songs is highly questionable, as it tends to mix up author and speaker, Hampton's analysis of some of the Dust Bowl songs provides helpful starting points which may lead to a deeper understanding of the songs.

In his discussion of "So Long It's Been Good To Know Yuh" and "Dust Storm Disaster," for example, that is, songs that configure the dust storms in the 1930s as a divine judgment, Hampton argues that "those [Guthrie] portrayed in these songs were more likely to perceive their plight in religious than in political imagery, and the great dust storms

35 Cf. Wayne Hampton, *Guerilla Minstrels: John Lennon, Joe Hill, Woody Guthrie, Bob Dylan* (Knoxville: U of Tennessee P, 1986).

36 Hampton 94.

37 Hampton 120.

38 Hampton 121.

were typically viewed in eschatological terms."[39] Yet, he does not explain *why* Southwesterners would view the storms as a sentence of the Almighty – it is the word "typically" that calls for further explanation. Likewise, in his discussion of "Do Re Mi," a song about the immigration of hundreds of thousands of Southwesterners to California in the second half of the 1930s, Hampton states that "to young Guthrie and the other 'dust bowl refugees,' California became the Promised Land, where they could escape the devastation and make a new beginning."[40] Starting from this observation, it would be interesting to find out *why* Guthrie would write about California as a paradise on earth. This can be done by reconstructing the cultural patterns that both shaped and were shaped by his song. Thus, a more comprehensive correlation of the songs with their cultural contexts is lacking in Hampton's study, which, one must add, he certainly had never intended to provide considering the overall topic of his book, which, very much in contrast to my endeavor, follows a more diachronic approach.

A similar (diachronic) approach to Guthrie and his oeuvre is provided by Bryan K. Garman, who, in his book *A Race of Singers*, analyzes the impact of Walt Whitman and his poetic conceptualization of a 'working-class hero' on protest singers from Woody Guthrie to Bruce Springsteen.[41] In his informative chapters on the Okie troubadour, his study traces the Whitmanesque in Guthrie, who was fashioned, and who fashioned himself, as the ideal protest (and prophet) singer as outlined in the poems and poetics of Whitman. Yet, apart from examining the significance of the Whitman legacy for Guthrie's development and for his songwriting, thereby hinting at another intertextual trace which might be worth pursuing, Garman also provides readings of at least some of Guthrie's most famous Dust Bowl songs in a chapter dealing with the "Politics of Cultural Memory."[42] Here, Garman explores the ways in which Guthrie is remembered and (re)fashioned in modern media and in tribute concerts, where the participating artists, as Garman argues, typically seek to disconnect Guthrie from his communist affiliation by performing only certain (apolitical) songs and, what is more, by changing lyrics which are considered to be too radical. However, just like Hampton's investigation, Garman's readings do not provide satisfactory contextualizations which

39 Hampton 121.

40 Hampton 122.

41 Bryan Garman, *A Race of Singers: Whitman's Working-Class Hero from Guthrie to Springsteen* (Chapel Hill & London: U of North Carolina P, 2000).

42 Cf. Garman, *A Race of Singers* 164-92.

reveal that Guthrie's songs already took part in shaping the collective memory of the Southwestern migrants in the 1930s.

Another contribution by Garman, entitled "The Ghost of History. Bruce Springsteen, Woody Guthrie, and the Hurt Song," also follows a diachronic approach to examine in how far both Guthrie and Springsteen employ the language and representational strategies of the 'hurt song,' which, according to Garman's definition, "express[es] the collective pain, suffering, and injustice working people have historically suffered, and articulate[s] their collective hopes and dreams for a less oppressive future."[43] As regards Guthrie, Garman points out that he "used such hurt songs as the rural blues and traditional ballad to connect his own pain and suffering with the downtrodden of the Depression, and to encourage them to join him in his pursuit of social justice."[44] Though Garman thus introduces a concept which is certainly apt to characterize Guthrie's oeuvre, and states that Guthrie might have been "the most celebrated singer and theoretician of the hurt song,"[45] he does not concentrate on the songs of the Dust Bowl balladeer. Rather does he gauge the impact of some of Guthrie's songs on Springsteen, predominantly examining Springsteen's rewritings and reinterpretations of Guthrie's original lyrics. Within this diachronic approach, Garman, time and again, adopts a more synchronic perspective and provides fruitful readings of a small number of Guthrie's songs, among them "John Hardy" and "Tom Joad." Yet, his major focus is the question of how Springsteen places himself in a particular musical and political tradition heavily influenced by Guthrie.

In his dissertation on *Dust Bowl Migrants in the American Imagination*, published in 1997, Charles J. Shindo analyzes the ways in which the image of the Southwestern migrant was configured in the works of Dorothea Lange, John Steinbeck, John Ford and Woody Guthrie.[46] In the case of Guthrie, he argues that "the lyrical demands of [his] *Dust Bowl Ballads* (1940) have combined to present a portrait of dust bowl migrants as the quintessential depression victims."[47] Like other artists or writers, Guthrie "placed the migrants in the position of victim, presenting an image filled with sympathy toward the displaced and oppressed,"[48] an image that has prevailed in the American consciousness until the present

43 Bryan Garman, "The Ghost of History: Bruce Springsteen, Woody Guthrie, and the Hurt Song," *Popular Music and Society* 20.2 (1996): 70-71.

44 Garman, "The Ghost of History" 71.

45 Garman, "The Ghost of History" 107.

46 Cf. Charles J. Shindo, *Dust Bowl Migrants in the American Imagination* (Kansas: U P of Kansas, 1997).

47 Shindo 2.

48 Shindo 3.

day. Though it is not the concern of the present study to discuss Guthrie's impact on the reception of the Dust Bowl migration today, Shindo's approach is still of interest, as it creates an awareness of the fact that Steinbeck, Lange, Guthrie and others have contributed to a cultural representation of the migrant experience, "in which," as Shindo puts it, "a mix of conflicting yet mutually reinforcing voices each seeks authenticity and authority."[49] It is the constructive nature of this migrant experience which is at the center of Shindo's thesis, and which I will also use as a starting point to analyze Guthrie's songs. Yet, quite in contrast to Shindo, who is chiefly concerned with the impact of Guthrie's songs on the public image of the Dust Bowl migrants *today*, I will try to find out in how far Guthrie's songs shaped his listeners' awareness of political and social conflicts in the second half of the Great Depression.

In his contribution, Shindo examines some of Guthrie's well-known Dust Bowl Ballads, yet his analysis merely hints at the contemporary (inter)texts referred to in Guthrie's songs without exploring them in detail through a close reading. In his discussion of one of Guthrie's songs about Jesus Christ, for instance, he argues that the Oklahoman minstrel "combined the outlaw legend with religion"[50] and adds in parenthesis that religion is "another traditional element in Okie culture,"[51] before he, in very short terms, hypothesizes about possible functions of that combination. However, in order to reconstruct the 'social energy' of the song, one needs to investigate the cultural paradigms that might have shaped and been shaped by Guthrie's song by means of an analysis of intertextual references to other contemporary literary and non-literary texts.

Correlating Guthrie's Songs with their Cultural Environment: Towards a Synchronic Contextualization of Guthrie's Songs

Apart from the biographical and the more diachronic approaches to Guthrie's oeuvre, there are only a few contributions that aim at correlating his songs with their cultural environment.[52] A scholar who, similar to

49 Shindo 3.

50 Shindo 179.

51 Shindo 179.

52 In addition to those discussed in detail there are: Guy Logsdon, "Woody Guthrie and his Oklahoma Hills," *Midamerica Folklore* (1991) 57-73, which is concerned with the history of a song rather than with its correlation with its cultural contexts; H.R. Stoneback's contribution to Guthrie research, predominantly focusing on the (intertextual) relation between John Steinbeck and Woody Guthrie, which will also be of importance for the present study (cf. Harry. R. Stoneback, "Songs of 'Anger and Survival': John Steinbeck on Woody Guthrie," *Steinbeck Quarterly* 23.1-2 (1990): 34-42. Cf. also Harry R. Stoneback, "Woody Sez:

Shindo, though with a more synchronic perspective, investigated into the religious imagery employed in Guthrie's songs, and in doing so, provided an explanation for his combining "the outlaw legend with religion,"[53] is Brad Lookingbill. In his essay "Dusty Apocalypse and Socialist Salvation," Lookingbill claims that "Guthrie's Dust Bowl ballads note the significance of spiritual belief and reflected the religious fundamentalism prevalent on the Southern Plains."[54] Yet, after having experienced the hardship of the Depression years, Guthrie "placed his hope in the secular religion of socialism which forecasted an apocalypse followed by a worldly paradise."[55] "To Guthrie," as Lookingbill puts it, "salvation from the dust could not be found in the old-time religion; only political action offered deliverance from the dusty judgment."[56]

Lookingbill's claim of a 'socialist conversion' is, at least at first sight, convincing, as it suggests a development in the character of Guthrie, who, after having become involved in socialist matters in the late 1930s, continued to be influenced by his fundamentalist upbringing on the Southwestern Plains – hence the fusion of Christian and socialist ideas in his later songs. Yet, such a 'conversion hypothesis' is doubtful, as it explains the imagery resorted to in Guthrie's songs in terms of a development of Guthrie's character. Thus, though Lookingbill's approach is promising in that it indeed takes the cultural patterns of the second half of the Great Depression into account, his 'conversion hypothesis' at least has to be modified.

James R. Curtis's essay on "Woody Guthrie and the Dust Bowl" is principally concerned with various "Dust Bowl themes,"[57] i.e., he cate-

Woody Guthrie and 'The Grapes of Wrath,'" *Steinbeck Newsletter* (Summer 1989): 8-9). A profound and illuminating study about the political and cultural contexts of New Deal America is Richard Nate, *Amerikanische Träume: Die Kultur der Vereinigten Staaten in der Zeit des New Deal* (Würzburg: Königshausen und Neumann, 2003). He also includes a chapter on Woody Guthrie (270-85), which provides promising starting points for a close analysis of Woody Guthrie's songs.

53 Shindo 179.

54 Cf. Brad D. Lookingbill, "Dusty Apocalypse and Socialist Salvation: A Study of Woody Guthrie's Dust Bowl Imagery," *Chronicles of Oklahoma* 72.4 (1994): 397. Contributions by Lookingbill which are less concerned with Guthrie, but more with the cultural environment of the Great Plains in the 1930s and are thus relevant for the present study as well are: "'A God-Forsaken Place': Folk Eschatology and the Dust Bowl," *Great Plains Quarterly* 14.4 (1994): 273-86, and "'The Living and the Dead Land': The Great Plains Environment and the Literature of Depression America," *Heritage of the Great Plains* 29.3 (1996): 38-48.

55 Lookingbill, "Dusty Apocalypse" 405.

56 Lookingbill, "Dusty Apocalypse" 406.

57 Curtis 256.

gorizes Guthrie's Dust Bowl Songs according to the topics dealt within them. Though his approach is helpful in putting Guthrie's songs in a chronological sequence, starting with songs about the "pre-Dust Bowl period," then continuing with the "description of the storms and subsequent destruction" and finally leading up to songs about "elements of migration and California,"[58] it lacks any detailed contextualization. Curtis points out himself that, "for the purpose of overall continuity, these themes will be dealt with in chronological sequence rather than on an individual-song basis"[59] and indeed, though his account contains a number of fruitful insights, there are no substantial close readings of texts and intertexts.

Robert Santelli and Emily Davidson's *Hard Travelin': The Life and Legacy of Woody Guthrie* contains at least two contributions that are relevant for the present approach to a contextualization of Woody Guthrie's songs about the Dust Bowl migration and the Great Depression. The first is an article by Craig Werner, which, though it does not contextualize the songs in detail, establishes an interesting argument focusing on the specific features of song in contrast to literature. In his article, Werner points out that "[i]t would be possible to make an argument for [Guthrie's] place in American literature based on the 'literary' qualities of 'This Land is Your Land,' 'Pastures of Plenty,' and 'Plane Wreck at Los Gatos (Deportees).'" "But there's no real point," he continues, "to confusing songs and literature."[60] Following from that, Werner argues that "lyrics almost always work better when they're sung than when they're read on the page."[61] In contrast to Bob Dylan's literary lyrics, "Woody [...] knew that [his] songs had to communicate clearly to an audience that was unlikely to pore over symbolism, pursue allusions, or ponder dense metaphors."[62]

Werner's conclusion addresses the social function of Guthrie's songs and thus hints at the mutual correspondence between them and their contexts. He states that the notion of the simplicity of Guthrie's lyrics should not lead to the assumption that "musical performance is inherently less complex than literature. The complexity, however, derives more from the

58 Curtis 257.

59 Curtis 256-57.

60 Craig Werner, "Democratic Visions, Democratic Voices: Woody as Writer," *Hard Travelin': The Life and Legacy of Woody Guthrie*, ed. Emily Davidson and Robert Santelli (Hanover, New Hampshire: UP of New England for Wesleyan UP, 1999) 71.

61 Werner 71.

62 Werner 71. Though I certainly agree with the importance of the communicative function of song that Werner elaborates on, I believe that Guthrie's audience would have understood the allusions he made, whether consciously or unconsciously.

context of performance and the shared energies of the group than from the text itself."[63] As an example, Werner refers to Guthrie's "Tom Joad," a rendering of selected passages from Steinbeck's novel *The Grapes of Wrath*, which, according to him, "functions both to spread the word and to expose the novel to an audience with relatively little access to the type of education needed to interpret Steinbeck's subtleties."[64] The assumption that songs function as a (re)integrating medium distributing and popularizing knowledge will be central to my contextualizing analysis of Guthrie's oeuvre.

Another illuminating point made by Werner, which is an immediate result of the first, and which will also have to be elaborated on in more detail in my theoretical considerations, is his discussion of the connection between music and literary texts. Referring to the theory of Ed Pavlic, a scholar of West African and African American culture, Werner states that

> [a] musical performance begins with the artist 'calling' to the audience by singing a line or playing a riff. Although the call is shaped by the leader – who frequently crafts it while separated from the community – the material of the initial call usually comes from a body of images familiar to most members of the community.[65]

Once again, Werner highlights the interdiscursive character of the sung word. Yet, what is more, he also hints at the 'shared experience' of a musical performance. "That Woody almost always used familiar melodies for his lyrics, reflects his understanding of this dimension of call and response,"[66] Werner observes in his application of the above-mentioned ideas to Woody Guthrie. Further, he points to the fact that "the response doesn't always have to be affirmative. Other voices [...] can agree, argue, redirect the dialogue, raise new questions."[67] Finally, Werner returns to his first suggestion of music as an integrating force, when he concludes that "[a]t its best, the call and response dynamic provides communities lacking access to the networks of official culture a way of comparing their experience and analyzing its meaning."[68] Thus, though he does not go into a detailed analysis of Guthrie's songs, Werner's general ideas both about the interdiscursive framework that Guthrie's

63 Werner 71.
64 Werner 71-72.
65 Werner 74.
66 Werner 74.
67 Werner 74.
68 Werner 75.

songs might provide and the collective experience of a musical performance are important for the contextualization of Guthrie's Dust Bowl songs.

Another contribution to Santelli and Davidson's collection of essays is Charles F. McGovern's "Woody Guthrie's American Century," which does not only explore "United States History in Guthrie's times, the better to understand the ways in which the momentous changes in America during his life made Woody's own voice and vision so compelling."[69] The article also reflects on Guthrie's impact in its specific historical context, an idea which is closely related to the New Historicist notion of the social and cultural productivity of literary texts. Yet, it is not so much McGovern's illustration of the social, political and economic conflicts of Great Depression America and his subsequent conclusion that "Guthrie's emergence in the 1930s as an entertainer and chronicler of the Dust Bowl and agricultural migrants was grounded in these larger battles" which are of interest.[70] What is highly relevant to this study instead, are his reflections on the 1930s' emphasis on plain folks' culture and the complementary documentation of social conditions that flourished in those days and generally affected American culture during that decade.

According to McGovern, this new focus on the common people "in part arose from a widespread popular curiosity that was fed by both the commercial culture industries – magazines, newsreels, movies, radio, serial fiction – and the state."[71] From that, he concludes that "since the 1930s, the rhetoric of portrayal representation and focus on common people has been central to the culture industries."[72] And Woody Guthrie, as McGovern argues, "was caught up in [this] shift in attention to the common people [and thus] participated in and benefited from the larger hunger in American life for understanding 'the people.'"[73] That is why, one may well conclude, the cultural productivity of his songs in the contexts of the 1930s must not be neglected. Like John Steinbeck or Dorothea Lange, Guthrie had an enormous impact on shaping the migrant experience and, thus, the contemporary discourses. McGovern's findings on the general concern for the common people provide one necessary key to understanding the impact of Guthrie's songs on the contemporary audience, which shall be further examined in my thesis.

69 Charles F. McGovern. "Woody Guthrie's American Century," *Hard Travelin'*, ed. Davidson and Santelli 111.

70 McGovern 118.

71 McGovern 123.

72 McGovern 124.

73 McGovern 124.

The most recent book on Guthrie's songs is Mark Allan Jackson's *Prophet Singer: The Voice and Vision of Woody Guthrie*. Jackson provides an erudite and well-informed study on an extensive selection of Guthrie's songs from the beginnings of his creative work in the mid-1930s to the 1950s. Understanding Guthrie's lyrics as a means to "voice his views on a wide variety of American historical realities,"[74] Jackson's contextualizing readings predominantly resort to biographical and historical data and reveal how Guthrie's socialization and the cultural contexts of the 1930s and 1940s shaped his songwriting. Jackson's study thus provides a number of fruitful insights into the cultural situatedness of Guthrie's oeuvre and, to a certain extent, we make similar observations in some of our analyses. In contrast to Jackson's book, my study, however, being indebted to the New Historicist 'science of the particular,' deliberately limits the selection of songs and redirects the analytical focus towards the intertextual interfaces between them and their contemporary contexts. Examining the cultural circulation and dissemination of the rhetorical, linguistic and compositional features employed in the songs, I thus attempt to gauge their cultural productivity. Moreover, by having taken a closer look at the musical and performative dimensions of Guthrie's songs which, as I argue, significantly contributed to their social energy, my readings significantly differ from Jackson's observation that Guthrie's lyrics "simply ride on the back of someone else's music"[75].

* * * * *

Though the overview of the scholarly contributions on Guthrie and/or his songs has not been exhaustive, it both hinted at some general tendencies of Guthrie research and revealed some gaps which the present study will hopefully be able to fill: First, some of those contributions that are indeed concerned with a correlation of Guthrie's songs with contemporary contexts still fall short in a close analysis of his lyrics and, what must not be forgotten, his music. In those cases in which Guthrie's songs are analyzed in more detail, they are predominantly considered mere reactions to particular socioeconomic, political or cultural circumstances or are correlated to Guthrie's biography. Thus, what still needs to be carried out is a detailed investigation into the intertextual references of his songs, which may point at a mutual correspondence between his songs and the con-

74 Mark A. Jackson, *Prophet Singer: The Voice and Vision of Woody Guthrie* (Jackson: UP of Mississippi, 2007) 6. It was only in the process of preparing this study for publication that Jackson's book appeared.

75 Jackson 7.

texts in which they were once performed. Such an investigation might also give substance to the claim that the songs were not only culturally produced in that they reacted to the sociopolitical and cultural contexts in which they were once written and performed, but also culturally productive in that they contributed to shaping contemporary discourses and perpetuated or undermined established elements and patterns of cultural knowledge. Second, the studies pursuing a more diachronic approach indeed provide some fruitful starting points for the analysis of the diachronic intertextual potential of Guthrie's songs, for example his imitation of Joe Hill's songwriting. However, this potential has not been analyzed in detail yet. Third, the more theoretically oriented contributions, which give possible reasons for the social and cultural significance of Guthrie's songs in the Depression contexts, are prolific in that they provide a step towards the explanation of the potential of the sung word, which shall also be taken into account and elaborated upon in the theoretical part of the present study.

2 Contextualizing Songs: Cultural Studies and New Historicism

Woody Guthrie's songs about the Dust Bowl migration and the Great Depression will, as already hinted at, neither be contextualized historically, i.e., read as reactions to a fixed historical background, as has been done in 'Old Historicist'[1] fashion in most of the works discussed above; nor will they be examined in a close reading which would merely concentrate on the text itself as a literary artefact without taking anything beyond it into consideration.[2] Instead, the songs will be correlated with other contemporary literary and non-literary documents in order to trace the origins of their linguistic, rhetorical and semantic elements in the contemporary culture and thus, as Corns has it, "return to [Guthrie's songs] the political potency they once possessed, by means of reanimating an awareness of those contexts which they engaged."[3]

That Guthrie's songs did possess such 'political potency,' which I am trying to rediscover and revive in my analysis, becomes evident as soon as one considers that they render one of the bleakest chapters in the history of the United States. Written at a time when the very foundations of American society were severely shaken – not only by the collapse of the capitalist system, but also by a series of devastating dust storms that turned the Southwestern states into a drought-stricken wasteland and thus contributed to a dramatic increase in the number of those in need –

1 The term 'Old Historicist/m' is put into single inverted commas, as it is not an official denominator for a certain theoretical school, but a label the New Historicists used in order to distinguish themselves from more traditional literary scholarship. The attribute 'Old' was used by the New Historicists, accusing their opponents not only of pretending to write an 'objective' history, which according to New Historicist ideas is simply impossible, but also of serving the bourgeois society by exclusively dealing with canonical texts, thus leaving behind any rejected text "in the darkened wings of history" (Volkmann 329).

2 New Critics regarded the text as a hermetically sealed entity which could be analyzed and evaluated according to a set of 'objective' laws. Actually, most of these analytical attempts fell victim to the rigidity of their own laws of interpretation (cf. Volkmann 328-29).

3 Quoted in Susanne Spekat, *Politische Straßenballaden im Zeitalter der Englischen Revolution (1640-1660): Eine kulturwissenschaftliche Untersuchung ihrer historisch-politischen, literatur- und mentalitätsgeschichtlichen Bedeutung* (Trier: WVT, 2002) 32.

Guthrie's songs were supposed to function as a means of articulating protest against the irresponsibility and thoughtlessness of those in power.

In order to come to a deeper understanding of his songs and to revive the social energy they were once charged with, it will be the task of this study to rehistoricize and repoliticize them by exploring and analyzing the cultural contexts in which they were written and sung. The frequent use of religious imagery and allusions in Guthrie's songs, to give only one example, can best be understood if the contemporary discourse of Protestant fundamentalism, particularly in the Southwestern states, is taken into consideration.

By reconstructing the cultural contexts of the second half of the Great Depression (1935-1941) and by correlating them to Guthrie's oeuvre, I hope to succeed in showing that his songs are not only products of this particular culture, but also contributed to maintaining and, presumably, to shaping it. Therefore, my investigation requires a theoretical framework that exceeds 'traditional' literary criticism: It will have to take a (re)orientation towards Cultural Studies[4] into account, which, over the past decade, have become increasingly influential in the humanities, particularly challenging orthodox literary scholarship and propagating an interdisciplinary approach which draws upon historiography, the social sciences and the humanities. One of the most prominent approaches that can be subsumed under the heading of Cultural Studies is certainly New Historicism, which I will draw on as a theoretical approach to contextualize Woody Guthrie's songs. In the following, I will outline the basic ideas and key concepts of Cultural Studies and of New Historicism and will eventually complete my theoretical design by including Jürgen Link's concept of interdiscourse analysis, concepts of intertextuality and considerations on the musical and performative dimensions of the sung word to make the New Historicist approach applicable for the analysis of Woody Guthrie's songs about the Dust Bowl migration and the Great Depression.

4 In the following, I will use the term "Cultural Studies" for a theoretical framework that, in German, would be referred to as "Kulturwissenschaftliche Literaturwissenschaft" and that, though it is, in many respects, similar to British and American Cultural Studies, does not share the strong ideological stance of its Anglo-American counterparts. The basic ideas of this "Kulturwissenschaftliche Literaturwissenschaft" are outlined in Ansgar Nünning and Roy Sommer, "Kulturwissenschaftliche Literaturwissenschaft: Disziplinäre Ansätze, theoretische Positionen und transdisziplinäre Perspektiven," *Kulturwissenschaftliche Literaturwissenschaft*, ed. Ansgar Nünning and Roy Sommer (Tübingen: Narr, 2004) 9-29.

2.1 Elevating the Popular: Cultural Studies as a Framework for the Analysis of Songs

Defining popular culture is certainly a challenging task. Lawrence Grossberg points out that it "has always been a rather paradoxical field; it is usually defined in explicit opposition to the 'legitimate' culture of the intelligentsia."[5] He adds that "it also stands ambiguously poised in relation to the actual culture of the dominant classes"[6] and goes on to explain that

> '[p]opular culture' exists within a complex series of terms (mass, elite, legitimate, dominant, folk, high, low, midcult) and oppositions (civilized versus vulgar, dominant versus subordinate, authentic versus inauthentic, self versus other, same versus different), which are, in various contexts, linked together in different ways.[7]

As Grossberg's account suggests, a single definition of the term 'popular culture' has not been agreed upon yet. According to him, the term is more likely to have a set of definitions that vary according to the criteria each of them is based upon. Thus, "[p]opular culture has been defined formally (as formularized), aesthetically (as opposed to high culture), quantitatively (as mass culture), sociologically (as the culture of 'the people') and politically (as resistant folk culture)."[8] It is the last definition mentioned by Grossberg that seems to provide the most appropriate concept of popular culture for this thesis, though I would argue that Guthrie's songs are also opposed to high culture and, in a way, belong to the culture of 'the people.' The difficulty of definitively assigning the attribute 'popular' to a particular cultural phenomenon, like Guthrie's songs, remains, as the boundaries between the various definitions are fluid and, what is even more, shifting. Thus, what was popular ten years ago, might have lost its popularity today, and what is considered high culture today, might become popular in a couple of years. Accordingly, whether one can categorize Woody Guthrie's Dust Bowl songs as part of 1930s popular culture largely depends on one's understanding of the popular, which, as we have seen, may indeed vary.

Consequently, whenever I use the term 'popular' to label Woody Guthrie's songs, I do so in order to indicate the songs' resistant potential, their appeal to the common people and, to employ Grossberg's words

5 Lawrence Grossberg. *We Gotta Get Out of This Place: Popular Conservatism and Postmodern Culture* (New York: Routledge, 1992) 75.
6 Grossberg 75.
7 Grossberg 75.
8 Grossberg 75-76.

once again, their oppositionality to the alleged high culture of those days. Popularity shall not be defined, as is often done, by the scale of consumption, as measured by sales figures and market indicators. Simon Frith points out that "even if such figures were accurate (which is doubtful), they provide no evidence as to why such goods are chosen by their consumers nor whether they are actually enjoyed or valued by them."[9] He states that "[i]n accounts of popular music, this [equation of popular culture with market choice] is to ignore the significant unpopularity of certain stars [...] and the popular influence of such market failures as Velvet Underground or Joy Division or Neil Young."[10] Following from that, one can assert that culture becomes popular not because it sells, but because it matters.

* * * * *

Analyzing and evaluating songs is not a completely new endeavor. At the beginning of the 1970s, a large number of dictionaries, articles and books that concerned themselves with the medium of song were published. As early as 1972, George H. Lewis, in his essay "Popular Music and Research Design: Methodological Alternatives," came up with a systematic framework of possible approaches towards popular music. He criticized the one-dimensionality of research designs involving the study of popular music and proposed a methodological model that was based on the concept of media as a social system. He developed an approach to the analysis of songs that did not only focus on a content analysis of the lyrics, but which also involved an investigation into the aspects of the song's creation, its production, its distribution, the effects of regulative agencies like censorship or radio station logs, the advertising agencies and the financial backing. Last but not least, he emphasized that an analysis of song structures was necessary to grasp the song's complexity and to uncover its didactic potential.[11] "There are alternatives," Lewis concludes at the end of his article, and suggests "that we attempt to employ them."[12] Indeed, in the immediate aftermath, sociologists, psychologists, and also literary scholars started to investigate a field that had long been

9 Simon Frith, *Performing Rites: Evaluating Popular Music* (1996; Oxford: Oxford UP, 2002)15.

10 Frith 15; cf. also Rainer Winter, *Die Kunst des Eigensinns: Cultural Studies als Kritik der Macht* (Weilerswist: Velbrück Wissenschaft, 2001) 205.

11 Cf. George H. Lewis, "Popular Music and Research Design: Methodological Alternatives," *Popular Music and Society*, 1.2 (1972): 108-15.

12 Lewis 114.

out of their traditional scope.[13] However, despite this growing interest in the study of songs among scholars from various disciplines in the 1970s, the analysis of what was sometimes understood as 'modern mass poetry'[14] more or less remained part of an alternative literary criticism that was, not seldom, frowned upon by orthodox scholarship.

However, over the past few years, Cultural Studies have gained immensely in popularity, even among a growing number of literary scholars, who have turned away from traditional literary criticism, which exclusively dealt with an established canon of authors and works. Said scholars are now moving towards more integrative approaches to literary and cultural phenomena, advocating not only an interdisciplinary (re)-orientation, but also a widening of concern. Though everybody, whether propagating or opposing this new development, feels somehow affected by what is commonly referred to as 'the cultural turn,' it is almost impossible to subsume the vast number of concepts that have already emerged under a single definition. This heterogeneity is partly due to the fact that Cultural Studies, though they actually can build on a long tradition,[15] are by no means an original theoretical approach, but resort to various theoretical and methodological approaches from other disciplines, which are pragmatically combined to provide a set of viable tools for the analysis of texts and contexts. Yet, from this multitude of ideas and concepts, at least three characteristic features can be distilled, which are shared by every theoretical approach that might be subsumed under the label of Cultural Studies and, what is more, which help to constitute a general theoretical framework for an analysis of Woody Guthrie's Dust Bowl songs: interdisciplinarity, a constructivist and semiotic concept of culture and a widening of concern.

Interdisciplinarity

According to orthodox literary criticism, presumably, Woody Guthrie's songs would not have been deemed worthy of analysis. The same goes for historiography, in which Guthrie's texts, if they are dealt with at all, are usually referred to as a source from which to extract information about the living and working conditions of the migrants and farm workers in the second half of the Great Depression.

13 Cf. e.g. Werner Faulstich, *Rock – Pop – Beat – Folk: Grundlagen der Textmusikanalyse* (Tübingen: Narr, 1978); cf. also Erwin Otto, "Flucht aus der Trivialität – Intention und Wirkungsästhetik politischer Popsongs," *anglistik & englischunterricht. Trivialliteratur* (1977): 151-71.

14 Faulstich 62ff.

15 Cf. Nünning and Sommer 13.

Thus, the interdisciplinary orientation of Cultural Studies is essential for the contextualization of Guthrie's songs in a twofold way. First, it provides a framework for the reconstruction and the analysis of the various sociocultural, ideological and political discourses of the 1930s with which Guthrie's songs are going to be correlated in order to reanimate their political potential. For this reason, my study will have to cross the borders of traditional literary analysis and move towards historiography and social sciences in order to reconstruct the great socioeconomic and political shifts of Guthrie's times, which are rendered and commented upon in his songs: The shattered belief in a laisser-faire economy after the stock market crash of 1929, which, backed by a Democratic President and his Keynesian policy of intervention, led to the renaissance of a socialist movement in the 1930s, is only one of a number of developments, then, which must be taken into account. Second, the interdisciplinary orientation also does justice to the problem of not being able to precisely assign the topic to a single academic discipline, as it is to be found in-between the research interests of the humanities and the social sciences.[16] Following from that, the necessity of taking an interdisciplinary approach is vitally important in order to fully grasp the dimensions of this study's subject matter.

Concept of Culture

Another characteristic feature of Cultural Studies which is of major relevance to the investigation of Woody Guthrie's songs and on which there is, in spite of the variety of Cultural Studies-oriented approaches, widespread agreement is the concept of culture: Culture is regarded as a socially constructed complex of attitudes, notions, norms and meanings that materialize in sign systems, i.e., texts.[17] This constructivist formula,

16 Cf. Ansgar Nünning, "Literatur, Mentalitäten und kulturelles Gedächtnis: Grundriß, Leitbegriffe und Perspektiven einer anglistischen Kulturwissenschaft," *Literaturwissenschaftliche Theorien, Modelle und Methoden: Eine Einführung*, ed. Ansgar Nünning (Trier: WVT, 1995) 177-78: "[Eine anglistische Kultur-wissenschaft] [rückt] kulturelle Problemfelder in den Mittelpunkt, die bislang vor allem deshalb wenig Beachtung gefunden haben, weil sie zwischen den Erkenntnisinteressen der Literatur- und Geschichtswissenschaft liegen und vom disziplinären Suchraster nicht erfasst werden." For a comprehensive discussion of the limits of academic disciplines and the possibilities of interdisciplinary approaches cf. Jürgen Mittelstraß,. *Wissen und Grenzen: Philosophische Studien* (Frankfurt a. M.: Suhrkamp, 2001).

17 Cf. Nünning and Sommer 18: "Demzufolge wird Kultur als der von Menschen erzeugte Gesamtkomplex von Vorstellungen, Denkformen, Empfindungsweisen, Werten und Bedeutungen aufgefasst, der sich in Symbolsystemen niederschlägt."

which owes a lot to cultural anthropology and cultural semiotics,[18] implies a tripartite division of culture into (1) a social dimension ("socially constructed") encompassing the users of the sign systems, i.e., individuals, institutions, or society in general, (2) a mental dimension, which encompasses the above mentioned attitudes, notions, norms and meanings as the conventional codes of a particular culture (mentefacts), and, finally, (3) a material dimension, i.e., texts in a semiotic sense, not only including literary artifacts which are usually referred to as 'high culture,' but also other literary and non-literary texts, even non-verbal texts like photographs, paintings, songs, rituals or modes of behavior that, in some way or other, make the underlying codes of a particular culture visible and observable.

As the concept of this threefold character of culture, which was originally outlined by Posner,[19] implies, strong interdependences exist between these three dimensions of culture, since the users of the sign system (social dimension) have to resort to certain codes (mental dimension) to be able to make sense of the material dimension of culture, which is the only facet directly accessible to us. Following from that, the examination of (literary) texts as elements of the material dimension of a culture might hint at its social and, first and foremost, at its mental dimension, at the "system of shared meanings, attitudes and values," which, by the analysis of "the symbolic forms (performances, artifacts) in which they are embodied,"[20] may be reconstructed. Consequently, the analysis of Guthrie's songs as cultural artifacts[21] may help us gain insight into the mental dispositions, attitudes and notions of his contemporaries. Yet, it is not so much the artifacts themselves that I am interested in. It is rather the relationship to their (extra-)literary contexts that will be focused on, since, as Meyer points out, "it is important to realize that any attempt to infer mental structures from literature has to

[18] Cf. Doris Bachmann-Medick, ed., *Kultur als Text: Die anthropologische Wende in der Literaturwissenschaft*, (Tübingen: A.Francke, UTB, 2004).

[19] Cf. Roland Posner, "Kultur als Zeichensystem: Zur semiotischen Explikation kulturwissenschaftlicher Grundbegriffe," *Kultur als Lebenswelt und Monument*, ed. Aleida Assmann and Dietrich Harth (Frankfurt a. M.: Fischer, 1991) 37-74.

[20] Peter Burke, *Popular Culture in Early Modern Europe*. London: Temple Smith, 1978) v.

[21] Fortunately, there are records of many of his songs available. Thus, the performative dimensions hinted at by Burke will, whenever possible, also be taken into consideration.

be complemented by the examination of other social phenomena, which may be of a textual or non-textual nature."[22]

Widening of Concern

The understanding of culture outlined above results in a widening of concern: Cultural Studies refrain from the exclusive treatment of authors and works that belong to an established literary canon, as has been practiced by traditional literary scholarship for decades and even centuries. In order to investigate a particular culture, it is by no means sufficient to analyze and interpret the works of its major authors. Often, this collection of seemingly important works, which we usually refer to as the 'canon,' is based on a selection that was made by the ruling elite of that particular culture. Undoubtedly, the claim that those works which happen to be part of the literary canon (and, of course, their respective authors) are representative of a particular culture is always ideologically biased.[23] To get to a more complex picture of what constitutes a society's cultural patterns, the advocates of Cultural Studies predominantly concern themselves with those (literary) texts that have been neglected or even excluded by orthodox literary scholarship, as they have been regarded as 'low culture,' not worth investigating at all. Yet, it is exactly the analysis of this 'low culture', of the voices of the unheard, that can reveal more about a particular culture than any interpretation of its literary canon, as 'low cultural' manifestations, as a rule, circulate widely and are thus far more representative of a culture than 'high culture' made for an intellectual elite.[24]

In contrast to Steinbeck's *The Grapes of Wrath*, which is written from a similar political perspective as Guthrie's, the songs of the Okie bard have neither received much attention nor have they been treated as 'true'

22 Friederike Meyer, "Literary History and the History of Mentalities: Reflections on the Problems and Possibilities of Interdisciplinary Cooperation," *Poetics* 18 (1989): 90.

23 Cf. e.g. Herbert Grabes, "Canon-Making and Cultural Memory: The Creation of 'English Literature' through the Writing of Literary Histories," *Journal for the Study of British Cultures* 10.1 (2003): 11-26.

24 Interestingly, in the United States, both scholarly and public interest in such 'low cultural' manifestations increased in the 1930s, as the Depression "cast a focus on everyday folks as both the victims of Depression and those who defied it" (McGovern 124). With his 'sung documentaries' of the Dust Bowl migration and the Great Depression, Woody Guthrie thus "participated in and benefited from the larger hunger in American life for understanding the people [and] forcefully and artfully staked a claim that America and the world should pay attention to the common folks' perspectives, dignity, and rights" (McGovern 124).

pieces of literature. Unlike Steinbeck's Pulitzer prize-winning novel, Guthrie's songs belonged to folk culture which has not been examined by literary scholars, as they did not regard it as worth analyzing. With the growing popularity of Cultural Studies in recent years, however, and with a more or less consistent theoretical framework emerging from the admittedly confusing variety of approaches, Guthrie's songs appear in a new light. Once the normative distinction between high and low culture is given up, they are, as a vital part of 1930s Dust Bowl culture, elevated into the realm of literary, or rather, cultural relevance, not only as objects of literary analysis, but also as historical fragments, the contextualization of which might help to reconstruct the beliefs, the attitudes and the mental dispositions of the past.

2.2 Singin' with the Dead: New Historicism and the (Re)Construction of Cultural Knowledge

In order to reconstruct the cultural framework which Woody Guthrie's songs were once tied to, I will have to correlate them with other textual manifestations of the late 1930s in order to trace aspects of its mental or social dimensions. Therefore, I will have to rethink the relationship between text and context, since I do not only want to show that (and how) Guthrie's texts provide insight into certain cultural patterns and discourses of his time, but that they have actually helped shape and perpetuate these patterns and discourses. To substantiate this endeavor theoretically, I will resort to the central ideas of New Historicism. Due to its strong focus on the dialectical relationship between text and context, it seems to be an especially adequate theoretical concept for an analysis which aims at deriving a particular culture's knowledge from songs and, at the same time, at reconstructing the songs' part in the formation process of this cultural knowledge.[25] Nevertheless, I will not stick to the New Historicist approach dogmatically, as I am well aware of the fact that New Historicism as a theoretical 'school' has not been immune to criticism over the past years. Thus, I will not only illustrate its key elements, which are supposed to theoretically frame the contextualization of

[25] Parts of my New Historicist approach to the contextualization of songs have already been outlined in Martin Butler, "The Power of the Sung Word: Reconstructing the Social and Cultural Significance of Songs," *Kulturelles Wissen und Intertextualität,* ed. Marion Gymnich, Birgit Neumann and Ansgar Nünning 165-81.

Woody Guthrie's songs, but also critically reflect on and – if necessary – modify them in the course of this chapter.

New Historicism, which has become one of the most well-established approaches in literary theory, emerged in the 1980s and was then a true challenge to the established modes of literary interpretation, in particular New Criticism, which had dominated literary scholarship in the 1960s and 1970s and, as already mentioned above, had regarded literary texts as artifacts that were interpreted without much consideration of the historical context.[26] It was New Historicism's aim to reintroduce the historical dimension of texts and to reactivate their political potential, to revive the social energy they once possessed in a particular context.[27] Interestingly, it was Stephen Greenblatt, the founder and certainly the most famous representative of New Historicism, who, soon after this new approach to literary criticism had increasingly gained attention, replaced the term 'New Historicism' with 'poetics of culture' or 'cultural poetics,' thereby hinting at the central idea of the approach more directly: According to Greenblatt, it is the literary scholar's task to relocate literary texts within the complex cultural surrounding in which they were written, performed and received and in which they once unfolded their political potential. In order to revive this potential, this "powerful energy" of the "written word [being] self-consciously embedded in specific communities, life situations, structures of power,"[28] Greenblatt suggests reconstructing the "extended borrowings, collective exchanges, and mutual enchantments,"[29] or, in other words, the 'negotiations' between the text and other manifestations of its cultural environment. Only then will one be

26 Cf. e.g. Ivor A. Richards, *Practical Criticism: A Study of Literary Judgement* (1929; New York: Harvest Books, 1956); William Empson, *Seven Types of Ambiguity* (1930; New York: New Directions, 1966); William K. Wimsatt and Monroe C. Beardsley, "The Intentional Fallacy," *The Verbal Icon: Studies in the Meaning of Poetry*, by William K. Wimsatt and Monroe C. Beardsley (Lexington: U of Kentucky P, 1954) 3-18.

27 I am well aware that New Historicism as such did not 'invent' the incorporation of context into the analysis and interpretation of literary texts. Already in the 1920s and 1930s, a number of approaches from the field of literary sociology considered extraliterary contexts to be important for the analysis of texts (cf. e.g. Herbert Schöffler, *Protestantismus und Literatur* (1922; Göttingen: Vandenhoeck, 1958); Levin L. Schücking, *Soziologie der literarischen Geschmacksbildung* (1923; Bern/München: Francke, 1961). Therefore, its general criticism of New Criticism and the 'Old Historicism' is, in many respects, an oversimplification and, as Volkmann has it, a mere "effort to gain attention" (Volkmann 329-30).

28 Greenblatt, *Renaissance Self-Fashioning* 7.

29 Stephen Greenblatt, *Shakespearean Negotiations: The Circulation of Social Energy in Renaissance England* (Berkeley: U of California P, 1988) 7.

able to gain insight into the complexity of a particular culture and its manifold, often contradictory, conceptions, which are both reflected and constructed in the literary document on hand.

Consequently, Greenblatt proposes "to look less at the presumed center of the literary domain than at its borders, to try to track what only can be glimpsed, as it were, at the margins of the text."[30] Though he admits that "the cost of this shift in attention will be the satisfying illusion of a 'whole reading,'"[31] he hopes to offer a compensation for this loss, namely "insight into the half-hidden cultural transactions through which great works of art are empowered."[32] In the New Historicist project, this "shift in attention" implies a redefinition of the relationship between the "literary domain" and its cultural surrounding, which is, in turn, based on a specific understanding of history, which the New Historicists adopted from modern historiography and made feasible for literary studies.

History, according to the New Historicist, is not a universally valid course of events which can be objectively analyzed and reconstructed, but an intellectual construction rendered in narrative. It is not, as Jean E. Howard points out, "a realm of retrievable fact,"[33] but, as he continues, "a construct made up of textualized traces assembled in various configurations by the historian/interpreter."[34] Thus, history is produced, not discovered, and its production, in any case, depends on the epistemological premises of the historian/interpreter, the theories and models he or she developed in order to analyze historical data and, last but not least, on his or her research interest, in short: on the ideological and methodological framework of the historian's/interpreter's own present. Indeed, historical facts, or, to speak in more general terms, historical 'reality' as

30 Greenblatt, *Shakespearean Negotiations* 4; cf. also Volkmann 333: "By reading between the lines, by taking into account the voices of other texts – be they fictional or non-fictional – the modern reader is in search of unwitting testimony, of the hidden flaws and fissures in the revealing silence of texts. Thus old sources are read in a new light to reveal secret, buried meanings of texts." In particular, Volkmann's phrase "to reveal secret, buried meanings of texts" is very much reminiscent of Greenblatt's famous opening sentence of his *Shakespearean Negotiations*: "I began with the desire to speak with the dead" (1).

31 Greenblatt, *Shakespearean Negotiations* 4.

32 Greenblatt, *Shakespearean Negotiations* 4.

33 Jean E. Howard, "The New Historicism in Renaissance Studies," *Renaissance Historicism: Selections from English Literary Renaissance*, ed. Arthur F. Kinney and Dan S. Collins (Amherst: U of Massachusetts P, 1987) 13.

34 Howard 13-14. The notion of history as a 'construct' was particularly shaped by Hayden White, whose ideas were taken up by the New Historicist approach. (cf. e.g. Hayden White, *Tropics of Discourse: Essays in Cultural Criticism* (1978; Baltimore: Johns Hopkins UP, 1987) 51.

a whole, is something neither the historian nor the literary scholar may have access to directly, as it is something that happened in the past and is thus irretrievably lost.[35] It is through texts then that history becomes accessible. Consequently, if we assume that every textual trace of history – as well as its interpretation – is characterized by a subjective perspective and is thus somehow ideologically biased, there cannot be one universal, linear history which may be objectively reconstructed, but only heterogeneous drafts of history, which are characterized by fragmentariness and discontinuity.

Starting from this idea that history is by no means transparent and objectively knowable, but a narrative construct based on the historian's interpretation of a network of rather arbitrarily chosen texts,[36] New Historicism claims that there is no such thing as a stable historical 'background' which might operate as a framework for the interpretation of literary texts. Rather is the New Historicist's endeavor guided by the notion that "the relative positions of text and context often shift, so that what has been the mere background makes a claim for the attention that has hitherto been given only to the foregrounded and privileged work of art; yet we wish to know how the foregrounding came about."[37] Thus, the binary distinction of a literary foreground and a historical 'background' loses its validity, as the 'background' of a text is understood to be made up of another set of interrelated texts and thus becomes the object of interpretation as well; the boundary between text and context is blurred, as "literature is part of history, the literary text as much a context for other aspects of cultural and material life as they are for it."[38]

The concept of context as a network of further texts is based on a semiotic definition of culture as text, which was originally introduced by cultural anthropologist Clifford Geertz, according to whom a particular culture is understood as a system of signs which does not only include literary documents, but also other cultural elements, such as pictures,

35 Hence Montrose's famous dictum of the 'textuality of history': "By the *textuality of history*, I mean to suggest, firstly, that we can have no access to a full an authentic past, a lived material existence, unmediated by the surviving textual traces of the society in question (20)".

36 Cf. White 81: "[A] historical narrative is […] necessarily a mixture of adequately and inadequately explained events, a congeries of established and inferred facts, at once a representation that is an interpretation and an interpretation that passes from an explanation of the whole process mirrored in the narrative."

37 Gallagher and Greenblatt 16.

38 Howard 15.

social practices, institutions or societal norms of behavior.[39] Once employed by the members of that particular culture as a means of communication, all these elements can be understood as texts, which can, as such, be correlated with the literary texts. By what Geertz calls 'thick description,' i.e., the endeavor "to construe all of culture as the domain of literary criticism," a text may thus be "perpetually interpreted," read as "an inexhaustible collection of stories from which curiosities may be culled and cleverly retold."[40]

Following from that, the concept of textuality in New Historicism is enlarged in that "both social and literary texts are opaque, self-divided, and porous, that is, open to the mutual intertextual influences of one another."[41] At the same time, the notion of 'culture as text' "expands the range of objects available to be read and interpreted."[42] Thus, though the binary division of literature into popular texts on the one hand and canonical texts on the other has not become completely obsolete, and though, according to Greenblatt,

> [m]ajor works of art remain centrally important, they are jostled now by an array of other texts and images. Some of these alternative objects of attention are literary works regarded as too minor to deserve sustained interest and hence marginalized or excluded entirely from the canon. Others are texts that have been regarded as altogether nonliterary, that is, as lacking the aesthetic polish, the self-conscious use of rhetorical figures, the aura of distance from the everyday world, the market status as fiction that separately or together characterize belles lettres.[43]

In this 'democratic universe of texts,' in which classic works of art, though they might have always been regarded as detached from their cultural surrounding, can be correlated to textual traces of various literary or non-literary kinds and in which minor pieces of literature are now objects of scholarly analysis, "there is no hierarchy of great texts and

39 Cf. Clifford Geertz, *The Interpretation of Cultures* (1973; New York: Basic Books, 2000). Geertz describes culture "as interworked systems of construable signs (what, ignoring provincial usages, I would call symbols) [...], [as] something to which social events, behaviors, institutions, or processes can be causally attributed; it is a context, something within which they can be intelligibly – that is, thickly – described" (quoted in Rainer Winter, *Der Produktive Zuschauer: Medienaneignung als kultureller Prozess* [München: Quintessenz, 1995] 77-78); cf. also Greenblatt, *Renaissance Self-Fashioning* 4.

40 Montrose 19.

41 Howard 15.

42 Gallagher and Greenblatt 9.

43 Gallagher and Greenblatt 9.

minor texts; all texts are equal as forms of cultural practice and as co-existing discourses, free to negotiate, to exchange and to circulate."[44] Undertood as one of those 'forms of cultural practice,' Woody Guthrie's songs are thus revaluated in the course of the New Historicists' "egalitarian enterprise [of] their leveling of texts, subjects and cultures."[45]

Following from this notion of a democratic 'market-place' of cultural manifestations, New Historicism promotes the idea of a dialectic relationship between texts and contexts, in which (literary) texts are no longer, as Elizabeth Fox-Genovese has it, mere "function[s] or articulation[s] of [their] context,"[46] but carry poietic[47] potential as well and are thus accorded real power, being agents in constructing a culture's sense of reality rather than passively reflecting it. As Montrose puts it, literary texts are not only a product of their sociocultural circumstances, but at the same time a *createur* of the discourses through which they have been shaped:

> Thus, to speak [...] of the social production of 'literature' or of any particular text is to signify that it is socially produced but also that it is socially productive – that it is the product of work and that it performs work in the process of being written, enacted, or read.[48]

On the one hand, a text's meaning is said to be inseparable from the circumstances of its making and its reception; thus "there can be no auto-

44 Volkmann 332.

45 Volkmann 333. It is, of course, questionable whether literary and non-literary texts should be dealt with in equal terms, since this would bear the risk of what Gallagher and Greenblatt call "a wholesale aestheticizing of culture" (12). According to Christoph Bode, literary texts belong to a special group of texts which is usually treated in a particular way: "Wenn man mit literarischen Texten so umgeht, dass sie primär eine fremde Gesellschaft, Kultur oder Zeit beleuchten oder illustrieren sollen, benutzt man sie wie jedes andere beliebige Sozialdokument nicht-literarischer Art, d.h. aber, man negiert die Tatsache, dass es sich dabei um *besondere* (epische, lyrische, dramatische) Texte handelt, um Texte eben, mit denen nicht nur in unserem Kulturkreis gemeinhin anders verfahren wird als mit nicht-literarischen" (Christoph Bode, "Anglistische Literaturwissenschaft und/oder Cultural Studies?" *Anglia* 114.3 [1996]: 409). In order to avoid levelling the difference between literary and non-literary texts completely, and in order to put emphasis on the specific characteristics of literary texts, I will resort to Jürgen Link's concept of literature as interdiscourse (cf. chapter 2.3.1).

46 Elizabeth Fox-Genovese, "Literary Criticism and the Politics of the New Historicism," *The New Historicism*, ed. Veeser 217.

47 The term 'poietic' is used to imply the creative and formative potential of (literary) texts, which is always included in their 'mimetic' or representational function.

48 Montrose 23.

nomous artifacts [...], no expression without an origin and an object, a from and for."[49] On the other hand, and more importantly, literary texts contribute to cultural discourses, may enhance or subvert certain ideological stances, and thus have "a privileged position in the continuing process of fashioning and refashioning consciousness, of defining possibilities of action, of shaping identities, and of shaping visions of justice and order."[50] Consequently, the interpretative task of the New Historicist must be to investigate "both the social presence *to* the world of the literary text and the social presence of the world *in* the literary text."[51]

The dialectic relationship of literature and society results from the fact that literary texts employ certain established cultural patterns of discourse in order to construct their models of reality. In doing so, these established patterns of discourse are thus communicated by the literary texts. As Montrose describes it, referring to Shakespeare's *A Midsummer Night's Dream* as an example,

> the fantasies by which the text of *A Midsummer Night's Dream* has been shaped are also those to which it gives shape. [...] [The play] also creates the culture by which it is created, shapes the fantasies by which it is shaped, begets that what it is begotten.[52]

Thus, (literary) texts must not be understood as merely reacting to the process of sociocultural change, but as active agents in this process. Once regarded as historical events in their own right, (literary) texts, according to New Historicism, exert a certain power on extraliterary structures, either substantiating the established societal order by containing any kind of resistance or subverting it by overt opposition. Following from this, I argue that as much as Shakespeare's comedy rendered, amplified and shaped established discourses, mental patterns, and ideological notions of Renaissance times, Guthrie's songs contributed to creating, perpetuating or challenging the American cultural knowledge of the 1930s, and it will be one focus of this study to find textual evidence for the ways in which his songs took part in the sociopolitical and cultural discourses during the Great Depression.

49 Greenblatt, *Shakespearean Negotiations* 12.
50 Fox-Genovese 222.
51 Greenblatt, *Shakespearean Negotiations* 5.
52 Quoted in Spekat 38.

2.3 Critical Evaluation, Methodological Specification and Modification of the New Historicist Approach

Stephen Greenblatt himself has never tired of stating that New Historicism is but "a practice – a practice rather than a doctrine,"[53] and he has also never tired of stressing that a theoretical conceptualization of the approach, which might turn it into a "repeatable methodology or a literary critical program,"[54] has not been worked out, and will, most probably, never be. Thus, though New Historicism certainly qualifies as an appropriate theoretical framework for an analysis of Woody Guthrie's songs, it still has its deficits which at the least have to be mentioned and, whenever possible, be supplemented by other concepts that might fill these theoretical gaps. Not only do the critical voices maintain that the concept of New Historicism is characterized by a methodological and theoretical heterogeneity which evokes an impression of pragmatic arbitrariness;[55] they also continue to claim that some of the New Historicists themselves do not stick to their own theoretical premises, as they, for example, still tend to exclude marginalized authors and rather focus on canonical texts to legitimize their endeavor. Moreover, critical voices continue to argue that the theoretical framework of New Historicism is rather vague and lacks methodological specification, which makes it difficult, if not even impossible, to apply it to the analysis of concrete texts.

Though New Historicism puts great emphasis on the dialectical relationship between text and context, which will be focused on in my analysis of Guthrie's songs, it does not provide appropriate methods to examine this relationship. The thesis that literary texts are not only culturally produced in their particular cultural contexts, but that they are also culturally productive in that they actively take part in shaping and changing contemporary discourses and patterns of cultural knowledge, has remained a mere theoretical dictum and, unfortunately enough, New Historicists seem to evade any further operationalizations which would make it applicable to literary analysis.

By resorting to Jürgen Link's concept of literature as an interdiscourse and by integrating appropriate concepts of intertextuality, I will try to specify one side of the coin, namely the songs' being culturally pro-

53 Stephen Greenblatt, "Towards a Poetics of Culture," *The New Historicism*, ed. Veeser 1.

54 Gallagher and Greenblatt 19.

55 This reproach of arbitrariness, which predominantly concerns the selection of textual material, might, at least to a certain extent, be weakened by Baßler's concept of the archive as outlined in the introductory chapter of this study (cf. chapter 1.2).

duced.[56] In order to specify their being socially and culturally productive, I will resort to the model of communication developed by representatives of the Birmingham School of Cultural Studies. Finally, I will include theoretical aspects related to the study of the musical and performative dimensions of the sung word, which, as I assume, significantly contributed to the songs' social and cultural potential and have thus to be taken into consideration as well.

2.3.1 Reconstructing Cultural Knowledge: Interdiscourse Analysis and Concepts of Intertextuality

Jürgen Link's concept of interdiscourse analysis[57] may help to specify the relationship between Guthrie's songs and contemporary discourses and to examine the patterns and elements of cultural knowledge rendered in the songs. In general, Link's approach distinguishes between specialized discourses, the development of which results from a continually growing functional differentiation of various branches of society,[58] and interdiscursive elements that contribute, as a kind of contrary force, to a reintegration of these separated societal spheres, at least to a certain extent. Though his approach is based on Foucault's concept of discourse, its focus is not so much on the specialized discourses as on the interdiscursive domain, which is characterized by discursive interferences and combinations of various discourses. Being highly selective, the interdiscursive elements systematically (re)integrate the specialized knowledge that has been gained in the various professional domains, and, by reducing the complexity of the original discourses, facilitate their distribution throughout society as a whole.[59] Link suggests that, apart from

56 Cf. Butler 170-73.

57 Cf. Jürgen Link, "Literaturanalyse als Interdiskursanalyse: Am Beispiel des Ursprungs literarischer Symbolik in der Kollektivsymbolik," *Diskurstheorien und Literaturwissenschaft*, ed. Jürgen Fohrmann and Harro Müller (Frankfurt a. M.: Suhrkamp, 1988) 284-307.

58 In his argument, Link uses the concept of discourse as outlined by Michel Foucault: "Mit Foucault können wir also vom juristischen, medizinischen, politökonomischen Diskurs usw. sprechen: jeder arbeitsteilig ausdifferenzierten und auf der Basis eigener pragmatischer Rituale gesondert institutionalisierten Praxisart entspricht dann ein spezieller Wissensbereich, den wir Diskurs nennen können" (288).

59 Link refers to these (re)integrative discursive constellations as "interdiskursive Sprachspiele": "Es leuchtet unmittelbar ein, dass die Tendenz zu wachsender Spezialisierung der Diskurse eine Herausforderung für die alltägliche Kommunikationsfähigkeit der Gesellschaft bedeutet: wie kann der Facharbeiter mit dem Arzt, die Hausfrau mit dem Mathematiker kommunizieren? Sie können kommunizie-

everyday language and journalistic texts, it is literature in particular which can be correlated to these 'interdiscursive dispositives.'[60] Therefore, literary discourse functions as a highly elaborate interdiscursive network paradigmatically selecting specific elements and structures from the specialized discourses and syntagmatically combining and integrating them in an innovative way.[61]

Guthrie's Dust Bowl songs are thus, to apply Link's concept to my thesis, understood as a kind of 'interdiscursive medley,' including and combining elements which have been generated from e.g. the religious, the sociopolitical and/or the economic discourses of Guthrie's time, which can, in turn, be considered as the 'raw material' for his song lyrics. Taking into account that, in times of utmost economic and political uncertainty, the majority of the population, particularly those at the bottom of society, felt a general need for information, his songs may indeed be said to have functioned as a reintegrating interdiscourse through which specialized knowledge could be and, as I am going to show, was mediated to his contemporaries.

According to Link's approach, interdiscursive elements, such as analogies, metaphors, topoi or stereotypes, which are taken from and represent spezialized disourses, occur recurrently and can therefore be regarded as characteristic of a particular culture.[62] They are, in his termi-

ren, weil es nicht bloß Spezialdiskurse, sondern – mit reintegrativer Funktion – auch *interdiskursive Sprachspiele* gibt. Ich zögere zu sagen: *einen* Interdiskurs oder *mehrere* Interdiskurse – und zwar aus folgendem Grunde: wir haben es zunächst mit einem *Gewimmel von Diskursinterferenzen und Diskursberührungen* zu tun" (288).

60 "Es gibt nun eine Reihe von Textsorten bzw. Genres, in denen die interdiskursive Funktion dominiert: das sind alle Textsorten der *Popularisierung*, vor allem journalistische und literarische im weitesten Sinne" (293). In contrast to journalistic texts, however, which, according to Link, may also function as reintegrating interdiscourses, literary texts particularly combine and configure *ambivalent* material (cf. 293).

61 Therefore, quite in contrast to what New Historicism claims, literary discourse can be distinguished from non-literary discourses, for it functions as an integrative force. The issues of paradigmatic selection and syntagmatic configuration are taken from Ricoeur's concept of mimesis. Cf. Paul Ricoeur, *The Rule of Metaphor: Multi-Disciplinary Studies in the Creation of Meaning in Language*, trans. Robert Czerny with Kathleen McLaughlin and John Costello (1975; London: Routledge 1978); cf. Paul Ricoeur, *Time and Narrative*, 3 vols., trans. Kathleen McLaughlin and David Pellauer (1983; Chicago: U of Chicago P, 1984).

62 Link describes the relationship between the various specialized discourses and the collective symbols as follows: "Die einzelnen Kollektivsymbole (bzw. die Symbolserien, etwa die *Maschinen*) repräsentieren bzw. konnotieren häufig

nology, referred to as 'collective symbols,' the analysis of which needs to take the synchronic contexts into consideration in order to gauge their social and cultural significance: Depending on the contemporary contexts, various symbols might be combined due to structural or semantic similarity or employed as oppositions and might thus be charged with new meaning and connotations. What is more, collective symbols can be used to articulate different discursive positions; they do not have a universally fixed meaning, but share a certain ambiguity, as one and the same symbol might be employed to express diametrically opposed ideas.

Being part of 1930s culture, there can be no doubt that Woody Guthrie's songs about the Dust Bowl Migration and the Great Depression contain such collective symbols, which will have to be analyzed in my thesis in order to sort out which discourses they can be associated with. Moreover, apart from the reconstruction of contemporary discourses, the investigation of the recurrent metaphors, images and analogies that constitute the interdiscursive patterns of his songs may hint at contemporary (collective) dispositions, which I will try to trace. Furthermore, I will also try to approach the question of whether the collective symbols that can be found in Guthrie's songs are used by different discursive positions and for what purposes.

In order to do so, I will have to embed the songs into a synchronic network of other texts from their cultural environment and to analyze their intertextual potential. As I will resort to a semiotic and constructivist definition of culture as the totality of dispositions, beliefs and attitudes of a particular age, which manifests itself in linguistic and extralinguistic sign systems, the texts I am going to correlate with Guthrie's songs will not only be literary, but also non-literary as well as non-verbal texts. Thus, it seems reasonable that my intertextual analysis needs to be based on the poststructuralist concept of intertextuality, which was predominantly shaped and developed by Julia Kristeva, who, drawing on Michail Bakhtin's categories of dialogism and polyphony as characteristic features of (certain) literary texts,[63] claims that "any text is con-

einen bestimmten *Spezialdiskurs* als Herkunftsbereich (die *Maschinen* etwa den Diskursbereich der Naturwissenschaften und ihrer Technologie; die *Krankheiten* den medizinischen Diskurs, die *Prozesse* den juristischen usw.). Das Symbolsystem scheint also wie ein 'Markt' zu funktionieren, auf dem verschiedene Spezialdiskurse bestimmte exemplarische Stereotypen 'umschlagen' können" (293).

63 Cf. Julia Kristeva, "Word, Dialogue and the Novel," *The Kristeva Reader*, ed. Toril Moi (Oxford: Blackwell, 1984) 24-33. Kristeva points out that "Bakhtin was one of the first to replace the static hewing out of texts with a model where literary structure does not simply *exist* but is generated in relation to *another* structure. What allows a dynamic dimension to structuralism is his conception of

structed as a mosaic of quotations; any text is the absorption and transformation of another."[64] In contrast to Bakhtin, however, who clearly distinguishes between dialogical and monological texts,[65] Kristeva radically generalizes the understanding of text in her semiotic approach, as she defines intertextuality as "cette inter-action textuelle qui se produit à l'intérieur d'un seul texte. Pour le sujet connaissant, l'intertextualité est une notion qui sera l'indice de la façon dont un texte lit l'histoire et s'insère en elle."[66] First of all, this definition implies that the dialogical is no longer an exclusive feature of specific (literary) texts, but characteristic of all texts.[67] Yet, what is even more, Kristeva's definition also underlines the semiotic notion that history or society respectively (have to) be read as texts, as it "situates the text within history and society, which are then seen as texts read by the writer, and into which he inserts himself by rewriting them. Diachrony is [thus] transformed into synchrony."[68] This idea of the '(inter)textuality of history' – to appropriate Montrose's dictum – allows me to correlate Guthrie's songs to other literary and non-literary (and even non-verbal) texts of the cultural archive of the 1930s.

Though I will predominantly focus on synchronic texts in order to position Guthrie's songs within the '(inter)textual universe' of his contemporary culture and thus to revive the social energy they once possessed, the examination of diachronic intertextual references of Woody Guthrie's songs to literary and/or musical traditions and conventions must not be neglected. Therefore, I will also have to resort to yet another and – as compared to the poststructuralist notion of intertextuality as a feature inherent to every verbal or non-verbal text – more narrow con-

the 'literary word' as an *intersection of textual surfaces* rather than a *point* (a fixed meaning), as a *dialogue* among several writings; that of the writer, the addressee (or the character) and the contemporary or earlier cultural context" (35-36, emphasis added). Though I will draw on her poststructuralist understanding of intertextuality, I will refrain from the notion that both a text's author and its addressee are but texts themselves.

64 Kristeva 37.

65 Bakhtin states that there are monological texts, which reflect the centralized and hierarchically structured society, and dialogical texts, in particular modern novels, which feature a 'microcosm of polyphony' (cf. Manfred Pfister, "Konzepte der Intertextualität," *Intertextualität: Formen, Funktionen, anglistische Fallstudien*, ed. Ulrich Broich and Manfred Pfister [Tübingen: Niemeyer, 1985]) 4. Thus, Bakhtin's concept may be referred to as intratextual rather than intertextual (cf. Pfister 4).

66 Quoted in Pfister 7.

67 Cf. Pfister 7-8.

68 Kristeva 36.

cept of intertextuality that enables me to trace intended allusions and intertextual references, an analysis of which might probably contribute "to enlarg[ing] and stratif[ing] [the] meaning [of Guthrie's songs]."[69] This concept of intertextuality, which is rooted in the tradition of hermeneutics, suggests that the author of a (literary) text deliberately refers to a specific pretext or various pretexts in order to create semantic surplus value. Though these pretexts are "always incomplete in the poem," as Riffaterre states, "they are either pointed to by textual signs or are fragmentarily actualized [...]. The original architecture of these 'other texts,' their grammar, the distribution of their lexicon, the sequence of their components, are nonetheless obvious to the reader, since they are part of his linguistic competence."[70] Thus, intertextuality is no longer understood as a general feature of any literary or non-literary text, but is regarded as a specific mode of constituting meaning in certain literary texts. In particular for an analysis of the diachronic intertextual references of Guthrie's texts both to individual texts, such as the Bible, or to structural patterns of certain literary or musical genres and traditions like the Blues or the Talking Blues, such a concept of intertextuality can be applied effectively.[71]

In order to fully grasp the intertextual dimensions in Woody Guthrie's songs, it seems worthwhile to combine these two approaches to intertextuality, which are by no means mutually exclusive, but represent a part-to-whole relationship in that the structuralist concept highlights specific kinds of intertextual references, which are included in the universe of intertextual relationships as propagated by the poststructuralist approach.

69 Ringbohm, quoted in Pfister 23. The enlargement and the stratification of meaning by analyzing intertextual references is, of course, limited to my analytical perspective. Whether there was an enlargement and a stratification of meaning for the contemporary audience is yet another question, which will have to be addressed separately (cf. chapter 2.3.2).

70 Quoted in Pfister 24.

71 As I draw on a semiotic understanding of culture (cf. chapter 2.1), 'intermusical' references will also be taken into consideration.

2.3.2 Constructing Cultural Knowledge: British Cultural Studies and the Active Audience Paradigm

> A song leaves your mouth just as soon as it leaves your hands. You've got to respect other people's rights to also have a message themselves. (Bob Dylan)[72]

As far as the analysis of the social and cultural productivity of Guthrie's songs about the Dust Bowl migration and the Great Depression is concerned, it may be helpful to employ the concept of the reception of popular media that was established by representatives of British Cultural Studies in the 1970s. Their findings, though they predominantly concerned the reception of popular television programs, might well be applied to an analysis of the impact of popular music on the cultural knowledge of its listeners.[73] Thus, in the following, both Stuart Hall's central ideas about the reception of popular media and the constitution of meaning and Simon Frith's approach to evaluating (the impact of) popular music, which takes up the model of communication developed by the Birmingham School, shall be outlined, as they may serve as additional theoretical approaches both to tackle the poietic potential of Woody Guthrie's songs and to create an awareness of the fact that all we may infer from the analysis of his oeuvre are *hypotheses* about the social and cultural functions of his songs.

Going against the mainstream of media research, which was and still is colored by the neo-marxist cultural pessimism of the Frankfurt School,[74] Stuart Hall, in particular, developed a model of mass communication which is based on the general assumption that the audiences of popular media, be it film, television or radio broadcast, are, by no means, monolithic blocs of passive recipients who absorb the messages spread by the "cultural entrepreneurs develop[ing] manipulative sales methods that ensnared [them] in self-delusion."[75] In contrast to Horkheimer and Adorno,

72 Quoted in Nat Hentoff, "Playboy Interview: Bob Dylan," *The Best of the Playboy Interviews 1962-1992* (Playboy Enterprises Inc., 1992) 55.

73 Scholars like Lawrence Grossberg or Simon Frith have already applied this concept of communication to the analysis of popular music.

74 The Frankfurt School, mainly represented by Max Horkheimer and Theodor W. Adorno, regarded popular culture as aesthetically worthless and, moreover, as a means to stabilize and reproduce the dominant ideology that, "while purporting to be democratic, individualistic and diversified, is in actuality authoritarian, conformist and highly standardized." (Chris Barker, *Cultural Studies: Theory and Practice* [London/Thousand Oaks: SAGE, 2002]) 45.

75 Frith 13.

who, in their theory of cultural industry,[76] degraded the consumers of mass media to mere objects of manipulation, assuming as they did that the "internal meanings are taken up by audiences in an unproblematic fashion,"[77] Hall, in his research on British television series, concerned himself particularly with the activities of reception among the viewers or listeners respectively. He introduced a concept which includes the reader of television texts in the process of constituting meaning and which might, at least retrospectively, be called the 'active audience paradigm.'[78] His approach starts with the assumption that media, in general, have the power to provide a framework of references with the help of which the members of a society perceive and interpret reality. It is thus responsible for "the provision and the selective construction of social knowledge, of social imagery, through which we perceive the 'worlds,' the 'lived realities' of others, and imaginarily reconstruct into some intelligible 'world-

76 Cf. Theodor W. Adorno and Max Horkheimer, "The Culture Industry: Enlightenment as Mass Deception," *Dialectic of Enlightenment*, by Theodor W. Adorno and Max Horkheimer (1947; New York: Continuum,1993).

77 Barker 45.

78 Cf. Barker 269ff. It should be added that Hall's findings are explicitly mentioned here because he was the first to elaborate on the idea of an active audience, which he summed up in his pioneering essay "Encoding/decoding" during his research at the Birmingham Centre for Contemporary Cultural Studies (CCCS) (cf. Stuart Hall, "Encoding/decoding," *Culture, Media, Language: Working Papers in Cultural Studies, 1972-79*, ed. Centre for Contemporary Cultural Studies [London: Hutchinson, 1980 (1973)] 128-38. Though I employ his concept of textual polysemy, I refrain from following his notion of class as the single decisive factor in the process of meaning constitution, which has been criticized and extended by other factors like cognitive, emotional or social competences as well in the works of other scholars (cf. e.g. David Morley, *The* Nationwide *Audience: Structure and Decoding* [London: BFI, 1980]). Hall's ideas were further developed and modified by others, e.g. by John Fiske in his *Television Culture* (London: Methuen, 1987) and Lawrence Grossberg. Furthermore, Barker points out that "[t]he active audience paradigm is not the 'property' of Anglo-Saxon cultural studies. McAnany and La Pastina's review of twenty-six telenovelas substantiates the argument that local organizational and cultural configurations mediate the understandings of soap operas generated by audiences" (270). What is even more, the 'active audience paradigm' is also a central idea in the tradition of hermeneutics and literary reception theory; cf. Hans-Georg Gadamer, *Philosophical Hermeneutics* (Berkeley, California: U of California P, 1976) and Wolfgang Iser, *The Act of Reading: A Theory of Aesthetic Response* (Baltimore: Johns Hopkins UP, 1978). With reference to literary texts, both Gadamer and Iser substantiated the view that "the relationship between the text and the audience is an interactive one in which the reader approaches the text with certain expectations and anticipations [...] involving not merely reproduction of textual meaning but *the production of new meaning by the readers*" (Barker 271).

of-the-whole,' some 'lived totality.'"[79] Hall concludes that there are various "world[s]-of-the-whole" which the members of society establish by consuming mass media, as the spectators, or listeners respectively, are regarded as active participants in the construction of meaning by reading (television) texts.[80] They decode the messages that were previously encoded by the producer of the text.[81] Therefore, Hall hypothesizes that "production and reception of the television message are not identical, but they are related: they are differentiated moments within the totality formed by the communicative process as a whole."[82]

This inclusion of the recipient in the process of communication means that the linear transmission of messages, as it is proposed in the traditional sender-receiver model, is not guaranteed; i.e., the meaning of a medial text is, to a large extent, constructed and constituted by the recipients, "produced in the interplay between text and reader so that the moment of consumption is also a moment of meaningful production."[83] Therefore, the meaning of a text may not only depend on its formal and historical relations to other texts, but also on the contexts of its reception.

Moreover, the texts' constructive character implies that language or texts respectively do not directly reflect reality. They rather, applying Paul Ricoeur's dynamic concept of mimesis, configure a reality, which, in turn, is integrated by the recipient into his or her individual cognitive and cultural contexts, into his or her "world of the whole."[84] Hall, quite similarly, points out that "discursive 'knowledge' is the product not of the transparent representation of the 'real' in language but of the articulation of language on real relations and conditions."[85] Following from that, it can be argued that the author's (or singer's) intention does not necessarily reach the recipients, as they, depending on their sociocultural, intellectual and cognitive competences, generate various meanings on the basis of one particular text.

Understood as 'meaningful discourse,' song texts, just like television texts, are thus always polysemous; i.e., "they contain the possibility of a number of different meanings which have to be realized by actual rea-

79 Hall, quoted in Winter, *Der Produktive Zuschauer* 83.

80 The understanding of television series as texts is, of course, one consequence of his semiotic approach.

81 Cf. Hall. It has to be added that the decoding of encoded messages only works under the premise that both text-producers and text-recipients share the same cultural codes (cf. Winter, *Der Produktive Zuschauer* 84).

82 Hall, quoted in Winter, *Der Produktive Zuschauer* 84.

83 Barker 11.

84 Cf. Ricoeur, *The Rule of Metaphor*, *Time and Narrative*.

85 Hall, quoted in Winter, *Der Produktive Zuschauer* 85.

ders who give life to words and images."[86] Thus it is impossible to simply infer audiences' meaning production from textual analysis. What "appears to be expressed in the lyrics, only form[s] the medium of which [listeners] make *active* use."[87] Or, as Frith has it,

> much of the argument that starts from lyrical content analysis assumes that the 'content' (or 'meaning') of songs as revealed by the analyst is the same as their content (or meaning) for other listeners. There is a very quick slippage in this analytic tradition from a summary of the lyrical content as revealed by academic survey to a moralist denunciation of the effects of pop songs on their listeners.[88]

Interestingly enough, it was Guthrie himself who recognized the value of active audience participation when he stated that "a song ain't nothing but a conversation where you can talk it over and over without getting tired of it. And it's this repeating over and over that makes it take hold."[89] In one of his notebooks, he elaborates on the idea that the meaning of a song is (also) constructed by its listener:

> Music talks, and it speaks differently in you than in me, because we are the same mirror, yet our reflections are not the same. If you and I were twins and had never lived apart a moment in our lives, still we would have looked into different corners and out [of] different windows, and our eyes would have seen the same room, yet different colors of paint and furniture, we would have looked at the same trees and seen different leaves, and when music brings your old hopes back to you and my own back to me, there would be spaces and distances and differences in us.[90]

Guthrie's notion of song as conversation is certainly based on his strong appreciation of Walt Whitman, who, quite similarly, developed the idea of an active recipient long before Cultural Studies or literary reception theory were established.[91] In an article about Whitman and Guthrie, Ron Klier argues that "Whitman refers to his readers as 'lovers,' and believ-

86 Barker 11. Again, I think it is legitimate to employ Hall's terminology – which was specifically developed to describe and analyze television texts – in the context of an analysis that is concerned with popular music.

87 Peter Wicke, quoted in Neil Nehring, *Popular Music, Gender, and Postmodernism: Anger Is an Energy* (London/Thousand Oaks: SAGE, 1997) 145.

88 Frith 164.

89 Quoted in Ron Klier, "Walt Whitman, Woody Guthrie, Bob Dylan, and the Anxiety of Influence," *The Midwest Quarterly* 40 (1999): 346.

90 WGA, Notebooks I, Notebook 26, 24-25.

91 For the impact of Whitman on Guthrie, cf. also Pascal or Garman, "The Ghost of History."

ing them so, seeks to transcend the page. He offers his readers the opportunity to engage themselves in what he has to say."[92] Then, Klier points out that "[w]hat he proposes is akin to contemporary reader-response criticism. He sets himself equal to the reader, understanding that he or she plays as much a part in the evolution of a work as he."[93] Indeed, in his *Leaves of Grass*, which Guthrie had most probably become acquainted with through his friend, actor Will Geer, at the end of the 1930s, Whitman addresses his audience and asks "[i]f you were not breathing and walking here where would they [the poems, the orations, the plays] all be?"[94] For him, as he included the audience in the process of meaning-production, the answer is obvious: "The most renowned poems would be ashes ... orations and plays would be vacuums."[95]

Following from all this, one must not forget that the reconstruction of the social and cultural productivity of Guthrie's songs in this study is, of course, done from a 21st-century perspective, supported by the knowledge and the analysis of a rather limited selection of textual material compared to the overall extent of the cultural archive of the 1930s. After all, one cannot be sure how Guthrie's contemporary listeners, conceptualized as active agents in the process of constituting meaning, actually made sense of his songs and how they integrated them into their knowledge of their 'worlds-of-the-whole.' However, what can and will be done in this study is to hypothesize about *possible* and *plausible* functions of Guthrie's songs within their specific cultural environment; about the ways in which they contributed to creating and shaping their listeners' cultural knowledge.[96]

92 Klier 346.

93 Klier 346.

94 Quoted in Klier 346.

95 Quoted in Klier 346.

96 One way of speculating about the ways Guthrie's songs were appropriated by his contemporary audience seems to be the consideration of his contemporary listeners' responses to them, which, of course, may also be found in the textual archive of the second half of the Great Depression in the form of reviews of his performances or records and which, though certainly not the major focus of the present study, shall be touched upon as well. Such textual records are, to be sure, hardly available. Guthrie's former colleague on the radio, Maxine Dempsey, holds a huge collection of fan letters; yet, as these letters are private issues, she was, most understandably, not willing to let me have a look at them. Moreover, the existing published reviews are highly conventionalized texts and thus not very telling. After completing an analysis of the political potential of the songs in the main part of this study (cf. chapters 3.1-3.7), I will, however, briefly reflect on the actual responses to Guthrie's Dust Bowl songs in the concluding part of this study.

2.3.3 Music, Performance and the Sung Word

In his analysis of female punkrock bands of the 1990s, Neil Nehring points out that "[m]ost of the work on popular music coming out of my field, literary studies, presents a sad contrast with [the] dialectical appreciation of the relation of sound and words."[97] He goes on to complain that the majority of approaches towards the analysis of songs are "entirely devoted to the thematic content of literary texts and lyrics, [though] differences do exist, to be sure, in the tonal and rhythmic possibilities of writing and verbal performance; writing in no way has the same range."[98]

Thus, in order to gauge the potential impact of Guthrie's songs on the contemporary audience, their "privileged position in the continuing process of fashioning and refashioning consciousness, of defining possibilities of action, of shaping identities, and of shaping visions of justice and order,"[99] or, in other words, in order to reconstruct their social and cultural productivity, it is also essential to reflect on their musical and performative elements, which, I assume, contributed a lot to their poietic potential.[100] It is not only the verbal signs of the lyrics, but also the non- or extraverbal signs, i.e., the rhythmic-melodic as well as the performative aspects, which have to be taken into consideration,[101] for, as Frith has it for Rap music, the "consciousness raising function lies in its aesthetic form, in other words, and vice versa."[102] The same might be true for the traditional protest song the form of which is in itself "a socio-symbolic

97 Nehring 143.

98 Nehring 143/140.

99 Fox-Genovese 222.

100 Cf. Butler 174-79. Of course, one could argue that the relationship between verbal texts and the extraverbal contexts can also be inverted in that the lyrics of the song might well be understood as contexts for the musical and performative 'texts.' Such a dialectical "interrelatedness [...] of all texts" (Volkmann 333), which can well be regarded as contextualizing each other, would certainly accord to the New Historicist framework of my approach. Yet, as I am working in the field of literary studies, I deliberately chose to put the focus of my analysis on the verbal texts, i.e., the song lyrics.

101 Cf. Grossklaus, in Faulstich 61. Under the category of verbal signs, Grossklaus includes syntactic, grammatical as well as lexical structures and literary aesthetic features of the song lyrics. Extraverbal signs are rhythmic and melodic patterns and musical aesthetic characteristics. Faulstich adds the dimension of the performative that includes audiovisual elements like gestures and mimics.

102 Frith 18. I am indebted to Frith's enlightening study on the analysis and evaluation of popular music, which, containing material from a number of his previously published articles, provides a comprehensive overview of the topic and frames my theoretical considerations of the musical and performative dimensions of the sung word.

message, or in other terms, […] is immanently and intrinsically an ideology in its own right."[103] Following from this, an investigation into the rhythmical and melodic patterns Guthrie employed in his songs should be included in a contextualizing analysis of his songs, as "the issue in lyrical analysis is not words, but words in performance. [...] Lyrics, that is, are a form of rhetoric or oratory; we have to treat them in terms of the persuasive relationship set up between singer and listener."[104] In this persuasive relationship, in which the singer establishes a communication with his listeners, "ordinary language [is] put to extraordinary use" (168); i.e., the performer employs such devices as variation of language and pronunciation, a particular rhythm and rhyme, emphases, sighs, hesitations and changes of tone, which then function as "material ways of organizing and shaping feeling and desire (169)". Therefore, to sing words indeed means "to elevate them in some way, to make them special, to give them a new form of intensity. […] [S]inging," as Simon Frith has it, "draws a different kind of attention to the words," which are, rather unnaturally, subjected "to a control that they're not used to: they have to take their part in a rhythmic and melodic frame" (172-73).

Unlike written poetry, which, being read, allows the readers to make their own decisions about the reading speed, about word stress or the overall tone, the performance of a song does not allow such flexibility, as the listeners are confronted with preset emphases, a given melody and a specific rhythm, which, in turn, may support or suggest a particular interpretation of the song. "The point is," as Frith sums up in a syllogism which epitomizes this semantization of the musical elements of a song, "that as speakers we create meaning through stress; music creates stress; therefore, music creates meaning" (181). Following from that, he concludes that "[t]he song becomes the preferred reading of the words […]. Song words work as speech and speech acts, bearing meaning not just semantically, but also, as structures of sound that are direct signs of emotion" (181).

In order to establish a heuristic framework for the analysis of the musical components of Guthrie's songs, which certainly contributed to their potential to disseminate and perpetuate cultural knowledge, it might be worthwhile to resort to the analytical categories provided by Werner Faulstich, who differentiates between the *rhythm*, the *melody* or *harmony*

[103] Fredric Jameson, *The Political Unconscious: Narrative as a Socially Symbolic Act* (Ithaca, New York: Cornell UP, 1981) 141.

[104] Frith 166. As most of the following quotations are taken from Frith, I will give the respective page number(s) in parentheses in the text.

and the *sound* of a song.[105] The first category, *rhythm*, might be approached by taking certain factors into account, such as forms and functions of beat variations or accentuations, unusual or irregular rhythmical structures, breaks or instrumental pre-, inter- or postludes. Moreover, an important rhythmical device that should also be taken into consideration is the tempo of, or the variation of the tempo of a song. The next category for the analysis of song, *melody/harmony*, focuses on the pitch range of the song's melody, on the segmentation of the song into different melodic sections and the relationship between the arrangement of these sections and the lyrics of the song.

Apart from analyzing a song's rhythmical and melodical patterns, it is the singer's voice which deserves particular attention, as it largely determines the *sound* of a song, which constitutes the third analytical category. Questions concerning the sound register, the choice of key or modulation, the tone color, the voice's pitch, specific modes of (over)articulating certain words, phrases and sentences and variations of the singing speed might be of relevance here. The voice in punk music, to give an example, is usually characterized by features associated with low prestige accents spoken in the south of England, like low-status pronunciations coupled with nonstandard grammatical forms, which have an assertive and aggressive effect and, what is more, aid identification with and by British working-class youth.[106] Likewise, Studs Terkel, in an interview with Woody Guthrie biographer Ed Cray, pointed out that he was not surprised that Guthrie could turn an Oklahoman accent on and off. "That's like so many others during that time," he said, "Harvard men who talked like working class people, the leader of The Animals in the 1960s speaking in a Cockney accent."[107] Just as the low-status pronunciation used in English punk music, Woody Guthrie's s adoption of the Southern drawl in his songs certainly contributed to his image as a companion in misfortune among his rural audiences and, consequently, to the potential for identification provided by his songs. At the same time, as Jeff Morgan argues, "the drawl [...] served to distinguish him from urban folk stylists, like Pete Seeger and Burl Ives, who performed with soft harmony and gentle intonations."[108]

105 Cf. Faulstich.

106 Cf. Peter Trudgill, *On Dialect: Social and Geographical Perspectives* (Oxford: Basil Blackwell, 1983) 154-55.

107 Studs Terkel, interview with Ed Cray, 8 Aug. 1998 (WGA, Accessions 2004, 67.4, Box I, Folder 13).

108 Morgan 12. Interestingly, in spite of the Southwestern accent Guthrie deliberately resorted to in a number of his songs to provide his listeners with a sense of

Yet, it is not only the musical components of a song that have to be considered in a contextualizing analysis of a song. Lyrics sung in front of an audience, as Simon Frith observes, also take part of their "meaning[s] and effect[s] [...] from the performing context, from the 'live' emotional atmosphere, the immediate pleasures of identification and suspense which are, in a sense, *tangible*. [...] The performance, in other words, [...], is a necessary aspect of [the song's] 'poetic' quality."[109] Any "'act' of singing is thus always contextualized by the 'act' of performing,"[110] and, as one may add, vice versa, considering the New Historicist notion of a mutual correspondence between text and context. This implies that the success of a performance, being a social or communicative process including the singer and an audience, can only be measured by the audience's responses and again, they might vary according to the social and cognitive background of the listeners:

> If the singer's voice makes public (makes manifest, makes available) the supposed sounds of private (personal, individual) feeling, then these public gestures are consumed privately, fitted into our own narratives, our own expressive repertoires. Similarly, if all songs are narratives, if they work as mini-musicals, then their plots are a matter of interpretation both by performers attaching them to their own star stories and by listeners, putting ourselves in the picture, or, rather, placing their emotions – or expressions of emotion – in our own stories, whether directly (in this situation, in this relationship, now) or, more commonly, indirectly, laying the performance over our memories of situations and relationships.[111]

Though Woody Guthrie continually toured California and performed his songs in front of migrant audiences in the FSA camps, his popularity was largely due to his appearance on KFVD. Still, his radio program did not lack the 'live' emotional atmosphere Frith claims to be an essential characteristic of songs, as Guthrie used to play his songs 'on air.' In any case, his singing and guitar-playing might have created something that Lawrence Grossberg, in his examination of the impact of rock music, describes as a kind of affective scope which "surround[s], enfold[s] and even invade[s] [the human body] within its own rhythms and textures. It incorporates its listeners into its own spaces, transforming passive reception into active production."[112]

shared identity, his recordings are usually characterized by a very clear and distinct articulation.

109 Frith 182.
110 Frith 211.
111 Frith 211.
112 Quoted in Winter, *Die Kunst des Eigensinns* 312.

Considering the aforesaid, it should now be clear that music itself is neither reactionary nor revolutionary. It is rather a way of rendering and expressing feelings in a strong, emotional manner which, in turn, might affect people's minds; thus "[m]usic cannot be used violently," but it may "instill empathy for the cause at hand and [...] inspire the participants' [the listeners'] consciousness."[113] By creating such an emotional atmosphere, by eliciting strong emotive effects, songs and sounds are able to draw us, as Frith put it, "into affective and emotional alliances,"[114] which, in turn, provide the listeners "with an intensely subjective sense of being sociable. Whether jazz or rap for African-Americans or nineteenth century chamber music for German Jews in Israel," Frith concludes, "it both articulates and offers the immediate *experience* of collective identity."[115]

In his book *Guerilla Minstrels*, political scientist Wayne Hampton argues along similar lines, as he points out that in a song "a few simple, repetitive symbols are used to project broad, abstract ideals designed to sway the collective consciousness."[116] Analyzing Joan Baez's legendary performance of "We shall overcome" at the Washington Monument, he illustrates that

> [h]er role was symbolic. She was performing a ritualistic act intended to stir the political imagination of the audience. The tangible effect was the collective swaying of one hundred thousand people, connected by clasped hands, forming a single reified entity, singing in one voice. At that moment, they all believed they could indeed overcome.[117]

Hampton's description of the scenario clearly hints at the song's potential to provide the audience with a feeling of collective identity, a feature of the sung word which is also highlighted by Frith.

Another element of Baez's song (and probably of political songs in general), which, though not directly linked with its musical and performative dimensions, enhances its potential to create a feeling of shared identity and thus should also be reflected on theoretically, is the use of the personal pronoun 'we.' Certainly contributing to the emergence of a collective consciousness among the listeners, the pronoun in first person plural, as one could well argue, functions as a 'communal voice' that clearly separates the oppressed from the oppressors, who are fashioned

113 Hampton 56-57.
114 Frith 273.
115 Frith 273.
116 Hampton 52.
117 Hampton 53.

as the collective Other. Likewise, in many of his songs, Woody Guthrie employs the first person plural, which, as one might well assume, has a similar function in his songs. Here is one example taken from his "Dust Storm Disaster":

> The storm took place at sundown, it lasted through the night,
> When we looked out next morning, we saw a terrible sight.
> We saw outside our window where wheat fields they had grown
> Was now a rippling ocean of dust the wind had blown.[118]

In her study *Fictions of Authority: Women Writers and Narrative Voice*, Susan Lanser established a typology of forms and functions of such communal voices.[119] Though she is concerned, as the title already suggests, exclusively with novels by women writers, her theses are, nevertheless, applicable to the analysis of other texts, including Guthrie's songs. She points out that, by employing a first-person plural pronoun, the narrator "begins to adopt a collective vision, a focalizing consciousness that represents itself in [this] plural 'we.' [...] In other words, the narrator reports perceptions and feelings as if she [or he] were authorized to represent the thoughts of other characters," thereby constituting what she calls a "plural perceptual consciousness."[120] This communal focalization of the narrative voice, which can be observed in a large number of Guthrie's songs, suggests a single group consciousness and certainly adds to their potential to create a collective identity among listeners.

Moreover, the verisimilitude of his accounts of the Dust Bowl migration is underlined by another narrative strategy that needs to be elaborated on briefly: Besides the communal 'we,' Guthrie also makes use of a communal 'I.' Lanser explains the function of the first-person singular narrative as follows: "These 'singular' communal narrators are constructed through subtle but important departures from autodiegetic practices, for while the narrators retain the syntax of 'first-person' narrative, their texts avoid the markers of individuality that characterize personal voice."[121] Though Guthrie quite often uses the first person singular to sing about

[118] Woody Guthrie, "Dust Storm Disaster," quoted in Harold Leventhal and Marjorie Guthrie, eds., *The Woody Guthrie Songbook* (New York: Grosset and Dunlap, 1976) 94. In the following, whenever quoting from one of Guthrie's songs, I will only give the respective source of the quoted song without mentioning Guthrie as the author each time.

[119] Cf. Susan S. Lanser, *Fictions of Authority: Women Writers and Narrative Voice* (Ithaca: Cornell UP, 1992).

[120] Lanser 249.

[121] Lanser 241.

the lives of migrants, those sung biographies do indeed "avoid the markers of individuality." They rather portray the life of a typical farmer, a typical migrant or a typical 'Okie' – typical, of course, from Guthrie's point of view. Yet, due to his Oklahoman origin, Guthrie seemed to be a reliable authority for most of his listeners. By employing the communal 'I,' he could emphasize his ideological alliance both to his narratees and his listeners.

Considering all this, I think it is appropriate to include an analysis of what Grossklaus called the extraverbal signs of song, i.e., the various musical elements Guthrie employed to intensify his lyrics as well as the performative contexts of his songs, be it on stage or 'on air.' To be sure, Guthrie's songs will neither be regarded as elaborate pieces of music nor will there be a close musical analysis of each and every song which is going to be discussed. Consequently, musicological considerations will be of minor importance. Yet, whenever it seems appropriate, the examination of the extraverbal contexts of music and performance will be integrated into the contextualizing analyses of Guthrie's songs.

* * * * *

So far, I have developed a theoretical and methodological design which will help me to tackle Woody Guthrie's Dust Bowl songs and to relate them to their cultural contexts. As a general theoretical framework, I resort to Cultural Studies, the major concepts of which, in particular its interdisciplinarity, its understanding of culture and the consequent widening of concern, help to make evident the cultural significance of Guthrie's songs.

Among the various approaches that can be found in the admittedly wide field of Cultural Studies, I opt for New Historicism as a theoretical basis for the contextualization of Guthrie's songs. Its concept of a dialectical relationship between text and context substantiates my endeavor to show that Guthrie's songs are not only a product of contemporary circumstances, but also an active agent in shaping them.

In order to make the New Historicist approach applicable for a contextualizing analysis of Guthrie's songs, I draw on Jürgen Link's interdiscourse analysis. Conceptualized as a reintegrating interdiscourse, Guthrie's songs are thus understood to relate and combine elements and structures taken from various specialized discourses, the reconstruction of which might not only stress the songs' having been culturally produced, but might also help to get insight into contemporary beliefs and dispositions.

In order to trace those discursive elements and structures, thus reconstructing the decade's cultural knowledge, I look for intertextual references made in the songs. Therefore, I resort both to a poststructuralist understanding of intertextuality, which allows me to correlate Guthrie's songs with textual manifestations of the 1930s, and a narrower concept of intertextuality that rather focuses on the deliberate allusions and references in his songs.

The 'active audience paradigm,' which includes the recipients of songs in the process of meaning constitution, helps to create an awareness of the difference between the songs' social and cultural *potential* and their *actual* impact on the contemporary audience and enables me to formulate plausible hypotheses about the different functions of the songs within their cultural environment.

Additionally, I concern myself with the extraverbal signs of songs, which have to be taken into consideration, as they, presumably, contributed to the songs' social and cultural potential as well. In this context, I predominantly resort to Simon Frith's and Lawrence Grossberg's idea of music as a means of creating a feeling of collective identity and Fredric Jameson's concept of the semantization of form. Further I use the categories of rhythm, harmony and sound as a heuristic framework to deal with the characteristics of the sung word. Referring to Susan S. Lanser's concepts of the communal 'I' and communal 'we,' I also hypothesize about the possible functions of the first-person pronouns 'I' and 'we' as characteristic features of Guthrie's songs.

3 Renderings of the Dust Bowl Migration and the Great Depression in the Songs of Woody Guthrie

3.1 "We thought it was our judgment, we thought it was our doom": Rendering Dust and Drought as Divine Punishments

Even before the 1930s, dust storms were not anything unusual on the prairies and farmlands of the American Southwest. However, the frequency and the intensity of the storms which began to haunt the drought-stricken plains in the first half of the 1930s were unprecedented and significantly contributed to the social and economic turmoil which the country had been suffering from since 1929. Woody Guthrie rendered this ecological disaster in a number of his songs, in which the dust storms are configured as a punishment from the Almighty. In a region where religious fundamentalism deeply affected the beliefs and dispositions of the people and thus constituted a central pattern of their cultural knowledge, the interpretation of the storms as a divine sentence was, as the following contextualizing analysis of Guthrie's songs reveals, widely disseminated. It eventually sedimented in Guthrie's songs, which, in turn, provided a narrative and interpretative frame that allowed both Guthrie and his listeners to make sense of the apocalyptic scenario they were confronted with and fostered, through the depiction of a shared fate, a feeling of shared identity.

In order to uncover the ties between Guthrie's songs about the dust storms and their cultural environment, this contextualizing analysis draws mainly on eyewitness reports, on the one hand, and sermons from Protestant and Catholic authorities, on the other. The closer investigation of these two types of (inter)texts attempts to make evident that the perception and interpretation of the storms as divine punishment was not only part of the religious folklore, but also officially disseminated by clerical institutions. Focusing on Guthrie's "Talking Dust Bowl Blues," the second part of this chapter then intends to reconstruct the symbolic significance of rainfall and, more importantly, the significance of its absence on the Southwestern Plains. In so doing, it reveals how his sung narrative picks up the extreme change of climatic conditions in the middle of the 1930s as a starting point to dramatize the drought and the subsequent migration. Finally, this chapter aims at examining both the lyrical and musical means Guthrie employs to criticize those who are held responsible for the ecological and economic disaster portrayed in his songs.

* * * * *

Before Woody Guthrie experienced the economic plight of the Great Depression and the ecological catastrophe on the Southwestern Plains, he went through a private disaster, as he witnessed the gradual disintegration of his family: His sister Clara died in a fire in 1919. His father, speculating in real estate, lost the major part of his portfolio in the bust season in Oklahoma. Their small house in Okemah burnt down in yet another fire and, most significantly, in 1927, his mother had to be admitted to the state asylum of Norman, Oklahoma, as she showed the first symptoms of Huntington's chorea,[1] the illness that also befell Woody Guthrie and eventually led to his physical and mental decay four decades later. Woody Guthrie had a "deep devotion"[2] for his mother, as a former neighbor of the Guthries in Okemah remembers, at least until the chorea began to disarrange her mind and she "turn[ed] into another person,"[3] as Guthrie himself later commented on her continuously changing behavior. "She would be alright for a while and treat us kids as good as any mother," Guthrie remembered, "and all at once it would start coming over her, and it come [sic] by slow degrees."[4] Despite his mother's growing physical and mental disintegration, which alienated her from the family, Guthrie was deeply affected by her tragic fate, as it was she who, time and again, had given him and his siblings emotional support in their otherwise shattered childhood – more often than not by singing traditional songs to and with them.[5] In his autobiography,[6] Guthrie recalls his mother lulling him to sleep when he was a little child:

> 'Sing to me,' I whispered to Mama. She had already been rocking me back and forth, humming the tune to an old song. 'What do you want me to sing?' 'That. That song.' 'The name of the song is "The Sherman Cyclone."' "Sing that.' And so she sang it:

1 Huntington's chorea is an inherited disease, which affects the central nervous system and results in movement disorder and progressive dementia.

2 Quoted in Cray 13.

3 Woody Guthrie, *Bound for Glory: The Hard-Driving, Truth-Telling Autobiography of America's Great Poet-Folk Singer* (1943; New York: Penguin, 1983) 136.

4 Guthrie, *Bound for Glory*136.

5 The biographical information is taken from Cray.

6 Guthrie, *Bound for Glory* 88.

You could see the storm approaching
And its cloud looked deathlike black
And it was through our little city
That it left its deathly track.

Nora Guthrie sang a song to her son which was then widely known as a traditional in Oklahoma. Some fifteen years later, in the middle of the Great Depression, Woody Guthrie wrote down the whole song in one of his notebooks. Let us consider the complete lyrics of "The Sherman Texas Cyclone" as put down by Guthrie:

The little Town of Sherman
A prosperous farming town
Its Fate was doomed to Scatter
Before the sun went down.

You could see the cloud approaching!
The storm looked death-like black
And thru our little city
It left its dreadful track.

The fathers warned their families
To shelter they must fly
This was the worst of cyclones
To ever fill the sky.

Their homes they built by farming
This fertile valley's land;
This storm it gave no warning,
Left many an empty hand.

You could see the storm approaching!
The cloud looked deathlike black;
It ripped apart their families
And left their homesteads wrecked.

O' when you count your Blessings,
Your loved Ones and your home;
You're never sure of living
To see the morning Sun.

A storm may overtake you,
Sometimes they never warn;
So build your house so solid
That you'll go thru the Storm.

You could see the storm approaching!
The cloud looked deathlike black!

Good friends ran out to shelter,
But some will never come back.[7]

From the perspective of one of its inhabitants, the song configures the fate of the little Texan town Sherman, which is haunted by a devastating cyclone. In an apocalyptic scenario, the "deathlike black" storm obscures the sun and, as phrases like "Its Fate was doomed to Scatter" or "O' when you count your blessings" imply, makes the speaker of the song think of the final judgment – hence, as one may argue, the allegorizing tone he adopts in the penultimate verse, which gives general advice on how to survive storms of any kind. The cyclone hits the prosperous farming town in the middle of a fertile valley without warning and ruins the basis for the people's livelihood by destroying their farmland and leaving "their homesteads wrecked." Moreover, by ripping apart families, it takes away the last institution which might have been able to provide protection and shelter in such a hopeless situation.

In his own notes on the song, which he probably used in order to introduce it when he was on the air, Guthrie elaborates on the context of the song. He points out that "in about 1895 one of the fiercest, blackest, most destructive cyclones in all history" all of a sudden "shattered and scattered the peaceful little farming town of Sherman, Texas, destroying everything in its wake, grinding all into its footprints, wrecking homes and killing untold numbers of pioneer settlers in that country."[8] Their "fertile valley's land"[9] was immediately turned into a desert, where no one could ever make a living again. Yet, interestingly enough, Guthrie does not get tired of stressing that after all this hardship caused by the cyclone, the city of Sherman "is a prosperous town [now], the home of many famous products and manufacturers, and famous for a number of things."[10] Adopting the allegorical tone of the song's last verses, Guthrie ends his comment by once again emphasizing that "the [personified]

7 WGA, Notebooks I, Notebook 4, 10. Guthrie's song might well be a variation of another well-known traditional called "Cyclone Blues," which is quoted in John Lomax, ed., *Cowboy Songs and Other Frontier Ballads* (New York: Macmillan, 1922) 294-95. Its lyrics are as follows: "I uster own the Double D; / I'm punchin' steers today, Because a cyclone comes along / And blowas my ranch away; / It struck the first of April, / An' as it's goin' hence, / It takes my barns and 'dobes / An' a mile er two of fence. / It takes the steers. I'm sayin', / An' my cows an' hawses, too, / It never leaves me nothin' / But the mortgage, which is due; / An' that's the why I'm punchin' / On the Lazy B today, / A-payin' fer the chattels / What the cyclone blowed away."

8 WGA, Notebooks I, Notebook 4, 10.

9 WGA, Notebooks I, Notebook 4, 10.

10 WGA, Notebooks I, Notebook 4, 10.

Faith and Energy got busy and built that little town back better than it was before the storm struck."[11] Yet, why would Woody Guthrie write down one of his favorite songs from his childhood, and why does he end his notes on a song about such a disaster with such an optimistic coda?

Guthrie's recalling the old song might well have been due to the series of devastating dust storms that had started hitting the Great Plains in the early 1930s, reminding him of the scenario portrayed in the song about the cyclone that struck the little Texan town of Sherman. These storms, which were caused by an exhaustion of subsoil moisture and, subsequently, a dramatic increase in topsoil erosion due to an unbroken drought starting in 1931, rolled over portions of western Kansas, southwestern Nebraska, southeastern Colorado, northeastern New Mexico and the Oklahoma and Texas panhandle. And the situation even worsened through the end of the 1930s. "Across eroding fields," historian Brad Lookingbill observes, "there were twenty-two dust storms in 1934 and as many as seventy-two in 1937."[12] "Between 1933 and 1938," as Frank L. Stallings puts it in his account of the Dust Bowl, "dust storms, especially in the spring, were so common that there was even a kind of resignation that it would be over 'someday.'"[13]

On April, 14th, 1935, one of the most terrible 'black dusters,' as the storms were often referred to, hit the area of eastern Colorado, southwestern Kansas, the Oklahoma and Texas panhandles, and northeastern New Mexico and destroyed over five million acres of wheat.[14] The day brought a calm dawn across the Southwestern Plains and most people started recovering from a number of previous storms, feeling assured that peace and safety had returned to their country. Yet, in mid-afternoon, the sun was eclipsed again and suddenly a horrible dust storm struck the already drought-stricken people. Though everybody, after weeks of dust since March 1st, prayed for rain, "there came a deluge of dust which rolled and boiled like the smoke of a gigantic oil fire," reported the

11 WGA, Notebooks I, Notebook 4, 10.

12 Brad D. Lookingbill, *Dust Bowl, USA: Depression America and the Ecological Imagination, 1929-1941* (Ohio: Ohio UP) 22. I am indebted to Brad Lookingbill's magnificent and enriching studies on Great Plains culture, especially on religious fundamentalism, as they give enlightening insights into the contexts of the 1930s and provide a lot of primary sources which were helpful for the contextualization of Guthrie's songs.

13 Frank L. Stallings Jr, *Black Sunday: The Great Dust Storm of April 14, 1935* (Austin, Texas: Eakin Press, 2001) 1.

14 Cf. Stallings 2; cf. also Donald Worster, *Dust Bowl: The Southern Plains in the 1930s* (1979; New York/Oxford: Oxford UP, 2004) 18ff.

Amarillo Daily News the following day.[15] "The impact is like a shovelful of fine sand flung against the face," Avis D. Carlson wrote in an article which appeared in the *New Republic*, rendering a horror scenario which could just as well be from the script of an Emmerich movie: "People caught in their own yards grope for the doorstep. Cars come to a standstill, for no light in the world can penetrate that swirling murk. […] It is becoming real. The poetic uplift of spring fades into a phantom of the storied past. The nightmare is becoming life."[16]

When the dust had cleared on the following day, *Associated Press* reporter Robert Geiger, writing for the *Washington Evening Star*, coined the term 'Dust Bowl,' pointing out that there were only "three little words achingly familiar on the Western farmer's tongue, [which] rule life in the dust bowl of the continent – if it rains."[17] However, it did not rain for the rest of the year, and the continuation of the dust storms shattered the hopes of the Southwestern farmers. Eyewitness Caroline Henderson describes the dust storm disaster in an article published in the *Atlantic Monthly*, shortly before it was sent to Henry A. Wallace, then Secretary of Agriculture, as a letter in July 1935:

> There are days when for hours at a time we cannot see the windmill fifty feet from the kitchen door. There are days when for briefer periods one cannot distinguish the windows from the solid wall because of the solid blackness of the raging storm. Only in some Inferno-like dream could any one visualize the terrifying lurid red overspreading the sky when portions of Texas are 'on the air.' This wind-driven dust, fine as the finest flour, penetrates wherever air can go. [...] 'Dust to eat,' and dust to breathe and dust to drink. Dust in the beds and in the flour bin, on dishes and walls and windows, in the hair and eyes and ears and teeth and throats, to say nothing of the heaped up accumulation on floors and window sills after one of the bad days.[18]

Henderson's mostly polysyndetic enumeration of the places where dust can be found instead of vital necessities like food, water and air puts emphasis on the desolate and hopeless situation, in which the dust has

15 Stallings 83.

16 <http://www.livinghistoryfarm.org/farminginthe30s/water_02.html>, 30 Aug. 2006.

17 Quoted in Lookingbill, *Dust Bowl, USA* 31.

18 Caroline Henderson, *Letters from the Dust Bowl*, ed. Alvin O. Turner (Norman, Oklahoma: U of Oklahoma P, 2001) 140-41. In the introduction to the collection of Henderson's letters, Alvin O. Turner states that "Caroline Henderson has been recognized for more than fifty years for the quality of her depictions of life on the Great Plains. A number of articles published between 1931 and 1937 in *Atlantic Monthly* and elsewhere drew national attention to the farmer's plight during the Depression and dust bowl era" (Henderson 3).

either destroyed or polluted what is essential for living.[19] Not only did it spoil the basic prerequisites for farming; it also caused numerous outbreaks of illnesses, such as measles, strep throat, and, first and foremost, bronchial diseases colloquially referred to as 'dust pneumonia,'[20] That the dust deeply affected private life and individual health is also depicted in one of Guthrie's songs, called "Dust Pneumonia Blues." Here is just the last verse, which, in a very ironic manner, reveals in how far the dust has replaced the essential necessities of life:

> Down in Texas my gal fainted in the rain,
> Down in Texas my gal fainted in the rain,
> I throwed a bucket o' dirt in her face just to bring her back again.[21]

Being a very rare occurrence, rain, as the first two lines imply, has become something that makes people faint, since they are not used to it anymore. Instead of water, they are now relying upon dirt, which, as the last line suggests, has become an adequate means to recover one's strength. The sense of comic relief expressed in Guthrie's song, in which nature is turned topsy-turvy, as the essential is exchanged for the unbearable, puts emphasis on the fact that such a serious disease as dust pneumonia has indeed become something people have learned to live with. Thus, though Guthrie resorts to a different rhetorical strategy, his highly ironic lines definitely take up the mood of Henderson's account of the Dust Bowl, in which the dust has become a constituent of everyday life.

However, Henderson's account is also interesting in yet another respect: her choice of words in describing the "raging" dust storm, comparing it to an "Inferno-like dream," implies that such a scenario of extraordinary scale must have been perceived as something supernatural. One of Woody Guthrie's sung descriptions of the storm of April 14th, 1935, called "The Dust Storm Disaster," interprets the natural disaster along similar lines:

> On the fourteenth day of April in nineteen thirty five,
> There struck the worst of dust storms that ever filled the sky;
> You could see that dust storm coming, it looked so awful black,
> And through our little city, it left a dreadful track.

19 Another of Henderson's letters implies that it was the dusty air that caused the most dramatic problems. In order to "avoid inhaling the irritating dust", she explains that they were "wearing [their] shade hats, with handkerchiefs tied over [their] faces and Vaseline in [their] nostrils" (Henderson 147).

20 Cf. Lookingbill, "Dusty Apocalypse" 405.

21 Michael Kleff, ed., *Hard Travelin': Das Woody Guthrie Buch* (Heidelberg: Palmyra, 2002) 252.

From Oklahoma City to the Arizona line,
Dakota and Nebraska to the lazy Rio Grande,
It fell across our city like a curtain of black rolled down,
We thought it was our judgement, we thought it was our doom.

The radio reported, we listened with alarm,
The wild and windy actions of this great mysterious storm;
From Albuquerque and Clovis, and all New Mexico,
They said it was the blackest that they had ever saw.

From Old Dodge City, Kansas, the dust had rung their knell,
And a few more comrades sleeping on top of old Boot Hill.
From Denver, Colorado, they said it blew so strong,
They thought that they could hold out, but didn't know how long.

Our relatives were huddled into their oil boom shacks,
The children they was crying as it whistled through the cracks.
The family it was crowded into the parlor room,
They thought the Lord was coming, they thought it was their doom.[22]

Guthrie's song is, most obviously, a rewriting of "The Sherman Texas Cyclone" cited above.[23] Following, in most respects, the mode of emplotment of the pretext, it describes the dreadful effects of the dust storm of April, 14th, on the Southwestern farmers, their land and their families. "Like a curtain of black rolled down" the storm suffocates everything in

22 Alan Lomax, Woody Guthrie and Pete Seeger, eds., *Hard-Hitting Songs for Hard-Hit People* (New York: Oak Publications, 1967) 218-19.

23 Guthrie even used the tune of the old song, a recorded version of which is still available in the online collection *Voices from the Dust Bowl. The Charles L. Todd and Robert Sonkin Migrant Worker Collection 1940-1941* at the American Folklife Center of the Library of Congress, <http://memory.loc.gov/cgi-bin/query/D?toddbib:6:.temp/~ammem_SBD8::e>, 30 Aug. 2006. The collection also holds another version of the lyrics as written down in 1940 by Jim Holbert, a migrant worker from the Farm Security Administration Camp in California: "Kind friends, if you will listen / A story I will tell / 'Tis of the great tornado / You all remember well. / It reached the town of Sherman / On the fifteenth day of May / And a portion of our city / Was completely swept away. / The people gay and happy / In their cozy little homes / They little thought so shortly / They'd be forced to meet their doom. / We saw the storm approaching / The cloud looked awfully black / And through our little city / It made a fearful track. / We saw the lightning streaming / And heard the thunder roar / It was the shortest moment / The story soon was told. / We heard the crash of timber / Of buildings tumbling down, / 'Twould melt the hardest-hearted / To hear the dreadful sound" (<http://memory.loc.gov/cgi-bin/query/r?ammem/todd:@field (DOCID +st101>, 30 Aug. 2006).

its way, leaves a track of destruction behind and forces the people to hide in buildings which they believe can withstand the strong wind.

However, in contrast to the model text Guthrie drew from, which predominantly employs a third person narrative that provides a rather distanced account of the events in Sherman, Guthrie manages to establish the feeling of collective experience by inserting a communal "we" or "our" respectively. Whereas in "The Sherman Texas Cyclone," the speaker only uses a first-person pronoun once, when he points out that the storm went "thru our little city"; the speaker of Guthrie's song uses a first-person plural pronoun whenever he refers to the little town he inhabits, describing, for instance, that "we thought it was our judgement, we thought it was our doom," or stating that "we listened with alarm." He is thus not an external observer, but a part of the community, one of those whose land was taken away and whose family had to suffer from the devastating storm. By employing a first-person plural pronoun, the speaker, as Susan Lanser puts it, "begins to adopt a collective vision, a focalizing consciousness that represents itself in [this] plural 'we.' [...] In other words, [the speaker] reports perceptions and feelings as if she [or he] were authorized to represent the thoughts of other characters," thereby constituting what Lanser calls a "plural perceptual consciousness."[24] This communal focalization of the narrative voice suggests a single group consciousness and certainly adds to the song's potential to create a collective identity.

Moreover, the collective experience of the dust storm rendered in Guthrie's song is no longer restricted to a particular town, as it was in the traditional pretext. Though the song's depiction centers on one "little town" in the American Southwest, it is made clear that the storm must have had enormous proportions, as it was seen and experienced in a number of cities and states, reaching "[f]rom Oklahoma City to the Arizona line, Dakota and Nebraska to the lazy Rio Grande," "[f]rom Albuquerque and Clovis, and all New Mexico," "[f]rom Old Dodge City, Kansas," to Denver in Colorado. That this enumeration of places was supposed to hint at the gigantic scope of the storm becomes evident as soon as we consider another version of the song, in which "our little city" in the first verse is replaced by "our mighty nation."[25] Thus, by configuring a collective experience which exceeded regional boundaries and which was not tied to a specific place, Guthrie's song certainly appealed to the majority of his (migrant) listeners, who, though coming from different areas of the American Southwest, shared the same lot.

24 Lanser 249.
25 Leventhal and Guthrie 93.

Therefore they could easily identify with the people from the 'little town' which, of course, could have been any town in the drought-stricken area of the Dust Bowl.

Besides emphasizing the collective experience of the storm, Guthrie's "Dust Storm Disaster" also features the people's interpretation of the natural catastrophe as a divine punishment. Thus, just like in its pretext, "The Sherman Texas Cyclone," the awful blackness and the gigantic proportions of the storm immediately make the people in the song think the worst: They interpret the ecological disaster in terms of St. John's revelation as foreboding their eventual doom. Though "The Sherman Texas Cyclone" also employs imagery that evokes visions of the final judgment, the apocalyptic scenario created in Guthrie's song cannot, however, be exclusively traced back to this particular pretext. As Caroline Henderson's statement above already implies, the interpretation of the dust storms as acts of the Almighty, seemed to be quite common among Guthrie's contemporaries. Thus, the day after the major storm on April, 14th, 1935, a *Kansas Liberal News* headline noted "Some People Thought the End of the World was at Hand when Every Trace of Daylight was Obliterated at 4:00 p.m."[26] Ruby Burke, an eyewitness from Beaver, Oklahoma, recollects her memories of the 'black duster' approaching her hometown:

> As I said, this was a beautiful Sunday afternoon, until this came up. Well, during the meantime, we had a church meeting for the elders at the church, and they became so frightened, one of my friends told me, she said, […] 'they thought it was the end of the world.'[27]

Fifteen-year-old Ida Mae Norman, another eyewitness who experienced the extraordinary dust storm in mid-April 1935, recalls the event and points out that "[she] was so frightened. [She] thought the world had come to an end"[28] and interpreted the dust storm as a "signal for Armageddon."[29] John Gikas remembers that he and his uncle "were up on the north plains, 12 miles north of Borger, hunting rabbits"[30] when the storm suddenly approached them: "It just looked like a curtain, a rolling cur-

26 Stallings 88.

27 Stallings 13.

28 Quoted in Lookingbill, "'A God-Forsaken Place'" 273.

29 Quoted in Lookingbill, "'A God-Forsaken Place'" 273. The biblical story of the seven angels pouring out their "vials of the wrath of God upon the earth" at Armageddon is found in Revelation 16.

30 John Gikas, interview with Ed Cray, 14 Mar. 1999 (WGA, Accessions 2004, 67.4, Box 1, Folder 11).

tain, coming toward us, [...] a rolling, black cloud coming across the prairie,"[31] Gikas elaborates and points out that they drove home immediately and, the moment they arrived, started to pray. He explains: "My uncle's family were very, very religious. They were Pentecostal. And they thought it was the end of the world. They surely did."[32] He recalls them saying: "Let's all gather around the bed, and pray to God for forgiveness of our sins."[33] Delores Marie Wilmot from the Oklahoma Panhandle recalled her experiences with the "deathlike black cloud," or, in Guthrie's words, with the "curtain of black rolled down," as follows:

> We thought the end of the world was surely coming, you know, because, well, we went to church all of the time and they had these traveling evangelists, and they preached the old fire and everything else was going to fall on you anytime; and I used to sit there bug-eyed and so scared of what the Lord was doing or going to do to us. And so I thought boy, here it's come. [...] And I wasn't the only one because, well, I was just a kid but there was a lot of adults that thought this was it.[34]

As the above reports imply, the notion that the dust storms were acts of divine judgment was indeed widespread among the people of the American Southwest, a region which has always been the epicenter of American Protestantism.[35] There, the people's perception of dramatic ecological and economical shifts was colored by a particular religious folklore, according to which social and natural misconditions were interpreted as punishments from the Almighty. "[I]ndividuals," as Brad Lookingbill put it, "saw omens of disaster as increasing trials which would precede the imminent return of Christ in judgment and salvation. [...] Scrambling for a piece of stable land, [they] often linked together the economic downturn and environmental hazards and recognized the dirty thirties as

31 John Gikas, interview with Ed Cray.

32 John Gikas, interview with Ed Cray. Pentecostalism is a radical Protestant movement, which highlights the emotional appeal of religion and puts a strong emphasis on miracles and supernatural gifts. Cf. James N. Gregory, *American Exodus: The Dust Bowl Migration and Okie Culture in California* (New York/ Oxford: Oxford UP, 1989) 200ff.; cf. also F.L. Cross and Elizabeth. A. Livingstone, eds., *Oxford Dictionary of the Christian Church*. (Oxford/New York: Oxford UP, 1983) 1062.

33 WGA, Accessions 2004, 67.4, Box 1, Folder 11.

34 Quoted in Lookingbill, "'A God-Forsaken Place'" 279.

35 The fact that April 14th was Palm Sunday, which is, according to Christian belief, the beginning of the Holy Week and a "commemoration of ritual sacrifice" (Lookingbill, *Dust Bowl, USA* 31), during which sinners were reconciled, might have strengthened many people's notion that the dust storm was a divine act.

the greatest tribulation of their lives."[36] Guthrie digested this attitude in his musical renderings of the storms. "That dry spell killed my crops, boys,"[37] he proclaims in one of his songs, implying that the ongoing drought on the Southwestern Plains is indeed something supernatural, something beyond man's control. Another of his songs, called "Dry Spell on the Plains," uses a similar imagery right from the beginning:

> I was a-grubbin' on a piece of land
> When this dry spell hit these plains,
> Raisin' up some crops t'pay my debts I owe;
> That ole dry dust-cloud come a-rollin';
> Wife, she prayed, and our kids all bawlin'
> When we fought this awful dry spell on the plains.[38]

The speaker of the song, a debt-ridden farmer, describes how the dust storms made his wife pray and his children cry,[39] as they faced the "dry dust-cloud" that approached their farm. Characterized as a "dry spell," the dust is translated into an image with metaphysical connotations, calling forth notions of the Great Plains as a god-forsaken, cursed place, where the lives of the people have become a never-ending and hopeless struggle against the forces of nature. And again, just like in his "Dust Storm Disaster," Guthrie utilizes a first-person perspective. This time, however, he uses the singular form, employing a speaker which might well be the prototypical farmer on the Southwestern Plains, whose farmland is taken away by the dust and the drought and whose family is both physically and mentally exhausted. Avoiding the markers of individuality, the song thus provides potential for identification with its listeners and emphasizes Woody Guthrie's ideological alliance both to his narratees and his audience.

Guthrie's "So Long, It's Been Good To Know Yuh"("Dusty Old Dust"), a song which was to become one of his most famous Dust Bowl Ballads, adds further dramatic potential to the people's general notion of the dust storms as indications of the imminent end of the world. In the song, friends and family members bid each other farewell, convinced that they may only meet again in the afterlife:

36 Lookingbill, "'A God-Forsaken Place'" 273-74.

37 "Dust Can't Kill Me" (Kleff 58).

38 Kleff 130.

39 According to the OED, "to bawl" means to cry loudly and roughly (<http:// dictionary.oed.com/cgi/findword?query_type=word&queryword=bawl&find.x=15 &find.y=14>, 22 Sept. 2006).

I've sung this song but I'll sing it again,
Of the place that I lived in the wild windy plains,
In the month called April, the County called Gray,
And here's what all of the people there say:

So long it's been good to know yuh;
So long it's been good to know yuh;
So long it's been good to know yuh.
This dusty old dust is a-getting' my home,
And I've got to be drifting along.[40]

Once again, the speaker of the song is not an external observer, but one of the local residents who also fell victim to the dust storm on April, 14th, 1935. That he, as such, seems to be a reliable authority whose renderings of the dust storms are based on personal experience, is already implied in the song's first line, which hints at the fact that he has repeatedly sung, or rather, has been requested to sing his song before. In the following verses, he gives an account of the people's first reactions to the storm, changing the first-person singular "I" to the plural form "we," thus underlining his affiliation to the local community:

We talked of the end of the world and then
We'd sing a song and then sing it again,
We'd set [sic] for an hour and not say a word,
And then these words would be heard: [...]

The telephone rang and it jumped off the wall
And that was the preacher a making his call
He said, 'Kind friend, this might be the end,
You've got your last chance for salvation of sin'

The churches was jammed, the churches was packed,
That dusty old dust storm blowed so black
That the preacher could not read a word of his text,
So he folded his specs, and he took up collection, said:

So long it's been good to know yuh;
So long it's been good to know yuh;
So long it's been good to know yuh.
This dusty old dust is a-gettin' my home,
And I've got to be drifting along.[41]

40 Lomax, Guthrie and Seeger 227.
41 Lomax, Guthrie and Seeger 227.

As the song suggests, even the church itself, represented by the preacher, proclaimed that the end of the world was nigh.[42] Resorting to the same farewell as the people in his parish, the preacher expresses his solidarity with his congregation and, at least implicitly, admits that he, just like the people he is supposed to take care of, is finally at a loss as to what to do next. The beginning of his sermon reveals that he interprets the storms as a punishment from the Almighty, which, in turn, implies that the people must have, in some way or other, deviated from proper Christian conduct. And indeed, in the aftermath of the April 14th duster, which can certainly be regarded as the climax of a seemingly never-ending series of black blizzards, evangelists never tired of emphasizing that the dust storms were self-inflicted. One minister of the Methodist Episcopal Church in Meade, Kansas, pointed out that, by the storm, "[w]e are reminded very forcibly of the greatness of our sin, and, at the same time, of the greatness of God's love and kindness toward us. [...] We also realize that we have deserved nothing but damnation on account of our sin."[43]

Already in 1932, a Southern Baptist convention resolution stated that "[t]he nations that forget God shall not prosper."[44] Another low church denomination that propagated the idea that the economic depression, including the dust storms in the American Southwest, was an act of divine judgment to punish the American people, was the so-called Moody fundamentalism. In their party organ, the *Moody Bible Institute Monthly*, they emphasized already in 1933 that "suffering, privations, depressions and all manner of catastrophies and troubles are to be taken as signs of the 'last days.'"[45] An attempt to make sense of the economic plight in the 1930s was provided by the following editorial written by a pious Methodist and entitled "Depression Tragedies," which appeared in a Kansas newspaper:

42 Whether the preacher really believes in this folk eschatology remains doubtful. One might well argue that he only exploits the common notion of a divine sentence in order to line his own pockets. Folding his specs under the pretext that he "could not read a word of his text" due to the dust that, assumedly, has also invaded the church, he starts to "[take] up collection". Cf. also Jackson 55-56, who quotes another version of the song, in which the preacher admits that he has "a cut rate on salvation and sin." However, it still seems plausible that not only the 'plain folks,' but also the clergical institutions might have interpreted the dust storms as a divine judgement, considering the cultural significance of religious fundamentalism on the Southwestern Plains (cf. Lookingbill, "Dusty Apocalpyse," "'A God-Forsaken Place,'" *Dust Bowl, USA*).

43 Quoted in Lookingbill, "'A God-Forsaken Place'" 278.

44 Quoted in Lookingbill, "'A God-Forsaken Place'" 278.

45 Samuel C. Kincheloe, *Research Memorandum on Religion in the Depression* (New York: Arno Press, 1972) 85.

> Man seems to have made a terrible failure, and sin and riotous spending, and living in pleasure, and forgetting God, has brought on God's judgments on our nation, by great areas of drought, and withholding rain, to add to the miseries of a great nation, full of pride, sin, adultery and forgetting God.[46]

The Southwesterners' "terrible failure" was explicated in further detail in an article published in the *Catholic Advance*, which admonished the farmers to revive traditional farming, since, as the article argues, they thoughtlessly employed destructive agricultural practices: by radically overplowing and overworking the God-given land they were turning it into a desert, which could well be compared to the "great Gobi desert in China [which] was once a fertile country."[47] Moreover, not only the Southwestern farmers, but the whole "nation, full of pride, sin, adultery," is said to have deviated from Christian doctrine, no longer leading a life abstaining from all "riotous spending," "living in pleasure," and, just like Cain, they are accused of having forgotten God. Interestingly enough, such accusations seemed to go hand in hand with contemporary sociological findings which claim that the economic depression of the 1930s was preceded by a religious one. Thus, already in 1929, Walter M. Horton observed that "[t]he rapid subsidence of the [First World] war spirit led to a wave of spiritual depression and religious skepticism, widespread and devastating,"[48] which, in turn, led to low church attendance and a low prestige of the church in the following years; "[r]eligion," as Robert T. Handy has it, "was often viewed with a negative if not a hostile eye,"[49] a phenomenon which eventually resulted in a kind of spiritual dryness that continued through the Depression years.

According to Reverend Mark A. Dawber, the drought of the 1930s was "a real test of Christian faith,"[50] which, as one may add, could only be passed if people simply went to church more often. And indeed, though mainstream Protestantism certainly suffered from an "internal Protestant depression," fundamentalist sects gained importance and membership grew rapidly in the 1930s.[51] Thus, Brad Lookingbill observes that "a few new Christian churches experienced dramatic surges in membership and participation. The Assemblies of God reached 148,043 members in the

46 Quoted in Lookingbill, *Dust Bowl, USA* 25-26.
47 Quoted in Lookingbill, *Dust Bowl, USA* 27.
48 Quoted in Robert T. Handy, *The American Religious Depression, 1925-1935* (Philadelphia: Fortress Press, 1968) 8.
49 Handy 9.
50 Quoted in Lookingbill, "'A God-Forsaken Place'" 275.
51 Handy 15.

entire Southwest by 1936, a 208 percent increase from 1926."[52] He concludes that "[b]y 1936, over one third of the total population of the southern Great Plains maintained church membership, and low church Protestant denominations dominated religious life there."[53] And it was these low church denominations, though certainly not all of them, which propagated what Lookingbill calls a 'folk eschatology,'[54] according to which the people on the Plains were to suffer from the wrath of God as a punishment for their misbehavior.

Yet, it was not only the people's forgetting God that had "brought on God's judgement on [the] nation."[55] God's anger was also stirred by their giving in to the pleasures of the 1920s boom years, symbolically dancing around the golden calf. Let us once again consider the editorial of the *Catholic Advance* cited above, in which the author alludes to yet another biblical precedent:

> The plagues that overran Egypt in the days of the stubborn Pharohs [sic] are classics in the Scriptures. God punished Egypt with the plagues because the Egyptians had made slaves of an entire race of people and because Pharoh would not accept Moses as God's prophet. We have Pharoh's [sic] today, too many of them, and nations which promote a bad species of slavery. For instance, all the so-called civilized nations of earth are slaves to money, slaves to power, slaves to pleasure.[56]

The pharaohs of today the author refers to may well be the then recently established land companies which represented an economic system based on the ideology of laisser-faire capitalism, which was, as it is insinuated, undoubtedly as inconsiderate as the Egyptian ruler. Just as the Pharaoh had made slaves of the Hebrew people in spite of their having lived peacefully in Egypt since Joseph's arrival, the capitalist order, based on money, power and the gratification of the baser instincts, is said to have enslaved the Southwestern farmers by exploiting their dependence on bank loans and by eventually depriving them of their land.

Another 'sin' that, according to many Southwestern farmers, might have stirred up the wrath of the Almighty was the agricultural program of President Roosevelt's New Deal, in particular the so-called Agricultural Adjustment Act (AAA) of 1933, which forced the farmers to destroy their crops and livestock in order to force an increase of prices for

52 Lookingbill, "'A God-Forsaken Place'" 275.
53 Lookingbill, "'A God-Forsaken Place'" 276.
54 Cf. Lookingbill, "'A God-Forsaken Place,'" "'The Living and the Dead Land.'"
55 Quoted in Lookingbill, *Dust Bowl, USA* 25-26.
56 Quoted in Lookingbill, *Dust Bowl, USA* 28.

agricultural commodities. Though the stated aim of this program was to stabilize the nation's agriculture, it was not well accepted, as the large-scale destruction of food in a time when a significant majority of the American people were suffering from poverty and malnourishment was a rather grotesque strategy. Such "unpardonable sins of destroying crops and livestock when millions were on the verge of starvation,"[57] as one Kansas farmer put it, most probably referring to the AAA, must have caused the divine uproar which, for most of his contemporaries, bore strong resemblances to a biblical plague.

It is the above quotation by the editor of the Catholic Advance which continues this analogy by suggesting a parallel between the migration of thousands and thousands of 'Dust Bowlers' to California and the Hebrews' exodus from Egypt. The dust that filtered into every house and settled on everything is thus interpreted as one of the Egyptian plagues, in which the dust became lice that settled on man and beast:

> And the Lord said unto Moses, Say unto Aaron, Stretch out thy rod, and smite the dust of the land, that it may become lice throughout all the land of Egypt. And they did so; for Aaron stretched out his hand with his rod, and smote the dust of the earth, and it became lice in man, and in beast; all the dust of the land became lice throughout all the land of Egypt.[58]

Making the night as black as the plague of darkness in Egypt and ruining the farmers' crops like the plague of hail, the dust storms carried enormous mythological potential, which was also drawn upon by Woody Guthrie, to come back to the Dust Bowl balladeer. He also hinted at the biblical dimensions of the black blizzards and, in an interview recorded for the Library of Congress, recalls his immediate response to the storm on April, 14th, 1935:

> A whole bunch of us was standing just outside of town. We watched the dust storm come up like the red sea closing in on the Israel children. It got so black, when that thing hit we all run into the house.[59]

Though Guthrie does not explicitly allude to the Egyptian plagues when talking about the storm, he nevertheless associates it with the relevant biblical passage about the exodus of the Hebrew people from the land of the Pharaoh. Just as they had been challenged by various dangers on their way to Canaan, the migrants are afflicted by hazardous incidents on

57 Quoted in Lookingbill, "'A God-Forsaken Place'" 282.

58 *The Bible: Authorized King James Version. With Apocrypha*, ed. Robert Caroll and Stephen Prickett (New York/Oxford: Oxford UP, 1998) Exodus, 8, 16-17.

59 Quoted in Partridge 48.

the way to *their* land of milk and honey, leaving behind a barren and infertile wasteland that, only about ten years before, had provided them with all they needed. In another of his Dust Bowl songs written, according to Guthrie's notes, "between June and August in the year of 1938," the Okie troubadour drives his point home more explicitly when he sings that "[i]n the jungle and the trees / day you melt and night you freeze / like the Christians in the Bible / We're the Dust Bowl refugees."[60]

One might well argue that the analogy between the migrants and the "Israel children" serves a similar purpose as did the interpretation of the dust storms as a divine act and reinforces the eschatological reading of the Dust Bowl disaster. Emplotted along the lines of the biblical story of the Hebrews' exodus from Egypt, the natural catastrophe and the subsequent migration were thus suggested to become comprehensible. At the same time, the identification of the migrants with the people of Israel certainly contributed to establishing a feeling of collective identity: The uprooted and dislocated farmers were thus provided both with a set of images and analogies taken from popular religious myths and with a comparatively stringent narrative that helped to explain, to understand and to overcome their plight on the Great Plains. Their religiosity provided them, as Garin Burbank puts it, "with a system of inherited ideas that was their habitual resort when they tried to explain the rights and the wrongs, the good fortune and the bad, the beauties and the terrors that they encountered in this life."[61] As an "enveloping ideology," Protestantism "gave meaning to the world of the country folk,"[62] and, as one might want to add, the necessary staying power to go through their distress.

And indeed, some people found the strength to cope with the almost hopeless situation, as they revised their fatalistic accounts of the storms and began to view them as a chance to overcome their spiritual dryness. "When I see a dust storm coming, I feel that it is God's will – so I try to like it," one pious woman stated.[63] Thus, along with the interpretation of the disaster as a divine punishment came the belief in eventual resurrection and the hope for a better future, for, as John L. McCarty had it in his "A Tribute to Our Dust Storms," "the God capable of such gigantic destructive demonstrations of nature can be just as calm and tender as

60 WGA, Songs I, Box 1, Folder 7.

61 Garin Burbank, *When Farmers Voted Red: The Gospel of Socialism in the Oklahoman Countryside* (Westport, Connecticut: Greenwood Press, 1977) 15.

62 Burbank 15.

63 Quoted in Lookingbill, "'A God-Forsaken Place'" 281.

[...] the bright day which follows"[64] – hence, as one may suggest, Guthrie's optimistic liner notes to his "Sherman Texas Cyclone."

Yet, for most of the Southwestern farmers who went on their journey west, brighter days were not to come too soon. Guthrie's song "Talking Dust Bowl Blues" portrays the farmers' exodus, giving a chronology of the events that forced them to their knees and made them leave their farms behind in order to make their fortunes elsewhere. The song is a variation of the so-called 'Talking Blues'-form, which Woody Guthrie used in a number of his songs. As the name of the form already suggests, the lyrics are, at least to a certain extent, spoken rather than sung, which often creates the impression of an extemporized free-verse performance. John Greenway hints at the African-American roots of the Talking Blues, pointing out that "there is no doubt that the form was originally Negro."[65] However, as he continues, "there is much in the talking blues that is not fundamentally Negro."[66] He goes on to explain that "the basic pattern of the talking blues stanza, a quatrain of four-accent lines, usually riming aabb (though some few use the alternate rime pattern, abab) and strongly iambic, is British."[67] Indeed, the original 'Talking Blues'-form, as Jeff Place has it, is "credited to an Anglo South Carolinian – Chris Bouchillon, who in April 1926 recorded the original 'Talking Blues.'"[68] Place adds that "[t]he recording director thought that Bouchillon had a good voice with limited singing ability, so he asked him to try talking while playing the guitar. The result was the talking blues."[69]

After Bouchillon's recording, the form disseminated and gave rise to a lot of varieties on a number of subjects. Interestingly, as Greenway points out, "a cascade of talking blues poured out of folk and sophisticated composers just before and after World War II, mostly on socio-economic inequalities,"[70] a thought that should be kept in mind when analyzing Guthrie's "Talking Dust Bowl Blues," which renders one of the bleakest episodes in American history. Its beginning, however, does not elaborate on the dust storms and the subsequent destruction of farmland, but recollects a prosperous past without sorrow and suffering:

64 Quoted in Lookingbill, "'A God-Forsaken Place'" 281.

65 John Greenway, "The Talking Blues," liner notes, *Folkways Records Album No. FH 5232* (New York: Folkways, 1958) n. pag.

66 Greenway, "The Talking Blues" n. pag.

67 Greenway, "The Talking Blues" n. pag.

68 Jeff Place, liner notes to Woody Guthrie's "Mean Talking Blues," *Hard Travelin': The Asch Recordings*, Vol. 3 (Smithsonian Folkways Recordings: Washington, D.C., 1998) 20.

69 Place, liner notes to "Mean Talking Blues" 20.

70 Greenway, "The Talking Blues" n. pag.

Back in Nineteen twenty seven
I had a little farm and I called that heaven.
Well, the price was up and the rain come down
And I hauled my crops all into town.
I got the money, bought clothes and groceries,
Fed the kids and raised a family.[71]

The speaker of the song, a Southwestern farmer and thus once again a representative of those who fell victim to the drought and the storms, elaborates on what his life was like before the Great Depression hit the country in 1929. "Back in Nineteen twenty seven," his farm yielded enough crops and, consequently, money to feed and clothe his family. Once again, biblical imagery is used; however, not in order to qualify the dust storms (which have not occurred yet), but in order to describe the farmer's situation: "And I called that heaven," the speaker proclaims in the third line, comparing his self-sustaining life on the Plains with an earthly paradise.

One may well argue that the first verse of Guthrie's song outlines the Jeffersonian idea(l) of a yeoman life close to nature, which, as the nineteenth-century version of the American Dream, "portrayed the agrarian frontier as the foundation of American Civilization."[72] At that time, agriculture was considered the basis of society and, accordingly, the farmer was regarded as "the cultivator of the earth, the husbandman who tilled his own acres," and eventually, "as the rock upon which the American republic must stand."[73] In 1851, Representative Julian outlined his view of the farmer in one of his speeches during the 2nd session of the 31st Congress:

> The life of a farmer is peculiarly favorable to virtue; and both individuals and communities are generally happy in proportion as they are virtuous. His manners are simple, and his nature unsophisticated. If not oppressed by other interests, he generally possesses an abundance without the drawback of luxury. His life does not impose excessive toil, and yet it discourages idleness. The farmer lives in rustic plenty, remote from the contagion of popular vices, and enjoys, in their greatest fruition, the blessings of health and contentment.[74]

It is "the blessings of health and contentment" that immediately remind us of the speaker in Guthrie's song pointing out that his simple and self-

71 Leventhal and Guthrie 218-19.

72 Henderson 4.

73 Henry N. Smith, *Virgin Land: The American West as Symbol and Myth* (Cambridge, Massachusetts/London: Harvard UP, 1978) 128.

74 Quoted in Smith 171.

sustained life could be "called heaven." Thus, one may well argue that Guthrie's emplotment of the farmer's life employs stereotypes of an agrarian ideal that had made its way into the American collective memory and was part of the Southwesterners' cultural knowledge. [75]

In the second half of the nineteenth century, this ideal of a self-sustained life on the frontier also reached the Great Plains, a region which had always been associated with a desert rather than with a garden suitable for agriculture.[76] As the continuous westward expansion of the frontier became an economic necessity, "the imaginative figure [...] of the stout yeoman who had for so long been the protagonist of the myth of the garden"[77] had to enter the Southwestern consciousness and adjust, if not revise the image of the Plains as a barren wasteland. And, according to Henry Nash Smith, "the crux of [this] matter was rainfall, since it was rainfall alone that distinguished the abundantly fertile prairies of eastern Kansas and Iowa from the bleak uplands farther west."[78] Consequently, Smith concludes that "the imaginative conquest of the desert accordingly took the form of a proliferation of notions about an increase of rainfall on the plains."[79] One of the narratives that contributed to this proliferation of the new image of the Southwest was Josiah Gregg's *Commerce of the Prairies*, which had already been published in 1844.

75 The deference to the prosperous, middle-class farmer was also digested in a number of songs, most of them focussing on the idea that "the farmer is the man who feeds them all." Here is the first verse of one of the most successful farmer-songs dating back to the post-Civil-War era, which not only displays the self-perception of the farmers, but also hints at their general acceptance as a key figure in America's economy: "When the lawyer hangs around and the butcher cuts a pound, / Oh, the farmer is the man who feeds them all. / If you'll only look and see, I think you will agree / That the farmer is the man who feeds them all" (John Greenway, *American Folksongs of Protest* [Philadelphia. U of Pennsylvania P, 1953] 213). Yet, as soon as we consider the chorus of the song, we realize that a farmer's life is far from being unproblematic, as his income is heavily dependent on the seasons and the weather, which forces him to take out loans in order to survive: "The farmer is the man, the farmer is the man, / Lives on credit till the fall; / Then they take him by the hand, and they lead him from the land, / And the middleman's the one who gets it all" (Greenway, *American Folksongs* 213). Such qualifications of the farmer's life might already hint at the fact that Guthrie's depiction in the first verse of his "Talking Dust Bowl Blues" is but an idyllic vision, which, as I will argue later on, serves a special purpose within the song's overall argument.

76 Cf. Smith's chapter "The Garden and the Desert" (Smith 174-84).

77 Smith 179.

78 Smith 179.

79 Smith 179.

The following excerpt reveals how the possibility of rainfall on the plains was promoted:

> The high plains seem too dry and lifeless to produce timber; yet might not the vicissitudes of nature operate a change likewise upon the seasons? Why may we not suppose that the genial influences of civilization – that extensive cultivation of the earth – might contribute to the multiplication of showers, as it certainly does of fountains? [...] At least, many old settlers maintain that the droughts are becoming less oppressive in the West. [...] Then may we not hope that these sterile regions might yet be thus revived and fertilized, and their surface covered one day by flourishing settlements to the Rocky Mountains?[80]

The prospect of rainfall and the hope for a time in which the dry surface of the Great Plains would turn into fertile and arable land made people stick to the Jeffersonian vision, though real living conditions, more often than not, did not correspond to the dreamlike scenario outlined above. Yet, according to another letter by Caroline Henderson of July, 26th, 1935, in which she recapitulates her life on the Great Plains, the dream seemed to have come true, at least for the year of 1926. Here is her enthusiastic and romanticizing account of the past:

> The wonderful crop of 1926 when our country alone produced 10,000,000 bushels of wheat – more, it was said, than any other equal area in the world – revealed the possibilities of our productive soil under modern methods of farming. I can shut my eyes and feel yet the rush of an almost painful thankfulness when we looked out over our fields that summer and watched our ripening grain bending, rising, bending again in golden waves swept on interminably by the restless wind. It seemed as if at last our dreams were coming true ....[81]

The idyllic vision that is depicted here seems to back up Guthrie's speaker comparing his life to heaven on earth – Henderson's feeling of a "painful thankfulness," and her poetic description of the "ripening grain [...] bending [...] in golden waves" suggest that she also regards her outstanding living conditions as a divine gift. Yet, the dream- or heavenlike situation respectively is only transitory, as the second verse of Guthrie's "Talking Dust Bowl Blues" makes evident right in the first line:

> Rain quit and the wind got high,
> And a black old dust storm filled the sky,
> And I swapped my farm for a Ford machine,
> And I poured it full of this gasoline.

80 Quoted in Smith 179.

81 Henderson 140.

> And I started, rocking and a-rolling,
> Over the mountains and out towards the old Peach Bowl.[82]

Unfortunately, the rain stops falling and turns the speaker's heaven into an unbearable hell of wind and dust. Thus, to quote Smith once more, "the crux of the matter is rainfall."[83] And, taking into consideration that rain had indeed been the essential ingredient in establishing the Jeffersonian vision of the Great Plains, the symbolic potential of the first two words of the second verse increases significantly. Now, it is not the prospect of rainfall which makes people bear up under the hard conditions on the prairie, but its absence which dramatically changes the situation of the farmer: "Rain quit and the wind got high," and the farmer's heavenly existence is obliterated by the "black old dust storm[s]" that started in the early 1930s. Separating the recollection of a prosperous past from the horrors of an insufferable present, Guthrie thus managed to capture both the extreme climatic changes of the times and the radical turn from the idealized vision of a self-sustained life at the frontier to spiritual dryness and human erosion.

Thus the outline of the Jeffersonian ideal in the first verse of the song serves as a foil against which the dust storm disaster and its consequences – as elaborated in the rest of the song – appear in their fullest dreadfulness. Guthrie achieves this remarkable effect by employing the prototypical pattern of a farmer's fortune to emphasize the destructive nature of the storms. Most interestingly, Caroline Henderson takes up the same strategy in her letter cited above, in which the recollection of a dreamlike past is supposed to highlight the terrors of the nightmarish present. Here is her letter once again – and indeed, her emplotment of the catastrophe bears a strong resemblance to Guthrie's song. After her nostalgic fashioning of 1926, her account of the present, significantly introduced with the word "yet," reads like a portrayal of the world turned topsy-turvy, of order disintegrated into utter chaos:

> The wonderful crop of 1926 when our country alone produced 10,000,000 bushels of wheat – more, it was said, than any other equal area in the world – revealed the possibilities of our productive soil under modern methods of farming. I can shut my eyes and feel yet the rush of an almost painful thankfulness when we looked out over our fields that summer and watched our ripening grain bending, rising, bending again in golden waves swept on interminably by the restlesss wind. It seemed as if at last our dreams were coming true ....

82 Leventhal and Guthrie 218-19.
83 Smith 179.

> Yet now our daily physical torture, confusion of mind, gradual wearing down of courage, seem to make that long continued hope look like a vanishing dream. For we are in the worst of the dust storm area where William Vaughn Moody's expression 'dust to eat' is not merely a figure of speech as he intended, but the phrasing of a bitter reality, increasing in seriousness with each passing day. Any attempt to suggest the violent discomfort of these storms is likely to be vain except to those who have already experienced them.[84]

Courtesy of the Woody Guthrie Foundation and Archives.

Another testimony which articulates the drastic change of conditions is a diary entry by Mary Knackstedt Dyck from Hamilton County, Kansas, who, after a dust storm struck her farm in early 1937, wrote down that "it cert[ai]nly seems like Par[a]dise yesterday, & to day it seems, as if we're in a different world."[85] The biblical image she employs to render the past brings us back to Guthrie's song, in which the transition from a heavenly life to an unbearable existence – which affects both the bodies and the minds of the Southwestern farmers, as Henderson's expressions like "physical torture," "confusion of mind" and "gradual wearing down of courage" suggest – is equally abrupt. After the rain has stopped, the speaker of the song is forced to sell his farm, because he fell victim to the perfidious strategy of the land owners and banks, who had given loans to the tenant farmers in the more prosperous years. Due to the boom-bust cycles of the Plains, those farmers were by no means able to pay back the loans after the dust storms had destroyed most of their harvest. Therefore, as Guthrie's cartoon[86] portrays, most of them sold their farms and bought a jalopy in order to head out for the "old peach bowl."

84 Henderson 140.

85 Pamela Riney-Kehrberg, ed., *Waiting on the Bounty: The Dust Bowl Diary of Mary Knackstedt Dyck* (Iowa City: The U of Iowa P, 1999) 52.

86 "You see, I lost the farm trying to finance the jallopie!" cartoon, WGA, Notebooks I, Notebook 2, 32.

In his Pulitzer Prize-winning novel about the 'Okie'-migration, *The Grapes of Wrath*, John Steinbeck epitomizes this dilemma of many Southwestern farmers in a dialogue between the ex-convict Tom Joad and the ex-preacher Casey:

> Joad said, 'What's the idear of kickin' the folks off?' 'Oh! They talked pretty about it. You know what kinda years we been havin'. Dust comin' up an' spoilin' ever'thing so a man didn't get enough crop to plug up an ant's ass. An' ever'body got bills at the grocery. You know how it is. [...] So they tractored all the tenants off a the lan'. [...] Well, the guy that come aroun' talked nice as pie. "You got to get off. It ain't my fault." 'Well,' I says, 'whose fault is it? I'll go an' I'll nut the fella.' "It's the Shawnee Lan' an' Cattle Company. I jus' got orders." 'Who is the Shawnee Lan' an' Cattle Company?' "It ain't nobody. It's a company."[87]

Deprived of all their property, yet full of hope, many of the Southwestern farmers believed that they could make a new start beyond the Rocky Mountains, in America's Golden State, California. In his "Talking Dust Bowl Blues," Guthrie tells the story of the farmers on their way westward, predominantly focusing on the hardship of the road – his talking the verses rather than singing them contributes to the narrative character of the song.

> Way up yonder on a mountain road,
> I had a hot motor and a heavy load.
> I was going pretty fast, I wasn't even stopping,
> A-bouncing up and down like a popcorn popping.
> Had a breakdown, a sort of a nervous bust-down of some kind.
> There was a fellow there, a mechanic fellow, said it was engine trouble.
>
> Way up yonder on a mountain curve,
> It was way up yonder in the piney woods,
> And I give that rolling Ford a shove,
> And I was going to coast as far as I could.
> Commenced coasting; picking up speed; (there) was a hairpin turn; I ... didn't make it.
>
> Man alive, I'm a-telling you
> The fiddles and the guitars really flew.
> That Ford took off like a flying squirrel
> And it flew halfway around the world.
> Scattered wives and childrens all over the side of that mountain.[88]

87 John Steinbeck, *The Grapes of Wrath* (1939; London: Penguin, 1992) 64.
88 Leventhal and Guthrie 218ff.

As the Talking Blues, according to John Greenway, was a form of expression both evolving in and dealing with "a cultural milieu of extreme meagerness,"[89] it was probably not by chance that Guthrie made use of it in describing the fate of the poor and dislocated migrants. Their trouble, as the verses reveal, does not start in California, but already on Route 66, the migrant road, which in many sections resembled a country lane rather than a highway. It led through the desert state of New Mexico and across the insurmountable mountains of Arizona, being "the path of a people in flight, refugees from dust and shrinking land, from the thunder of tractors and shrinking ownership […], the mother road, the road of flight."[90] We can easily picture that it is here that the speaker of Guthrie's song, underestimating a "hairpin turn," loses control of his vehicle. It is typical both of Guthrie's facetiousness and of the ironic undertone characteristic of the Talking Blues that the speaker of the song deals with the damage of his property – "The fiddles and the guitars really flew" – in the same way as he deals with the injuries his family suffers. The speaker's wife and his children are "scattered all over the side of that mountain" like discarded household goods.

Yet, though the description of the speaker's scattered belongings might be ascribed to the humorous nature of the Talking Blues form and creates a sense of comic relief, it still carries serious overtones, as it once again calls forth the destruction of property and the breakdown of social ties during the ecological disaster that caused the farmers' exodus. And indeed, Guthrie used the participle "scattered" in a similar context in an undated letter to his sister Mary Jo to characterize the situation of the poor, uprooted Southwesteners, stating that "[t]he poor folks don't own anything. They are scattered, wandering, broke, hungry, dirty, ragged, hungry-looking, and all of that."[91] The "poor folks" are, in other words, as gone with the wind as the Old Testament's chosen people, having to seek refuge in lands whose inhabitants are predominantly hostile. In his *The Grapes of Wrath*, Steinbeck elaborates on these disastrous conditions on the migrants' way to the new Eden, which would, for the better part of them, remain a dream that would never come true:

> The people in flight streamed out on 66, sometimes a single car, sometimes a little caravan. All day they rolled slowly along the road, and at night they

89 Greenway, "The Talking Blues" n. pag. Greenway, back in 1958, explicitly referred to the cultural milieu of the African-American community in his characterization of the "Talking Blues."

90 Steinbeck, *Grapes* 160.

91 Woody Guthrie, *Pastures of Plenty: A Self-Portrait*, ed. Dave Marsh and Harold Leventhal (New York: Harper Perennial, 1992) 31.

> stopped near water [...] Two hundred and fifty thousand people over the road. Fifty thousand old cars – wounded, steaming. Wrecks along the road, abandoned.[92]

Such an Odyssey undertaken with hopelessly run-down cars is in many ways reminiscent of the toil the Hebrew people suffered on their flight from Egypt. Consider the last verse of Guthrie's "Talking Dust Bowl Blues":

> We got out to the West Coast broke,
> So dad gum hungry I thought I'd croak,
> And I bummed up a spud or two,
> And my wife fixed up a 'tater stew
> We poured the kids full of it.
> Mighty thin stew, though; you could read a magazine right through it.
>
> Always have figured that if it had been just a little bit thinner
> some of these here politicians could have seen through it.[93]

Naturally, the poor condition of the cars and the devastating state of the roads endangered the success of the journey. Moreover, the malnutrition added to the refugees' despair. Having invested all their money in their Model Ts and saving the little that remained for gasoline, most of them could not afford anything but "tater stew," which furthered the general malnutrition of the migrants. Yet, unlike most of the migrants who, according to Guthrie, believed in the rich folks' "radio programs, sermons, moving pictures, books, magazines, and all sorts of advertising"[94] which deceived them with promises of better work at better pay, he attacks "these here politicians" for having neglected their duties by only furthering the interests of the monied class instead of providing relief to the impecunious. By lengthening the word "politicians" in his rhythmical talking and deliberately overemphasizing the plosive /t/, Guthrie assumedly underlines his extreme rage and frustration about their irresponsibility and carelessness. Thus, by nuancing just one word, as Guthrie biographer Klein observes, the last line of his song actually became more effective than "a dozen radical pamphlets."[95]

However, it is not only his over- or mispronouncing the word "politicians" which emphasizes the critical tone of the song's coda. Since its

92 Steinbeck, *Grapes* 165.
93 Leventhal and Guthrie 220.
94 Guthrie, *Pastures of Plenty* 31.
95 Klein 86.

satirical tone is a characteristic feature of the Talking Blues,[96] Guthrie's choice of the musical form was, one might argue, in itself a political statement substantiating the criticism articulated in the lyrics. Considering both John Greenway's observation that "the talking blues were first performed by Negroes for Negroes as an in-group vehicle of anti-white satire"[97] and Serge Denisoff's radical claim that the "folkish 'talking blues' is the most indicative American genre of Brechtian style of propaganda,"[98] one could well argue that Guthrie used a musical form which was ideologically charged and, due to its satirical potential, particularly apt to provide its migrant listeners with a feeling of collective identity.

Interestingly enough, the last verse of Guthrie's "Talking Dust Bowl Blues," which critically hints at those responsible for the plight of the migrants and thus in charge of coming up with a solution, seems to be a later addition to or a rewriting of the original version of the song, which can be found in one of his manuscripts. According to Guthrie's own notes on this original version, the song portrays "the story of our radeo kayreer in poem style. Hit dont ryme, but neighther did our kayreer" (sic).[99] Strikingly enough, this remark is crossed out. On the left side of the page, we can find another annotation documenting that he wrote down this version for publication on Victor Records, the record label on which his whole set of *Dust Bowl Ballads* was to appear in 1940. Yet, as the crossed-out lines at the bottom suggest, the lyrics on the manuscript page were never recorded. Here is the last verse of this version:

> Got to L.A., didn't have no dough,
> Commenced a sangin' on the Radeo!
> Signed up a contract one year long –
> Cause you folks liked Old Time Songs!
> Oklahoma Yodelin – playin' the fiddle!
> Lefty Lou come along done all the hard work!
> You got behind us – Dearly Beloved!
> That's what saved us! Shore fine people!
> Must of come from Down South![100]

96 Cf. Greenway, "The Talking Blues."

97 Cf. Greenway, "The Talking Blues."

98 Denisoff, R. Serge, *Sing a Song of Social Significance* (Bowling Green, Ohio: Bowling Green U Popular P, 1972) 25.

99 WGA, Songs I, Box 1, Folder 5. Guthrie uses the first-person plural, as he refers to Maxine Dempsey, born Crissman, also known as "Lefty Lou," his accompanist on his radio program at the Los Angeles radio station KFVD.

100 WGA, Songs I, Box 1, Folder 5.

The politicians are not mentioned at all, nor is the tater stew which was too thin to feed the speaker's starving family. Instead, the speaker of the song, who can now be clearly identified as Guthrie, informs the listeners of the happy ending of his horrible odyssey to California. Thus, taking this early version of the song into consideration, the critical implications of the later, published version as cited above become even more conspicuous.[101] By replacing the account of his career on the radio with a narrative which is not characterized by obvious autobiographical markers, Guthrie's account of the exodus from the Southwest to the Golden State becomes representative of the fates of thousands of 'Okies,' 'Arkies' and 'Mizoos.' Just like the speakers of his "Dust Storm Disaster" or his "So Long, It's Been Good To Know Yuh," the speaker of his "Talking Dust Bowl Blues" could thus well be characterized as "retain[ing] the syntax of 'first-person' narrative, but, at the same time, "avoid[ing] the markers of individuality that characterize personal voice."[102] Following from that, Guthrie's sung biography, which does indeed "avoid the markers of individuality," portrays the life of a typical Southwestern migrant farmer on his way to the Golden State – and not necessarily his own, as the earlier version of his song suggests. The song thus provided its listeners with the opportunity to identify with the speaker both through its lyrics and, one may argue, by employing the ideologically charged form of the Talking Blues.

101 Of course, it is hard to find out whether it was Guthrie himself who decided to record the 'new' version of the song or whether he was influenced by the record company or his producer, Alan Lomax. In his "Hard Travelin'," Jeff Morgan observes that Alan Lomax contributed a lot to the fashioning of Guthrie as a political bard. It was he who decided on the selection of songs for the Guthrie recordings. One might be tempted to argue that it was Lomax, too, who had a say in the final version of the lyrics which were to be put on record.

102 Lanser 241.

3.2 "Unwelcome travellers and other brave men": Fashioning the Outlaw as a Hero of Great Depression Oklahoma

> I never stopped to think of it before, but you know – a policeman will jest stand there an let a banker rob a farmer, or a finance man rob a workin man. But if a farmer robs a banker – you would have hole dern army of cops out a shooting at him. Robbery is a chapter in ettiquette (Woody Guthrie)[1]

It was not only through its extreme climatic conditions that the 'Great American Desert' in the Southwest gained its reputation as a region one had better avoid going to or settling in; besides being haunted by drought and dust on a regular basis, it was said to be the home territory of outlaws of various kinds. From Calamity Jane to Jesse James, the line of lawless bandits and outcasts who wreaked havoc in the region could well be traced back to the early nineteenth century. A number of Woody Guthrie's songs render the life, the deeds and, occasionally, the deaths of some of these outlaws. Probably his most prominent outlaw song, which was later recorded as one of his *Dust Bowl Ballads* released by Victor Records in 1940, is his "Pretty Boy Floyd." It deals with the Oklahoman criminal Charles Arthur Floyd, who went raiding in the states of the American Southwest in the late 1920s and early 1930s and was soon after said to have helped the impoverished farmers by distributing his loot among them. After his death in 1933, numerous yarns and tales shot up like mushrooms and contributed to Floyd's reputation, who eventually became a cultural icon[2] for those who suffered most from the ecological and economic turmoil that had struck the country.

Using Guthrie's ballad about Floyd as a point of departure, this chapter aims to reconstruct the medial creation of the Oklahoman outlaw as a modern Robin Hood by investigating newspaper accounts and (alleged) eyewitness reports, which, owing to their particular myth-making quali-

1 Woody Guthrie, *Woody Sez*, ed. Marjorie Guthrie, Harold Leventhal, Terry Sullivan and Sheldon Patinkin (New York: Grosset & Dunlap, 1975) 14ff.

2 By 'cultural icon,' I mean an exemplary figure who, as a representative of a particular culture, can be instrumentalized for various cultural, social or political purposes and who usually serves to establish a feeling of shared identity among those who belong to the culture represented by him or her. In general, the term 'cultural icon' can either be applied to literary or mythological types or to historical people (cf. Bernd Engler and Isabell Klaiber, "Kulturelle Leitfiguren: Prozesse und Strategien ihrer Funktionalisierung," *Kulturelle Leitfiguren – Figurationen und Refigurationen*, ed. Bernd Engler and Isabell Klaiber [Duncker & Humblot: Berlin, 2007] 9-28).

ty, helped to shape the legend of Pretty Boy Floyd. Moreover, the chapter examines how Guthrie's sung genealogy of the outlaw participated in the contemporary discourse on Floyd and contributed to him being fashioned as an ally of the poor. In order to illustrate the forms and functions of the rhetorical and aesthetic devices and techniques Guthrie employs to configure the outlaw's life and deeds, this chapter also glimpses at some of his other outlaw songs,[3] correlating them with the strong tradition of English and Scottish outlaw ballads prevalent in the American Southwest.

* * * * *

On April 16th, 1931, Charles Arthur Floyd and Willis Miller, also known as Billy the Killer, were spotted in Bowling Green, Ohio, accompanied by their newly acquired girlfriends, Beulah Baird and Rose Ash. Police officials were alerted immediately and presumed them to be robbers casing a bank on South Main Street. As Bowling Green Police Chief Carl Galliher and Officer Ralph Castner slowly drove down Main Street to find out what was going on, they spied the amorous quartet entering a shop in order to buy some dresses for the ladies. The two policemen stopped, climbed out of the squad car and approached the two suspects. Tommy Vail, another police officer, who later joined his two colleagues, recalled the confrontation: "The 'gangsters' were accompanied by their girl friends, Rose Ash, 23, and Beulah Baird, 21, sisters from Kansas City. When the police got out of their car, that is when the shooting started. It was quite a thing."[4] In the gunfight, Miller was hit in the stomach and collapsed dead on the street. Though Beulah Baird was seriously wounded by a bullet that struck her head, her life could eventually be saved. One of the policemen, Ralph Castner, was also severely wounded, yet continued to fire his gun at Charles Floyd, who tried and finally succeeded in getting out of the situation, though he was pursued by Castner's colleague Galliher. Shortly after the incident, Castner was rushed to a hospital, but could not rally from his gunshot wound and died.

3 For a discussion of an extensive selection of Guthrie's outlaw songs including "Pretty Boy Floyd" cf. also Jackson (166ff.), who makes similar observations in some of his readings.

4 The reconstruction of the gunfight in Bowling Green, Ohio, is taken from Michael Wallis, *Pretty Boy: The Life and Times of Charles Arthur Floyd* (New York: St. Martin's Press, 1992) 209ff. I am indebted to Wallis's informative study on the life of Floyd and the contexts of rural Oklahoma in the 1920s and 1930s, as it provided a number of contemporary texts which I work from in this chapter.

Charles Arthur – or Pretty Boy[5] – Floyd's notoriety instantly grew after the gunfight on Main Street in Bowling Green, Ohio. Not only was he charged with the murder of a police officer, there was also a one thousand dollar reward for his apprehension. Headlines in local and regional newspapers featured the name 'Pretty Boy Floyd' in bold type for the first time and, by retelling the story of Bowling Green again and again, contributed to the creation and the shaping of the myth of the infamous outlaw. Moreover, in the following days "rumors and alleged sightings of the desperado popped up quicker than sunflowers in a manure pile," as Michael Wallis has it in his biography of Floyd.[6] By giving a summary of the various reports on Floyd, he demonstrates their sometimes absurd inconsistency:

> On April 18 in Toledo, it was thought Pretty Boy Floyd was the one who had held a pistol to the head of taxi driver Robert Robinson and had stolen his cash and cab. The following day, Robinson's hack was found abandoned near Monroe, Michigan, where that same afternoon another cab driver was victimized by a lone gunman identified as Floyd. The nervy bandit was seen at restaurants, movie theaters, and even church services. Witnesses swore on a stack of Bibles that it was Pretty Boy himself who had attended a marathon dance contest. He reportedly surfaced here and there throughout the Midwest. All of a sudden, Pretty Boy was everywhere at the same time, a media creation of these bleakest Depression years.[7]

Yet, it was not only the reports of alleged eyewitnesses and the numerous articles in the newspapers that retold and thus refashioned the story of the outlaw, who eventually even became a "popular hero among the children," as a contemporary newspaper reported in 1933.[8] With his song "Pretty Boy Floyd," which was written in the second half of the 1930s[9]

5 Charles Arthur Floyd got this nickname from the mother of Wallace and William Ash, who were believed to be killed by Floyd and Miller, as they had been affiliated with Beulah and Rose and thus were the only obstacle in the criminals' pursuit of the girls. Shortly after the Bowling Green incident, mother Ash was interviewed by the press and her first reaction, that would make Floyd's nickname popular, was the question: "Did they get Pretty Boy?"(cf. Wallis 211).

6 Wallis 213.

7 Wallis 213.

8 Quoted inWallis 145.

9 Unfortunately, the exact date of composition is not known. Yet, what we know is that a first, slightly different version of the song was written down by Guthrie during his time at KFVD in Los Angeles on 12 Mar. 1939 (WGA, Songs I, Box 3, Folder 21). On the manuscript page, Guthrie notes that he "made up the words and the tune to this ballad on march twelfth, nineteen thirty nine, in Los Angeles, Calif."

and recorded during his Library of Congress sessions in 1940, folksinger Woody Guthrie, a contemporary of Floyd's, unequivocally contributed to the "media creation" of the Floyd legend.[10] The song provides a genealogy of the outlaw by chronologically rendering both pre- and post-criminal stages of Floyd's life. Here are the first five verses, which configure the incident that eventually turned him into an outcast:

If you gather round me children
A Story I will tell,
About Pretty Boy Floyd, the outlaw,
Oklahoma knew him well.

It was in the town of Shawnee
On a Saturday afternoon
His wife beside him in the wagon
As into town they rode.

There a deputy sheriff approached[11] him,
In a manner rather rude,
Using vulgar words of anger,
And his wife she overheard.

Pretty Boy grabbed a log chain,
And the deputy grabbed a gun,
And in the fight that followed
He laid that deputy down.

He took to the trees and timbers
And he lived a life of shame,
Every crime in Oklahoma
Was added to his name.[12]

Right at the beginning of the song, Guthrie's direct address to his audience of children and his disclaimer that he is going to tell them a story, makes evident that his sung biography of Floyd is more of a yarn than a 'true' historiographic account. Moreover, Guthrie declares in his liner notes to the song that "[i]t *tells* of *tales* I *heard* concerning his life and what kind of man he was."[13] Thus, from the outset, Guthrie makes no

10 In his liner notes to the song, Guthrie points out that he "talked to lots of folks that knowed him personal" (Lomax, Guthrie and Seeger 114). He even claims to have been on the same freight train with Floyd while travelling with his uncle.

11 Another version of the song has "reproached" instead of "approached," which slightly changes the line's tenor, as "reproached" adds emphasis to Guthrie's overall notion that Floyd was unjustly accused of crimes (Lomax, Guthrie and Seeger 115).

12 Kleff 112.

13 Lomax, Guthrie and Seeger 115, emphasis added.

secret of the fact that his narrative about Floyd's life and deeds is based only on 'second-hand information.' And indeed, compared to the presumably more accurate narrative of Michael Wallis's biography of Floyd, the distortion becomes obvious: Guthrie's rendering of Floyd's encounter with the deputy sheriff is – most probably – based on the Bowling Green homicide of police officer Castner as outlined above, though Guthrie's choice of the setting does not seem to fit into this correspondence at first sight. Yet, as soon as one takes into consideration that Floyd and his accomplice Miller, according to Floyd biographer Michael Wallis, spent some time in the Shawnee area in Oklahoma shortly before they headed off to Ohio, it makes perfect sense to assume that the people Guthrie listened to would, time and again, mix up these places when telling the story of Pretty Boy Floyd.

The portrayal of the confrontation with the police in the second and third verse separates the good from the bad: The deputy sheriff's rude manner and his "vulgar words of anger," which even embarrass Floyd's wife, expose him as an aggressive lout. Floyd, on the contrary, is fashioned as a gentleman of integrity: he is married, and, being a good husband, he has taken his wife out on a Saturday afternoon for a trip to town. Unarmed as he is, Floyd "grab[s] a log chain," which was supposedly stored in the back of his wagon, and calls the deputy sheriff to account for his rude manner of approaching him and his wife. The "fight that follow[s]" is unfair, as the deputy's gun seems to be the more effective weapon; yet Floyd manages to lay him down in defending his life and restoring his wife's honor. Though the verses do not fade out Floyd's criminal and violent potential entirely, as it is him who resorts to physical violence first, they certainly contribute to shaping the ideological dispositions of the opponents, portraying the representative of law and order as an instrumentalized and corrupt person, whose prejudiced opinion leads to his unjustified cornering of Floyd, who is, though not whitewashed, fashioned as morally superior.

As a consequence of the homicide, Floyd, as the fifth verse of the song tells us, was forced to live in the "trees and timbers" and is, though he regretted what he had done, unjustly blamed for "every crime in Oklahoma."[14] Now, at the very latest, the analogy Guthrie draws in his song

14 As Wallis argues, the outlaw was indeed blamed by both federal and state authorities for a lot of crimes he did not commit. Yet, Wallis does not whitewash Floyd but states that he was one of the cruellest criminals of the Depression era. Thus, though he had certainly become a scapegoat for J. Edgar Hoover (326ff.), the degree of moral integrity that is attributed to Floyd in Guthrie's song is nevertheless questionable.

has become obvious: Floyd, whose moral standards were certainly not as high as portrayed in Guthrie's song, as his criminal record makes evident,[15] is fashioned as a modern Robin Hood, living a hidden life in the forest. Just as the popular old English outlaw, whose exploits with his band of 'Merry Men' in Sherwood Forest were rendered in numerous songs and ballads, Charles Arthur Floyd is depicted as a gallant bandit who steals from the rich in order to give to the poor. The next verses of the song continue to fashion Floyd as a modern version of the medieval outlaw:

> Yes, he took to the trees and timbers
> On that Canadian River's shore,
> And Pretty Boy found a welcome
> At many a farmer's door.
>
> There's many a starvin' farmer,
> The same old story told,
> How this outlaw paid their mortgage,
> And saved their little home.
>
> Others tell you 'bout a stranger,
> That come to beg a meal,
> And underneath his napkin
> Left a thousand dollar bill.
>
> It was in Oklahoma City
> It was on a Christmas Day,
> There come a whole car load of groceries,
> With a letter that did say:
>
> 'You say that I'm an outlaw,
> You say that I'm a thief,
> Here's a Christmas dinner
> For the families on relief.'[16]

Floyd is pictured as an ally of the poorest part of the Oklahoman population, the farmers, who, at that time, had to cope with enormous financial problems, as the prices for agricultural products dramatically decreased in the first years of the Great Depression. As a consequence, many small farmers were not able to pay their bank loans anymore, which they had taken out a few years before, when a growing demand had necessitated

15 Cf. Jeffery S. King, *The Life and Death of Pretty Boy Floyd* (Kent, Ohio/London: The Kent State UP, 1998) 150ff. Among the crimes listed on the criminal record are robbery, highway robbery, vagrancy and, above all, murder.

16 Kleff 112.

investments into new machinery. According to the song, Floyd, just like his Sherwood predecessor, managed to support those in need by taking from the rich – of course, one may add, outlaws stole from the rich, as robbing the poor would not have made much sense anyway. Interestingly, the crimes Floyd must have committed in order to provide the farmers with the money necessary to redeem their credits and to make their living are not mentioned at all. By deliberately focusing on those who benefited from Floyd's illegal activities and by neglecting his victims, the song again contributes to him being fashioned as a morally superior caretaker of the poor.

Whereas Floyd's image as a supporter of the needy seems to be unquestioned in the rural parts of Oklahoma, some people in the urban region of its capital still have to be convinced of his righteousness, as the last two verses cited reveal. With a "whole car load of groceries" and a covering letter addressing those who still believe him to be a downright criminal, Floyd tries to rehabilitate his reputation. That the outlaw's package for "the people on relief" arrives on Christmas Day adds to the symbolic potential of his generous gift and makes him appear as a benevolent altruist without any malicious intent.

However, even ignoring the crimes he was unjustly blamed for, Floyd displayed a considerable degree of malicious intent, as he had robbed a number of banks in the region. As Eugene Gum, then secretary of Oklahoma's bankers' association, stated, these robberies supposedly included "so called 'Robin Hood' acts of charity. In return, the persons to whom he gives financial aid, shield him from the law."[17] One of his robberies took place in Okfuskee County in east central Oklahoma. Floyd was identified in photographs that were taken while he, accompanied by two fellows, looted $2600 from the First State Bank in Castle, a small community located only seven miles northwest of Okemah, where Woody Guthrie was born.

It is not only due to the local affiliation with Floyd that Guthrie would write a song about him 23 years later. Nor is Guthrie's fashioning the outlaw as a Robin Hood-type of criminal originally his idea, as Eugene Gum's statement above already revealed. The worshipping of Floyd in his song rather represents a certain aspect of Oklahoman mentality that evolved at the beginning of the 20th century: Oklahoma, which achieved statehood only in 1907, had long been considered the last frontier of the outlaw, "a true refuge for the lawless and untamed."[18] Yet, interestingly enough, the criminal deeds of outlaws like Henry Starr, the Daltons, the

[17] Quoted in Wallis 233.
[18] Wallis 36.

Youngers or, above all, the infamous Frank and Jesse James were, by many at least, not regarded as morally wrong, but as forms of political protest. Bank robberies were considered a means of striking back at the establishment which, to a large extent, dominated the lives of the rural citizens, i.e., the Oklahoman farmers. "Starting in 1910," as Michael Wallis has it, "there had been a steady rise of what became known as 'social banditry,'"[19] the rationale of which he explains as follows:

> To the tenant farmers and sharecroppers scrambling to dig a living from the earth, there was little wrong with a man who had the guts to rob a bank. It was the ultimate expression of protest. Bankers, like the big railroad barons who had fenced off grazing land, were the enemy as far as the poor folks were concerned. They believed the banks cheated them every chance they got.[20]

Following from that, these 'social bandits,' very much in the tradition of Robin Hood, were regarded as morally superior to the "bankers" and "big railroad barons" by a surprisingly large number of Oklahomans. The fact that, in 1912, Oklahoma led the nation in bank robberies and, of course, the numerous mythologizing tales about the James brothers, Belle Starr and others underline this widespread appreciation of the outlaw.

In the course of the Great Depression, the number of Southwestern farmers in need dramatically rose, which, in turn, led to a renewed appreciation of social banditry, and Charles Arthur Floyd entered upon the inheritance of his infamous predecessors. Pretty Boy, who soon became a cultural icon, personified a particular spirit of revolt, as he, though illegally, redistributed the goods of the rich among the poor and thus fought social injustice that had been caused by the capitalist system. At least for the majority of rural Oklahomans, who, ever since the beginning of the twentieth century, had become adherents of a grass-roots socialist ideology, Floyd had become the archetypal partisan in a fight against those who were responsible for social misconditions in the Depression – i.e., the bankers and landlords, as the following excerpt from the *New Century* implicitly indicates:

> School has begun in the towns but the children of the tenant farmers of Oklahoma are in the cotton field. For two months more they will be there. In the meantime the children of the bankers and the landlords are getting the benefit of the best educational advantages obtainable. The workers pay for

19 Wallis 113.
20 Wallis 113.

> these facilities, but through rents, interest, and profits their children are kept from their enjoyment.[21]

Taking such disparities of condition into account, it is not surprising that the outlaw Floyd, who was said to pay the farmers' mortgages and thus "sa[ve] their little homes," would soon gain immensely in popularity among the rural poor. Relating the success of the Floyd myth to the devastating living conditions and the general frustration among the rural Oklahomans in the 1930s, *Oklahoma News* reporter Vivian Brown concluded that

> [t]he papers were full of Floyd. The depression was having its demoralizing effect upon society and many of the destitute admired the boy who could go out and take money from the bankers. When banks in our territory began failing, when industry slowed down and farm prices dropped near nothing, public temper was ripe for Floyd to catch the public fancy.[22]

The "public temper" of Depression Oklahoma seemed to be conducive to the emergence of social bandits like Pretty Boy. In particular for the disenfranchised farmers, this type of outlaw symbolized justice and moral integrity in a country in which injustice, at least for those at the bottom of society, seemed to be gaining the upper hand. On January 22nd, 1933, the headline of the *Wichita Beacon* read "Pretty Boy Floyd – Oklahoma's Enemy or Robin Hood?" The article nicely summarizes the opposite points of view that are implied in its headline:

> To peace officers he is Oklahoma's public enemy No. 1 with the price of $2000[23] on his head, dead or alive. [...] But to another class that is composed of many law-abiding citizens of Oklahoma he is a far different person, a modern Robin Hood who robs only those who can afford to lose, who helps those in need and distress, who has a happy smile and a cheery word of greeting for his friends [...].[24]

Only two months before, the *Literary Digest* featured a story that added to the Floyd myth, characterizing him as the "bandit king of Oklahoma, the latest of that state's long line of outlaw chiefs."[25] In 1934, the aforementioned Vivian Brown, the only journalist who ever managed to conduct an interview with the living legend, summarized her impression in

21 Quoted in Burbank 17.

22 Quoted in Wallis 275.

23 The state's $1000 reward had been doubled by the Oklahoma Bankers' Association in 1932 (cf. Wallis 238).

24 Quoted in Wallis 145.

25 Quoted in Wallis 291.

an article stating that "[t]here is so much to support the picture of Floyd as a modern Robin Hood. Like the famed marauder of the English forests, he took money from those who had it – the banks – and divided the proceeds of his raids with the poor."[26]

However, the renaissance of the outlaw was a phenomenon not exclusively found in Oklahoma. In 1938, Hollywood produced a still famous movie adaptation of the tale of Robin Hood starring Errol Flynn, which reached a nationwide audience. It definitely reached Woody Guthrie, who, in one of his manuscripts, recalls one of his tours through the country:

> We froze up over the hump past Bakersfield, Fresno, and up past Marysville, on up to the Sacramento River bottom five or six miles west of the town called Chico. The oak forests here are the prettiest in the world, this is where Errol Flynn rode and robbed to make the movie of Robin Hood.[27]

As the modern version of the medieval outlaw, Charles Arthur Floyd thus represented the moral standard of a predominantly rural society that blamed capitalist banking for the foreclosures of their farms. For Guthrie, Charles Floyd "had the right idea but he had the wrong system,"[28] as he ironically comments in his notes to the song. In one of his notebooks, Guthrie points out that "we ain't never had a governor down there that was half as popular as Pretty Boy," and, in his notoriously ironic manner, adds that "[Pretty Boy] tried and done it wrong, [but] the governor won't even try."[29]

Given this considerable media coverage of Floyd and his deeds, it is not surprising that already by the year 1932, the myth of Floyd had disseminated throughout the region. Floyd gossip could be heard in almost every Oklahoman household and "[c]hildren at play had vied to take the role of Pretty Boy during games of cops and robbers."[30] Even Ma Joad, a character of Steinbeck's *The Grapes of Wrath*, resorts to the legend of Pretty Boy Floyd in a conversation with her son Tom, who, as a fugitive, is in a similar situation as the Oklahoman outlaw: "I know'd Purty Boy Floyd's ma," she tells her son, "[h]e wasn't a bad boy. Jus' got drove in

[26] Quoted in Wallis 278.

[27] "Woody Guthrie by Woody Guthrie," Smithsonian Center for Folklife and Cultural Heritage, Ralph Rinzler Folklife Archives and Collections (RRFAC), Washington, D.C., *Woody Guthrie Papers,* Box 3, Folder 6, 10.

[28] Smithsonian, RRFAC, *Woody Guthrie Papers*, Box 1, Folder 6.

[29] Smithsonian, RRFAC, *Woody Guthrie Papers*, Box 1, Folder 6.

[30] Wallis 269.

the corner."[31] Then she warns him: "Tom, they'll drive you, an' cut you down like they done to young Floyd."[32]

Most probably, Woody Guthrie not only listened to friends of his talking about Floyd's deeds, but also read one or the other of the numerous newspaper articles that contributed to the creation of the Floyd myth. To what a stupendous extent Guthrie, time and again, was inspired by newspaper articles as a basis for his songwriting, can best be illustrated by considering another of his outlaw ballads about the famous female criminal Belle Starr. Though it is a song that was written only in the second half of the 1940s, a short discussion of it might be worthwhile, as it lets us understand better what Guthrie means when he points out that his songs "tell of tales [he] heard." Here are the lyrics of the song, which provide insight into the outlaw's love life:

Belle Starr, Belle Starr, tell me, where have you gone
Since old Oklahoma's red sandhills you roamed?
Is it Heaven's wide street you now tie the reins?
Are you singlefootin' somewhere below?

Your Cherokee lover, Blue Duck was his name,
He kissed you in the sandhills before your great fame,
Blue Duck stopped a bullet in eighteen eighty-five,
And Blue Duck's no longer alive.

Cole Younger was your first man, he fathered your girl,
The sweet name you picked for your daughter was Pearl,
Cole robbed some bank and he drawed the lifeline,
I heard he got pardoned after twenty years time.

You took Jim Reed to warm your wedding bed,
Out of your love was born your boy, Ed,
Some pal killed Jim Reed by the dark of the moon,
Your son, Ed, got blowed down in a drunken saloon.

Bob Younger came next, and you loved him well,
Bob rode with them James boys off down this long trail,
Bob was caught in Minnesota with all of the gang,
Bob died down in jail by the long rusty chain.

You made love to William Clark Quantrill,
And Clark's Civil War guerillas in Missouri's bluehills,
Quantrill hit Lawrence, Kansas, he fought 'em deadstill,
And when he rode out, two hundred lay killed.

31 Quoted in Harry Thorton Moore, *The Novels of John Steinbeck: A First Critical Study* (Port Washington, New York: Kennikat Press, 1968) 72.

32 Steinbeck, *Grapes* 571.

You tell me you could have, you tell me you might
Have loved Franky James a couple of nights,
Frank fought the Midland Railroad almost to death,
'Round nineteen fifteen Frank drew his last breath.

Belle Starr, Belle Starr, my time's getting late,
I've told you all eight, I've told you their fate,
Your man, Jesse James, had one wife and son,
Jess got shot down at home by the Ford brothers' gun.

Eight men, they say, combed your black wavy hair,
Eight men knew the feel of your dark leather waist,
Eight men loved your tan leather circling skirt,
Eight men heard the bark of the guns that you wore.

Belle Starr, Belle Starr, tell me, where have you gone …[33]

By elaborating on Belle Starr's eight lovers and their dramatic deaths, the female outcast is fashioned as a tough lady, who seems to be downright unflappable. What is even more, her toughness is stressed by the description of her outward appearance – her black hair, her leather clothing and, last but not least, the guns she wears portray her as a femme fatale possessing quasi-masculine attributes and attitudes. Yet, it is not so much the content of the song that is interesting, but the fact that the song was configured according to a one-page feature about Belle Starr entitled "More Deadly Than the Male," which appeared in the *Sunday News* on December, 2nd, 1945. Here is the article in its original format:[34]

[33] Kleff 232ff.

[34] "More Deadly Than the Male," *Sunday News* 2 Dec. 1945: 2. The article is taken from the Ralph Rinzler Folklife Archives and Collections at the Smithsonian Center for Folklife and Cultural Heritage, Washington, D.C.

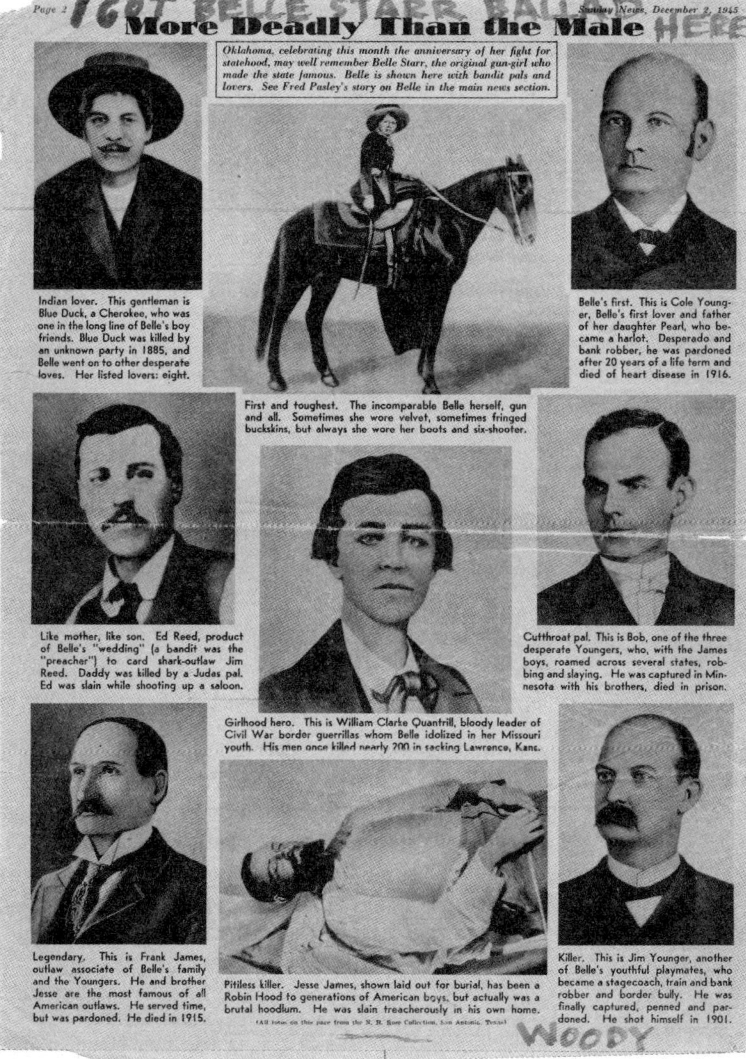

Page 2 I GOT BELLE STARR BALLAD HERE Sunday News, December 2, 1945

More Deadly Than the Male

Oklahoma, celebrating this month the anniversary of her fight for statehood, may well remember Belle Starr, the original gun-girl who made the state famous. Belle is shown here with bandit pals and lovers. See Fred Pasley's story on Belle in the main news section.

Indian lover. This gentleman is Blue Duck, a Cherokee, who was one in the long line of Belle's boy friends. Blue Duck was killed by an unknown party in 1885, and Belle went on to other desperate loves. Her listed lovers: eight.

Belle's first. This is Cole Younger, Belle's first lover and father of her daughter Pearl, who became a harlot. Desperado and bank robber, he was pardoned after 20 years of a life term and died of heart disease in 1916.

First and toughest. The incomparable Belle herself, gun and all. Sometimes she wore velvet, sometimes fringed buckskins, but always she wore her boots and six-shooter.

Like mother, like son. Ed Reed, product of Belle's "wedding" (a bandit was the "preacher") to card shark-outlaw Jim Reed. Daddy was killed by a Judas pal. Ed was slain while shooting up a saloon.

Cutthroat pal. This is Bob, one of the three desperate Youngers, who, with the James boys, roamed across several states, robbing and slaying. He was captured in Minnesota with his brothers, died in prison.

Girlhood hero. This is William Clarke Quantrill, bloody leader of Civil War border guerrillas whom Belle idolized in her Missouri youth. His men once killed nearly 200 in sacking Lawrence, Kans.

Legendary. This is Frank James, outlaw associate of Belle's family and the Youngers. He and brother Jesse are the most famous of all American outlaws. He served time, but was pardoned. He died in 1915.

Pitiless killer. Jesse James, shown laid out for burial, has been a Robin Hood to generations of American boys, but actually was a brutal hoodlum. He was slain treacherously in his own home.

Killer. This is Jim Younger, another of Belle's youthful playmates, who became a stagecoach, train and bank robber and border bully. He was finally captured, penned and pardoned. He shot himself in 1901.

(All fotos on this page from the N. H. Rose Collection, San Antonio, Texas)

WOODY

Courtesy of the Ralph Rinzler Folklife Archives and Collections, Smithsonian Institution.

Guthrie collected the article and obviously used it for his outlaw ballad, as his handwriting on the page suggests, saying: "I got Belle Starr Ballad here." And indeed, the article introduces the reader to the lives and deaths of the *eight* lovers of the female outlaw in a very concise manner, providing a photograph of each of them. The parallels between the article and the song concerning form and content are striking and allow us to assume that Guthrie also used one or the other of the numerous newspaper features that regularly appeared in the Oklahoman newspapers when writing "Pretty Boy Floyd."

Taking the general perception of Floyd as a Depression hero into consideration, the social energy of Guthrie's song about the "Sagebrush Robin Hood"[35] increases dramatically. His retelling of a story that was part of the cultural knowledge of the Oklahoman population certainly reaffirmed its moral standards. In order to drive his point home, the Okie bard generalizes his social criticism in his song's last two verses, which are among his most famous:

> Now as through this world I ramble,
> I've seen lots of funny men,
> Some will rob you with a six gun,
> And some with a fountain-pen.
>
> But as through this life you travel
> And as through this life you roam,
> You will never see an outlaw
> Drive a family from its home.[36]

Once again, yet on a more general level, the 'good robber' is clearly distinguished from the bad one, not only by his choice of weapons, but also by his moral standards. Whereas a robber like Floyd respects certain values, as he would never "drive a family from its home," the banker, as it is implicitly suggested, does not stop at anything and is thus morally inferior to the 'social bandit.' By providing such a subversive concept of integrity, according to which the outlaw's crimes can be morally legitimized as mere acts of charity and, at the same time, the banker's capitalist ambition is condemned as a vicious flaw, the last two verses epitomize the song's polemic attack on the capitalist system.

Thus, it perfectly mirrors the moral attitude of (rural) Oklahomans outlined above. Interestingly enough, the son of George Birdwell, another

[35] Wallis 269.

[36] Kleff 112. An unpublished version of the last verse reads: "I've known lots of outlaws, but I have never known / An Oklahoma outlaw to drive a family from their home" (WGA, Notebooks I, Notebook 5, 17).

infamous Oklahoman criminal and Pretty Boy's accomplice in a number of robberies, remembered his father teaching him the same lesson when he was a little child. He recollected that he could still hear his father when he was "sitting on his knee in an old Model T Ford working the gas for him and he'd tell me about what to expect from life. He said way back then that there were two kinds of people who robbed – some who did it with a gun and some with an ink pen."[37]

Guthrie's "Pretty Boy Floyd" continued the tradition of numerous outlaw ballads that had been sung and listened to on the Southern Plains since the late 1800s, when economic recession hit the land in a similarly severe way as it hit in the 1930s. In the following decades, songs fashioning the myths of people like Jesse James, Henry Starr, the Daltons and Billy the Kid, who had become archetypes of resistance and moral integrity and had thus, as cultural icons, made their way into the collective memory of the Southwesterners. "You hear songs everywhere springing up about these fellers, springing up like flowers in the right early spring," Guthrie mentioned in his annotations to "Pretty Boy Floyd."[38] He contributed to this collection of songs about outcasts and criminals, thereby participating in the discourse on moral integrity and, subsequently, shaping contemporary attitudes towards the distinction between the good and the bad. One of Guthrie's contributions to this 'archive' of outlaw songs is his version of what might probably be considered the most famous outlaw story in American culture:

> Jesse James and His Boys rode that Dodge City Trail
> Held up that Midnight Southern Mail
> And there never was a man with the law in his hand
> That could keep Jesse James in a Jail.
>
> It was Frank and Jesse James that killed a many a man [sic]
> But they never was Outlaws at Heart
> I wrote this song to tell you how it come
> That Frank and Jesse James got their start.
>
> They was living on a farm in the old Missouri Hills
> With a silver haired Mother and a Home
> Now the Railroad Bullies come to chase them off their land,
> But they found that Frank & Jesse wouldn't run.
>
> Then a Railroad Scab he went and got a bomb
> And he throwed it at the door

37 Quoted in Wallis 224.

38 Smithsonian, RRFAC, *Woody Guthrie Papers*, Box I, Folder 6.

And it killed Mrs. James asleeping in her bed,
So Jesse grabbed a big 44.

Yes, Frank and Jesse James was men that was game
To stop that high rollin' Train
And to shoot down the rat that killed Mrs. James
They was 2 Gun Frank and Jesse James.[39]

Very much like Charles Arthur Floyd, the James brothers, according to Guthrie's song, seem to be victims of corruption and violence. Their becoming outlaws is shown to be the result of an unscrupulous attack by a mean "railroad bull," who did not only "come to chase them off their land," but also "killed Mrs. James asleeping in her bed." Thus, Frank and Jesse James were "never [...] Outlaws at Heart," but only reacted to the railroad bull's actions. In his liner notes to the song, Guthrie makes clear who is to be made responsible for the James's careers as outlaws: "It was the Railroad Buyers that sent the bullies down to push folks off of their farms in the country that the new railroad was a coming through – but some folks just naturally don't push so easy,"[40] but, as one may add, react. Yet, the reactions of the James brothers would not remain without consequence, as is revealed in the last three verses of the song, which dramatize the death of Jesse James:

Now a bastard and a coward called little Robert Ford
He claimed he was Frank and Jesse's friend
Made love to Jesse's wife, and he took Jesse's life,
And he laid poor Jesse in his grave.

The people was surprised when Jesse lost his Life
Wondered how he ever come to fall

39 Smithsonian, RRFAC, *Woody Guthrie Papers*, Box 1, Folder 5. Guthrie's version of the Jesse James story goes back to numerous songs about Jesse and Frank James, which are all very similar in form and content. Four of them can be found in John Lomax, *Cowboy Songs* 152-58. Moreover, as Guthrie explains in the liner notes to the song, he "got some of the ideas [in the song] from the picture show. It showed the life of Jesse James and his boys a raising Sam Hill through the Missouri Mountains, and the Kansas Badlands, and all over the Country" (Smithsonian, RRFAC, *Woody Guthrie Papers*, Box 1, Folder 5). Guthrie also points out that he "was on a CBS Broadcast […] with Burgess Meredith, Franchot Tone, Walter Huston, and a big orchestra – they put on the life of Jesse James" (Smithsonian, RRFAC, *Woody Guthrie Papers*, Box 1, Folder 5). Thus, just like for the case of "Belle Starr," his writing the Jesse James-song was also influenced by other contemporary media dealing with the topic.

40 Smithsonian, RRFAC, *Woody Guthrie Papers*, Box 1, Folder 5.

Robert Ford it's a fact, shot Jesse in the Back
While Jesse hung a picture on the wall.

They dug Jesse's Grave and a stone they raised,
It says, Jesse James lies here
Was killed by a man, a bastard and a coward,
Whose name ain't worthy to appear.[41]

The rendering of the insidious murder of Jesse James, shot in the back while hanging a picture on the wall, once again portrays Jesse as a victim. He had no chance to defend himself – if he had had one, he would certainly have won the fight against Robert Ford, as the song implies by putting emphasis on the people "wonder[ing] how he ever come to fall." Both the story of his mother being violently murdered and his being killed by a "bastard and a coward" underline Jesse James's moral superiority. Like "Pretty Boy Floyd," Guthrie's song "Jesse James and His Boys" thus suggests a subversive moral concept that criticizes the established socioeconomic order – it is not the James brothers but the "Railroad Buyers" who, as representatives of the capitalist system, are morally wrong.

However, the creation of modern Robin Hoods and their prominent part in the Southwestern collective memory might not only have been a consequence of worsening socioeconomic conditions. The analogies drawn between the American outlaws and their medieval predecessor might have also been fostered by the fact that, at least in some Southern states, a certain repertoire of traditional English ballads was still in use. Woody Guthrie became acquainted with these songs when he was a child. Then, his mother Nora

> sang him the songs [she] had brought from Tennessee, songs that had come over on the boats from England and Ireland and that had been passed from mother to daughter (men, by and large, thought them too sappy) ever since. She sang of murders and jealous lovers and natural disasters. She sang about the woman who left her family to run off with the dashing outlaw, about the town that had been crushed by a cyclone, about families wrecked by bad luck.[42]

Unfortunately, there is no evidence that there was a traditional Robin Hood ballad among the songs Guthrie's mother sang to lull her son to sleep, which eventually might have influenced his composition of "Pretty Boy Floyd." Yet, there is no doubt that traditional English ballads had a certain impact on his songwriting, as the story of "the woman who left her family to run off with the dashing outlaw" was rendered in his ver-

41 Smithsonian, RRFAC, *Woody Guthrie Papers*, Box 1, Folder 5.
42 Klein 14.

sion of an old English traditional that is known by numerous titles, for example "The Gypsy Laddie," "Black Jack Davie" or "Amos Furr."[43] In this song, a landlord's lady leaves her husband to spend her life with an infamous outlaw in the woods. In the middle of the night, the desperate husband decides to follow his adulterous wife and finds her sitting at a campfire, singing songs with her new love. What follows is a dialogue between husband and wife, in which he tries to persuade her to come back home. Here is the argument as rendered in Guthrie's song that was, most probably, written in 1938:[44]

> Have you forsaken your house and home?
> Have you forsaken your baby?
> Have you forsaken your husband dear
> To go with the Gypsy Davy?
> And sing with the Gypsy Dave
> That song of the Gypsy Dave?
>
> Yes I've forsaken my husband dear
> To go with the Gypsy Davy.
> And I've forsaken my mansion high
> But not my blue-eyed babe,
> Not my blue-eyed babe.
>
> She smiled to leave her husband dear
> And go with the Gypsy Davy;
> But the tears come a-trickling down her cheeks
> To think of the blue-eyed babe,
> Pretty little blue-eyed babe.

43 According to the *Frank C. Brown Collection of North Carolina Folklore*, "The Gypsy Laddie" was widely known and sung in a number of Southern states, including Massachusetts, Tennessee, North Carolina, Arkansas, Missouri and Indiana (cf. Henry M. Belden and Arthur Palmer Hudson, eds., *The Frank C. Brown Collection of North Carolina Folklore, Vol. 2: Folk Ballads of North Carolina* [Durham, North Carolina: Duke UP, 1952] 161). As Alan Lomax argues, Guthrie's version is a combination of Texan and Oklahoman texts. (cf. Alan Lomax, ed., *The Penguin Book of American Folk Songs* [Baltimore: Penguin, 1964] 112).

44 In an unpublished manuscript that is dated April 1938 and that is called *Woody and Lefty Lou's One Thousand and One Laffs and Your Free Gift Of One Hundred and One Songs*, Woody wrote an introduction to the song: "Wimmens hearts is like guitars – and here is the song and tale of a woman who decided to leave her husband and wealth and go with a Gypsy Davy, and she loved all the songs played on the strings of her heart – except one string. She couldn't bear the thoughts of leaving her purty little Blue-Eyed Baby. I don't reckon they [sic] is anybody knows how old this song is. I've heard it all my life" (quoted in Jeff Place, liner notes to "Gypsy Davy," *This Land is Your Land: The Asch Recordings*, Vol. 1 [Smithsonian Folkways Recordings: Washington, D.C., 1998] 17).

Take off, take off your buckskin gloves
Made of Spanish leather;
Give to me your lily-white hand
And we'll ride home together,
We'll ride home again.

No, I won't take off my buckskin gloves,
They're made of Spanish leather.
I'll go my way from day to day
And sing with the Gypsy Davy,
That song of the Gypsy Davy,
That song of the Gypsy Davy,
That song of the Gypsy Dave.

In his strategy of persuasion, the landlord, or "boss" as he is called in Guthrie's version of the ballad, tries to appeal to his wife's bad conscience by enumerating the standards for a 'good' wife's behavior: he hints at her responsibility for house and home, for her baby, and, last but not least, for her husband. And, at first, it seems that his strategy is successful, for she starts crying as she thinks about the child she is going to leave behind. Yet, she is eventually able to overcome her social obligations and decides to stay with the Gypsy Davy. Just like Guthrie's "Pretty Boy Floyd," though on a different level, his "Gypsy Davy" thus undermines established moral concepts by romanticizing a lawless life beyond any social restraints and conventions. In this respect, the song very much fits the context of Oklahoman outlaw culture in the years of the Great Depression.

What catches one's eye or ear respectively is that Guthrie's version of the song about the "Gypsy Davy" contains a number of formal and lyrical features which are characteristic of the traditional folk ballad. One formal element which immediately reminds us of the long tradition Guthrie's song is indebted to is the repetitive structure at the beginning of the first verse, the so-called 'incremental repetition,' which is employed in order to enumerate the things or people abandoned by the woman.[45] Another formal feature which hints at the traditional pretext(s)

45 Würzbach defines 'incremental repetition' as "an overt kind of repetition and variation [...], which ranges all the way from the similar to the contrastive" (Natascha Würzbach, "An Approach to a Context-Oriented Genre Theory in Application the the History of the Ballad: Traditional Ballad – Street Ballad – Literary Ballad," *Poetics* 12 [1983]: 54). She points out that the semantic correlation between the repeated elements "often reinforces syntgamatic correlations in the narrative such as those based on chronological sequence, logic of events, or dialogue structure" (Würzbach 54). The latter, one may argue, is the case for Guthrie's "Gypsy Davy."

of Guthrie's ballad is the postposition of adjectives in expressions like "my husband dear" or "my mansion high" in the second or third verse respectively. Finally, the image of the woman's "lily-white hand" Guthrie employs in the fourth verse of the song is a lyrical commonplace often employed in traditional English and Scottish ballads.

That Guthrie was well aware of the long tradition of English and Scottish popular ballads and included a considerable number of them in his repertoire shall be illustrated by the analysis of yet another example, which will reveal that the subversive concept of moral integrity promoted in Guthrie's outlaw songs was also associated with the Christian concept of charity. In his song "The Unwelcome Guest," Guthrie configures the life of the Englishman Richard Turpin, which was also led beyond any restraints and conventions and that, from the beginning of the eighteenth century onwards, has been fashioned in numerous songs and stories. Born at Hempstead in Essex in 1705, Turpin was apprenticed to a butcher, but soon turned to illegal activities like cattle-stealing in order to make a living, before he later turned to highway robbery. His illegal deeds were first fashioned in William Harrison Ainsworth's romance *Rockwood* (1856), which deals with Turpin's ride on his horse Black Bess from London to York.[46] It seems that it is in this connection that Turpin's name was remembered. The story of the ride spread as far as the American Southwest, particularly the Indian territory, where it was rendered in a song which is said to have been particularly popular among cowboys.[47]

Written in 1940, Guthrie's "The Unwelcome Guest" was certainly inspired by the tales and songs about the English outlaw circulating in the American Southwest. It fashions Turpin as an outlaw who only takes from the rich and does not even think of robbing those who are at the bottom of society.[48] Following the standard pattern of fashioning the out-

46 William H. Ainsworth, *Rockwood. A Romance* (New York: 1873 Press, 1999 [1856]).

47 The song "My Bonnie Black Bess," which deals with Turpin's ride, can be found in Albert B. Friedman, ed., *The Viking Book of Folk Ballads of the English-Speaking World* (1915; New York: Viking Press, 1976) 369.

48 Kleff 389: "To the rich man's bright lodges I ride this wind / On my good horse I call you my shiny Black Bess / To the playhouse of fortune / To take the bright silver/ And gold you have taken from somebody else. / [...] / I've never took food from the widows and orphans / And never a hard working man I oppressed / So take your pace easy, / For home soon like lightning / We soon will be riding, my shiny Black Bess. / [...] / I don't know, good horse, / As we trot in the dark here / That robbing the rich is for worse or for best / They take it by stealing and lying and gambling / And I take it my way, my shiny Black Bess."

law as an ally of the poor and oppressed, the lyrical I, Turpin, claims that he neither "took from the widows and orphans," presumably the most innocent and helpless members of society, nor did he oppress "the hard working man." It is only the rich who have to suffer from his forays. Though he is not sure whether his criminal activities are "for worse or for best," Turpin justifies his crimes with the observation that the rich have acquired their wealth by "tak[ing] it from somebody else." And they did so illegally, as they took it "by stealing and lying and gambling."

As the second to last verse of the song reveals, Turpin seems to be well aware that his crimes will, sooner or later, lead to his being caught and killed by those whom he had robbed. Yet, he is already sure that somebody will enter upon his heritage and continue to support the poor by robbing the wealthy:

> Yes, they'll catch me napping one day
> And they'll kill me
> And then I'll be gone but that won't be my end
> For my guns and my saddle will always be filled
> By unwelcome travellers and other brave men.[49]

Turpin's strong belief that his "guns and his saddle will always be filled / By unwelcome travellers and other brave men" implicitly emphasizes that 'social banditry' is a recurrent phenomenon which is closely related to the political and economic situation in a particular region or country. Thus, as already argued above, it was not by chance that stories and myths of outlaws would flourish in the American Southwest during the Great Depression.

Interestingly, the song's last verse introduces a notion which further backs the concept of moral integrity promoted both in "The Unwelcome Guest" and in the other outlaw ballads discussed:

> And they'll take the money and spread it out equal
> Just like the Bible and the prophets suggest
> But the man that go riding to help these poor workers
> The rich will cut down like an unwelcome guest.[50]

Turpin legitimizes his deeds and the deeds of his successors through a reference to the Bible, for he claims that "unwelcome travellers and other brave men […] take the money and spread it out equal / Just like the Bible and the prophets suggests." The passage of the Bible to which

49 Kleff 389.
50 Kleff 389.

the verse's lines corresponds, is found in the Acts of the Apostles, which promotes, just like the song's verse, an equal distribution of goods:

> And they continued stedfastly in the apostles' doctrine and fellowship, and in breaking of bread, and in prayers. And fear came upon every soul: and many wonders and signs were done by the apostles. And all that believed were together, and had all things common; and *sold their possessions and goods, and parted them to all men, as every man had need.* And they, continuing daily with one accord in the temple, and breaking bread from house to house, did eat their meat with gladness and singleness of heart, praising God, and having favour with all the people. And the Lord added to the church daily such as should be saved.[51]

One may well argue that it is not by chance that Guthrie's version of Turpin's story contains a hint at a biblical intertext. The reference rather expresses the general reappreciation of basic Christian values in a time when the majority of the American population suffered from unemployment and poverty. In the course of the Great Depression, the renaissance of the idea(l) of Christian solidarity and charity was pressed ahead by the upcoming labor movement, the adherents of which preferred a very literal reading of the Bible and interpreted it as an early manifesto of socialist thinking. Being an archetype of the righteous, the outlaw personified these ideals of just and fair distribution, of a life led according to fixed moral principles, quite in contrast to the rich, whose moral integrity, as we have seen, was portrayed as corrupted by avarice and greed.[52]

Whereas it is obvious both by their topic and their form that Guthrie's "Gypsy Davy" and his "The Unwelcome Guest" were modeled after traditional English and Scottish folk ballads, the traditional traces of "Pretty Boy Floyd," are not quite as evident. That his song also resorts to compositional features of traditional ballad writing, might best be illustrated by a closer look at its beginning:

> If you gather round me children
> A Story I will tell,

[51] *The Bible*, ed. Caroll and Prickett, Acts of the Apostles, 2, 42-47, emphases added.

[52] For the appropriation of the religious idea of charity in the socialist discourse cf. chapter 3.6 of this study. Following from this notion, it is probably not by chance that in Guthrie's "Pretty Boy Floyd," the outlaw's act of charity takes place on the birthday of Jesus Christ: "It was in Oklahoma City / It was on a Christmas Day, / There come a whole car load of groceries, / With a letter that did say: / 'You say that I'm an outlaw / You say that I'm a thief, / Here's a Christmas dinner, / For the families on relief'" (Kleff 112).

About Pretty Boy Floyd, the outlaw,
Oklahoma knew him well.

The speaker's request to "gather round" him in order to listen to what he has to say imitates the topical introduction of English street ballads or street ballad-variations of folk ballads.[53] Let us examine, for example, the first verse of the Middle English song "A Gest of Robyn Hood":

Lythe and listin, gentilmen,
That be of frebore blode
I shall you tel of a gode yeman,
His name was Robyn Hode.[54]

Another song entitled "A True Tale of Robin Hood" starts off in a similar way, the first two verses reading

Both gentlemen, or yeomen bould,
Or whatsoever you are,
To have a stately story tould,
Attention now prepare.

It is a tale of Robin Hood,
Which I to you will tell,
Which being rightly understood,
I know will please you well.[55]

As hinted at above, one cannot be sure whether Guthrie was aware of any Robin Hood ballads; nor is his begging for the audience's attention an exclusive feature of his outlaw songs.[56] However, the formal and topical analogies outlined above suggest that Guthrie's songwriting was indeed influenced by the English and Scottish folk *and* street ballad traditions.

53 For a comprehensive analysis of the forms and functions of rhetoric devices and strategies used in traditional English street ballads cf. Spekat 272ff. Other characteristic elements of a traditional ballad which can be found in Guthrie's song are its "concentration on a central, conflict-loaden incident" (Würzbach 48) or its focus on a single character as "a principle of textual coherence" (Würzbach 47).

54 Francis J. Child, ed., *The English and Scottish Popular Ballads*, Vol. 3 (New York: The Folklore Press in association with Pageant Book Company, 1956) 56.

55 Child 227.

56 The "Come all ye"-structure is a prominent feature in a number of protest songs in order to catch the audience's attention. Thus, the assumption that Guthrie's use of it was exclusively stirred by his knowledge of Elizabethan ballads is indeed vague. Still, its being rooted in the English and Scottish ballad tradition is of major significance for gauging the intertextual potential of Guthrie's songs.

Yet, the opening lines of "Pretty Boy Floyd" are interesting in quite another respect, as they, by suggesting a close connection between the song's speaker and his listeners,[57] hint at the oral tradition of ballad-singing and thus at the fact that singing, in general, is a performative act which requires an audience.[58] Without listeners, the song of the outlaw would not be worth performing, as the audience plays an important part in the communal experience of singing. Presumably, Guthrie performed the song on KFVD in California, where he would reach the ears of the Southwestern migrants.[59] Taking into consideration that Pretty Boy Floyd, as a vital part of the Southwesterners' collective memory, had become, for most of the migrants, a cultural icon symbolizing their democratic heritage, Guthrie's song might have "instill[ed] empathy for the cause at hand […] and inspire[d] [the listeners'] consciousness."[60] What is more, the shared memory of the outlaw myth might have created what Frith would call an "affective and emotional alliance"[61] among the audience, who were thus provided with an "intensely subjective sense of being sociable."[62]

By drawing on a topic that had deeply shaped the Oklahoman collective memory ever since the state's economy began to bust at the end of the 19th century, the song did not only articulate, but also offer a feeling of shared identity among its (potential) migrant listeners. And indeed, when the manager of the FSA migrant camp in Marysville, California, complained about the migrants' general hatred for the law and their refusal to accept certain restraints in the Camp Report of August 29, 1936, he pointed out that he was shocked by their "idolizing Pretty Boy Floyd and other criminals," concluding that the migrants were characterized by an "outlaw psychology," an observation which once again emphasizes the assumption that the numerous outlaw myths and their un-

57 Cf. Spekat 274: "[D]ie straßenballadentypische Adressatenanrede [stellt] schon zu Beginn des Vortrags […] einen engen Bezug zwischen Erzählinstanz und Rezipient [her]." In addition, as Jackson argues, the speaker's addressing children points to the fact that the story of Floyd "should be handed down to another generation" (181).

58 Cf. Würzbach 53.

59 We might deduce that from the fact that another draft of the song which carries a note that reads "Original Song Woody Guthrie KFVD 3-12-39" (WGA, Notebooks I, Notebook 4, 101).

60 Hampton 56-57.

61 Frith 273.

62 Frith 273. The frequent use of the word "Oklahoma(n)" in one of the unpublished versions of the song might put empasis on this assumption (WGA, Notebooks I, Notebook 4, 101).

derlying concept of moral integrity was deeply engrained in the cultural knowledge of the Southwestern migrants.[63] Even when the Depression years were gone and the American economy began to recover, the myth of the outlaw remained vivid in the Oklahomans' collective memory and, at least to a certain extent, it was Guthrie's song that kept it alive.[64] Thus, in July 1942, Guthrie received a letter from his producer, Alan Lomax, who informed him about the reception of his songs in public, pointing out that "on picnics and beer parties the songs that they've liked the best have been Pretty Boy Floyd and then Pretty Boy Floyd all over again."[65]

63 Quoted in Walter J. Stein, *California and the Dust Bowl Migration.* Westport (Connecticut: Greenwood Press, 1973) 172.

64 Cf. Jackson 181.

65 WGA, Correspondence II, Box II, Folder 17.

3.3 "Believe it or not, you won't find it so hot": (De)Constructing the 'Californian Dream'

> The best of all funny songs have got a mighty sincere backbone. (Woody Guthrie)[1]

The image of California as a place of plenty and abundance, where the sun always shines and everyone is able to make his or her fortune, has become an integral part of the collective memory in the United States and beyond. Even today, California's reputation as a place where fortunes are made and opportunities abound seems to attract people from everywhere within and outside the United States. In the times of the Great Depression, this image lured thousands of impoverished migrants to the Golden State, after they had been forced to leave their farmlands in the Dust Bowl region of the American Southwest. Woody Guthrie took in the migrants' hardships on the road and rendered this large-scale migration to California in a number of his songs.

This chapter examines how Guthrie configures California, the migrants' favorite destination, in his songs about the Dust Bowl Migration. My contextualizing analysis will show the ways in which Guthrie's songs (re)-negotiate the clichés of the 'Californian Dream': on the one hand, they draw from a rather traditional stock of images to fashion the state on the American west coast, and, on the other hand, they question the reputation of California as a place of prosperity by deliberately distorting and undermining these images.

After briefly outlining the changing patterns of interstate migration to California in the Great Depression, the following chapter centers on a close analysis of Guthrie's "Do Re Mi," using it as a departure point to explore both the origin and the contemporary distribution of the imagery he utilizes by reconstructing the stages of the medial creation and dissemination of what is commonly referred to as the 'Californian Dream.' By correlating Guthrie's song to its historico-political contexts, this chapter also ponders on the political implications of Guthrie's distortion, or deconstruction, of the 'Californian Dream,' which was used as a political statement on the radically discriminating immigration policy of the Californian administration in the second half of the 1930s.

* * * * *

[1] Letter to Alan Lomax, 19 Sep.1940 (WGA, Correspondence I, Box 1, Folder 39).

Interstate migration to California before the 1930s was nothing unusual at all. It followed, as James N. Gregory has it, "the standard logic of American Westward movement."[2] He goes on to explain that "[h]istorically, people usually moved west not out of desperation but in response to the perceived attractions of opportunity-filled new settings."[3] In the pre-Depression decades, Southwesterners, mostly townsfolk and modestly prosperous farmers, had settled in the Golden State, the majority of them in the big cities, particularly in the communities of Greater Los Angeles. For the 'middling classes,' the West had always been the land of new beginnings and opportunities and moving westward was quite a normal business.

The majority of these migrants were, socially and economically, well-off; thus, the migration to California did not cause any severe problems. Yet, in the middle of the 1930s, when America's economy was shaken by the Great Depression, the previous patterns of westward migration changed dramatically. Now, the majority of migrants came from the impoverished agricultural areas in the Southwestern states of Oklahoma, Texas, Arkansas and Missouri in order to find new jobs in California. What had only been a significant minority compared to the overall number of migrants at the beginning of the 20th century soon became a major concern. Already in 1926, a journalist reported that "Oklahoma farmers in their second-hand flivvers, piled high with furniture and family [...] have been pouring through the divides by the hundreds."[4]

About a decade later, this image of the Southwestern migrants, arriving at the Californian border in an old jalopy packed with their belongings and which, in most of the cases, the migrants could only afford by selling their farm back home, would become standard. Most of the Southwesterners called the San Joaquin Valley their new home, which would later become the "most publicized destination of the Dust Bowl Migrants,"[5] as the press began to call them in the middle of the 1930s. Thus, migration became a major concern for the Californian population. Gregory points out that

> [c]ontemporaries decided that they witnessed something unprecedented in the history of white Americans: a large-scale refugee migration, a flight from pri-

2 Gregory 7.
3 Gregory 7.
4 Quoted in Gregory 9.
5 Gregory 9.

> vation of the sort Americans read about elsewhere but hoped never to see in their own land.[6]

A part of this "large-scale refugee migration" is rendered in Woody Guthrie's song "Do Re Mi," which was probably written in 1937 and first appeared in *Woody and Lefty Lou's Favorite Collection of Old Time Hill Country Songs.*[7] It deals with the experience of the migrants arriving at the Californian border after their long and exhausting journey from the regions in the American Southwest:

> Lots of folks back east, they say,
> Leavin' home ev'ry day
> Beatin'the hot and dusty way
> To the California Line.
> 'Cross the desert sands they roll
> Getting out of that old dust bowl,
> They think they're going to a sugar bowl,
> But here's what they find:
>
> Now the police at the port of entry say:
> 'You're number fourteen thousand for today! Oh, [...][8]

The first verse briefly summarizes the story of thousands of farmers that were forced to leave their homes in the Southwestern states.[9] In California, the song suggests, they expect the opposite of what they had to leave behind – a sugar bowl, a term which immediately calls forth an idea of cornucopian prosperity. However, the dream of wealth and abundance vanishes into thin air, as the migrants at the border are confronted with a police officer telling them that they are not the first to come up with the idea of settling in the Golden State. The chorus of the song makes the officer's policy obvious:

6 Gregory 10.

7 Cf. Smithsonian, RRFAC, *Woody Guthrie Papers*, Box 2, Folder 4.

8 Leventhal and Guthrie 81-82.

9 It is important to point out that among the masses of the so-called Dust Bowl migrants, less than 16,000 people from the Dust Bowl proper ended up in California, which is only six percent of the total from the Southwestern States. According to Gregory, "journalists are to blame for this misunderstanding. Confusing drought with dust, and assuming that the dramatic dust storms must have had something to do with the large number of cars from Oklahoma and Texas seen crossing the California border in the mid-1930s, the press created the dramatic but misleading association between the Dust Bowl and the Southwestern migration" (11).

Oh, if you ain't got the do re mi, folks,
If you ain't got the do re mi,
Why, you better go back to beautiful Texas,
Oklahoma, Kansas, Georgia, Tennessee,
California is a garden of Eden,
A paradise to live in or see.
But, believe it or not,
You won't find it so hot,
If you ain't got the do re mi.[10]

According to the officer, the migrants will only be allowed to cross the border if they have got the "do re mi," another word for "dough," a contemporary colloquial expression for cash money, which they would need to support themselves.[11] Moreover, as the musical term "do re mi," denoting the beginning of the c-major scale, suggests a harmonious arrangement of sounds, another, more metaphorical reading of the expression suggests itself: Accordingly, the police officer's words imply that the migrants will never be able to live in tune with the Californians' attitudes and to conform with their way of life, let alone be able to afford doing so, which immediately brings us back to the first reading of "do re mi."[12] The officer, correct in assuming that the migrants do not have any money, tells them to return to their home states and mocks the migrants' conception of California as "a paradise to live in or see," for, most probably, they will never be able to enjoy it, since it is a paradise for the monied class only.

Once again, the extraordinary living conditions which can be found in California are highlighted. It is fashioned as another "garden of Eden," an image which invokes a land where "the earth [brings] forth grass, and herb yield[ing] seed after his kind, and the tree yield[ing] fruit"[13] and provides an abundance of gold and precious gems. By contrast, the territory of the migrants "back East" is a wasteland devoid of all the features

10 Leventhal and Guthrie 82-83.

11 The significance of the musical term 'do re mi' is highlighted by its appearance in a song, thus becoming, in a way, a self-reflexive element which attracts the attention of the listeners.

12 Interestingly, Kleff's German translation of the term 'do re mi' is based on the metaphorical reading: "Wenn ihr nicht in unserer Tonart singt, Freunde, / wenn ihr nicht unser Do Re Mi singt, / dann geht ihr besser zurück ins schöne Texas, Oklahoma, Kansas, Georgia, Tennessee. / Kalifornien ist ein Garten Eden, eine Augenweide, ein Paradies, wenn man dort lebt, / aber du kannst es glauben oder nicht: / Wenn du nicht in unserer Tonart singst, wirst du alles nicht mehr ganz so schön finden" (95).

13 *The Bible*, ed. Caroll and Prickett, Genesis, 1, 12.

Eden in its fertility displays – as the metaphor of the "sugar bowl," in direct contrast to the "old dust bowl," suggests.

The origin of this biblical imagery, which is fused with the prospects of material wealth and thus used to portray California as a place of plenty, where everyone can easily make his or her fortune, goes back to the times of the Gold Rush, when California gained its reputation as a state of abundance. "[B]lessed with a remarkable climate and a wondrous array of natural resources," as Gregory argues, "California's pecuniary attracttions had [then] been fused with equally compelling images of exceptional beauty."[14] The Gold Rush spawned songs, tales and wishful dreams about California. At the same time, these songs and tales contributed to the image of California that would become a constituent part of American collective memory as of the middle of the 19th century. Consider the first verse and the chorus of a song entitled "The Race to California," which was written in 1849 and which certainly contributed to the creation of the 'Californian Dream':

> Oh, the good time is come at last, and each succeeding day, Sir,
> Inventions, curiosities, new novelties display, Sir,
> But pow'r of steam and light of gas, and electricity, Sir,
> Are naught to California's wealth, that great and last discovery –
>
> [Chorus]:
> Gold, Gold, Gold.
> Ev'rybody's running after Gold, Gold, Gold.[15]

The steam-engine and the electric light bulb are "naught to California's wealth," the attraction of which is emphasized by the frequent repetition of the word "Gold" in the chorus, which, in turn, creates the impression of a frantic enthusiasm about the state on the American west coast. Alluding to the American myth of the frontier and the never-ending spirit of moving westward in order to expand economically, California's wealth is said to be "that great and last discovery." Embodying progress and industriousness, the 'Golden' State thus soon became the major destination for migrants not only from the other American States, but from all over the world, as the next verse suggests:

> Ten thousand ships they're building now to cross the wide Atlantic,
> And all are on their way to reach those golden shores romantic;

[14] Gregory 8.

[15] Irwin Silber, ed., *Songs from the Great American West* (New York/London: Macmillan, 1967) 7.

Butchers, bakers, leave their work, cobblers and 'Navvies' too, Sir,
And even lawyers emigrate. Oh dear, what shall we do, Sir?[16]

People with various social backgrounds from everywhere around the world seek their fortune in California. All of them, as the song has it in the fourth verse, "go with the same intent, the hope of gaining wealth, Sir / Nor do they stop to eat or drink, regardless of their health, Sir." And, as the song further suggests, even the poorest of the poor will eventually come to terms in California:

Soldiers desert, no wonder, since the means of getting rich, Sir,
Is open to the poorest man by scraping in a ditch, Sir.
Their officers now make their beds, and cook their meals we hear, Sir,
But soon they must betake themselves to scrape *there* too, we fear, Sir.[17]

Along with the Gold Rush came the necessity to feed the hundreds of thousands of settlers who believed themselves able to make their way 'from rags to riches' in California. Thus, in the second half of the 19th century, agriculture succeeded mining as the most important economic branch of the state.[18] When immigration to the Golden State reached its first peak, the boom in California's agriculture seemed to be limitless. Soon, with the state's flatlands and foothill fields covered with orchards, vineyards, citrus groves, vegetable and all kinds of cereal crops, California's image changed to that of a green idyll providing the resources necessary to feed the growing population.

What is more, with the actual transition of California's economy to agriculture, an extensive marketing campaign fostered the paradisiac image of plenty and abundance, which soon spread all over the United States. In 1907, a citrus promotion campaign was initiated in order to increase the national sales of citrus fruits: A special orange train was sent to Iowa, promoting "Oranges for Health – California for Wealth."[19] The same year, one of the most successful trademarks in history was established, which, like no other trademark before, coined the image of juicy oranges and sunny California: Sunkist.

16 Silber 7.

17 Silber 7.

18 For the following considerations about Californian agriculture and its marketing, I predominantly draw from Kevin Starr's illuminating study *Inventing the Dream: California Through the Progressive Era* (New York/Oxford: Oxford UP, 1985).

19 Starr, *Inventing the Dream* 162.

In the following years and decades, the local demand grew and spread eastward, as the transcontinental railroad and steamship systems opened up new opportunities for marketing Californian fruits and vegetables. In need of an effective way to identify and advertise a product for customers who lived thousands of miles away, the Californian packing companies employed wooden shipping boxes about 12" x 12" x 27", and used labels about 10" x 11" fixed on the boxes' ends. These brightly colored, attractively designed paper labels soon proved to be a key ingredient in the national marketing scheme of Californian agricultural products. Thus, one might well assume, it is no coincidence that in 1915, Edward James Wickson, in his book *California Garden*, fashioned the Golden State as the "garden of America," and declared that "the orange [...] was the premier fruit of California, in itself a symbol of California's call to civilized rural life."[20]

Orange crate labels

In the 1910s and 1920s, the "orange crate labels" even emerged as an artistic from of expression throughout the art deco era and were thus perfected, now conveying their most explicit image of the Golden State.[21] California's landscape was idealized as a place apart, as a Mediterranean idyll and a land of fantasy and dreams. As Peter Gould, one of the first geographers to work on the images of places in the collective consciousness, observed, "perceptions of places [are] derived from people's information flow, such as newspapers, magazines, books, movies, television, and other forms of media."[22] Thus, though it is, most probably, impossible to really gauge the impact of these orange crate labels,

20 Starr, *Inventing the Dream* 139-40.

21 The orange crate labels are taken from <http://www.labelframes. com>, 4 Sept. 2006; another online collection of crate labels can be found at: <http://www.california-historicalsociety.org/exhibits/past_ex_big_orange. html#>, 4 Sept. 2006.

22 George O. Carney. 1994. "Music and Place," *The Sounds of People and Places*, ed. Carney 212.

one might well assume that these highly stylized images, bearing titles like "Miracle" or "Full o' Juice," or, even more explicitly, "California Dream," spread their message of California as a place of extraordinary wealth and agricultural abundance and thus contributed to the nation's collective image of the state on the American west coast.

As these 'mental maps'[23] people develop in order to conceptualize certain regions or locations vary "with the individual's past experiences and present attitudes acting through values, needs, memories, moods, social circumstances, and expectations,"[24] it is not surprising that, in the second half of the Great Depression, the potential of the 'Californian Dream' as a 'pull'-factor increased dramatically, especially for the Southwestern migrants, who, traumatized and dislocated, hoped to find new opportunities in the Golden State.

And indeed, it was the image of California as a place of plenty and abundance most of the migrants from the Southwestern states had in mind when they traveled on Route 66 to the west coast, as the following excerpt from a conversation with Mrs. J.W. Becker from Oklahoma, recorded on August, 16th, 1940, reveals. Mrs. Becker reflects on her reasons for coming to California:

> Long about 1912, the people started talking about California and they made it so flowery that the people talked California [sic]. Maybe people came out here and started trading land, especially here in the San Joaquin Valley [...] And there's one man came out here and he traded thousands of acres of land. And then he came back to Oklahoma [...] Well, he was well acquainted and was telling the people about sunny California.[25]

In his novel *The Grapes of Wrath*, John Steinbeck lets one of his protagonists, Ma Joad, express her expectations about going to California. Her speech is loaded with cliché-ridden images that could have also been used in one of the advertisements mentioned above:

> But I like to think how nice it's gonna be, maybe, in California. Never cold. An' fruit ever'place, an' people just bein' in the nicest places, little white houses in among the orange trees. I wonder—that is, if we all get jobs an' all

23 For an outline of the concept of 'mental map' cf. Peter Gould and Rodney White, *Mental Maps* (Boston, Massachusetts: Allen & Unwin, 1986).

24 Carney, "Music and Place" 212-13.

25 Quoted in *Voices from the Dust Bowl. The Charles L. Todd and Robert Sonkin Migrant Worker Collection 1940-1941* at the American Folklife Center of the Library of Congress the Farm Security Administration Camp, <http://memory.loc.gov/cgi-bin/query/D?toddbib:193:./temp/~ammem_rmrp::>, 2 Sept. 2006.

> work maybe we can get one of them little white houses. An' the little fellas go out an' pick oranges right off the tree.[26]

The migrants' expectations are also revealed in a number of poems and songs, some of which were published in the newspapers of the Farm Security Administration Camps, which were run by the government and temporarily housed thousands of migrants during the late 1930s and early 1940s. Those testimonies drew from a number of expressions and phrases deriving from the 'orange crate pastoralism' outlined above in order to describe California's beauty, like "California where the sun always shines," or "the shining of your sun / the beauty of your orange groves."[27] Moreover, they also expressed the economic concerns of the migrant workers who were looking for new job opportunities, as the following four lines by an unknown composer reveal:

> When I first came to California
> Was in the year of thirty-seven,
> From what I read in papers,
> I thought it was poor man's heaven.[28]

Another example is a song written by Jack Bryant, which was recorded in a migratory labor camp near Firebaugh:

> You've all heard the story
> Of old Sunny Cal
> The place where it never rains
> They say it don't know how.
> They say, 'Come on, you Okies,
> Work is easy found
> Bring along your cotton pack
> You can pick the whole year round.'[29]

Obviously, the image of "old Sunny Cal" that was invented and successfully distributed by the media starting at the end of the 19th century, also

[26] Steinbeck, *Grapes* 124.

[27] Quoted in Gregory 20.

[28] Quoted in Gregory 20. In some respects, my analysis of the poems cited follows Gregory's examination, in which he refers to the poems as "source[s]" which shall give evidence of "the range of concerns and attractions which brought people to California" (20). I will, however, refer to the poems as intertexts for the contextualization of Guthrie's songs in order to explore the circulation and dissemination of particular patterns of cultural knowledge both in various media and various genres.

[29] Quoted in Gregory 20.

reached the Southwestern states, where California would soon become the last resort, or, as the anonymous writer has it in her poem quoted above, "poor man's heaven." In his autobiography, Guthrie remembers a letter from his aunt Laura from California he received when he was still with his uncle Jeff Guthrie in Texas. Trying to convince her nephew to come to California, she, as well, resorts to an argument that fuses natural beauty with the prospects of prosperity. She points out that

> when Texas is so dusty and bad, California is so green and pretty. You must be twenty-five by now, Woody. I know I can get you a job here in Sonora. Why don't you come? Your aunt Laura.[30]

And Guthrie came. According to his recollections, it was this letter that eventually made him travel to the west coast in 1937. Yet, before he left, he went to the general store in Pampa, where he bought some postcards he would later sent to his friends and relatives. Still in the store, he wrote on the cards: "Greetings from the Land of Sunshine and just plenty of Good Fresh Air."[31] Taking into account that Guthrie is retrospectively fashioning himself and the Dustbowl experience in his autobiographical recollections, we might assume that he used elements like the letter and the text on the postcards to capture the contemporary notion of California as the "Land of Sunshine."

In the course of the Dust Bowl migration, thousands of families were lured to the Golden State. Yet, in contrast to Guthrie, who deliberately toured the country, "hittin' the road"[32] whenever possible, the majority of the migrants came because they did not have any other option. Guthrie's song called "Willy Rogers Highway" configures the migrants' traveling on Route 66 to California:[33]

> My Sixty-Six highway, this Will Rogers road,
> It's lined with jalopies just as far as I can see;
> Can you think up a joke, Will, for all o' these folks
> From New Yorker town down to Lost [sic] Angeles?
>
> Ten thousand lost families I count every day
> Caught under my bridges and under my trees;

30 Guthrie, *Bound for Glory* 191.
31 Guthrie, *Bound for Glory* 194.
32 Guthrie, *Bound for Glory* 191.
33 Route 66 was named after Will Rogers, who, in the 1930s, was to become the most popular and best loved entertainer of his time. He went to Hollywood in 1918 and starred in many features in silent cinema and became, after the advent of sound, the most popular male actor in Hollywood.

> Can you make up a joke that'll win them a job
> From New Yorker town down to Lost Angeles.[34]

The additional "t" in "Lost Angeles" hints at the shady sides of the alleged 'Californian Dream' the majority of the "lost families" still believed in when they were on their way to the American west coast. Unfortunately, most of the migrants who eventually made it to the Golden State would not find a job, neither in Los(t) Angeles nor in the San Joaquin Valley. If they found one, they were exploited as cheap labor by the Californian agricultural companies which paid them ridiculously low wages. With advertisements, the companies were easily able to persuade Southwestern farmers and sharecroppers to migrate to the Golden State. "I seen in the papers how they want folks to come an' pick grapes an' oranges an' peaches,"[35] Ma Joad tells her son Tom in Steinbeck's novel. At the same time, she refuses to follow the advice of people coming from California warning the Joads that their 'Californian Dream' might turn into a nightmare. One of the people they meet tries hard to convince the Joads that their great expectations might not come true, as they will be exploited by the Californian agricultural companies as soon as they enter the state:

> 'Look,' said the man. 'It don't make no sense. This fella [the Californian grower] wants eight hundred men. So he prints up five thousand of [the folded handbills] an' maybe twenty thousan' people sees 'em. An' maybe two-three thousan' folks gets movin' account a this here han'bill. Folks that's crazy with worry.'[36]

Apparently, the result of the grower's strategy was, as already hinted at above, an enormous decrease in wages. Yet, most of the folks came nevertheless, as they were not only "crazy with worry" due to their poor living conditions, but also crazy about California, where they believed to find new opportunities. Consider the description of the Joads' arrival in California suggesting that, despite all contradictory messages they might have heard on their journey, they seemed to be reluctant to develop a skeptical attitude towards the alleged 'Californian Dream,' as it seemed, if only at first sight, to be coming true:

> They drove through Tehachapi in the morning glow, and the sun came up behind them, and then—suddenly they saw the great valley below them. Al jammed on the brake and stopped in the middle of the road, and, 'Jesus Christ!

34 Kleff 154.

35 Steinbeck, *Grapes* 122-23.

36 Steinbeck, *Grapes* 259, additions mine.

> Look!' he said. The vineyards, the orchards, the great flat valley, green and beautiful, the trees set in rows, and the farm houses. [...] The peach trees and the walnut groves, and the dark green patches of oranges.[37]

In his sung adaptation of Steinbeck's novel, called "Tom Joad," Woody Guthrie also rendered the scene of the Joads' arrival in California:

> They stood on a mountain and they looked to the West,
> And it looked like the promised land,
> That bright green valley with a river running through
> There was work for every single hand, they thought,
> There was work for every single hand.[38]

As in his "Do Re Mi," Guthrie draws on biblical imagery, summing up the beautiful features of California in the phrase "It looked like the promised land." Again, the beauty of the land is combined with the prospects for "work for every single hand," which contributed to the attractiveness of the Golden State. Yet, there were even more popular singers, such as Country star Jimmie Rodgers, who also resorted to this image of California as a plentiful idyll in a number of their songs. Rodgers became the first nationally known star of country music and had a considerable influence on many later performers.

In November of 1927, he published four songs, among them "'T' for Texas," which was to become a great success and one of only a handful of early country records to sell a million copies.[39] Due to such large-scale reception it might well be argued that this song also served to spread the myth of the land where, as Rodgers puts it, "the water drinks like cherry wine." Here is an excerpt of the lyrics of his most successful song:

> Well, 'T' for Texas, 'T' for Tennessee
> 'T' for Texas, 'T' for Tennessee
> 'T' for Thelma, the gal that made a wreck out of me. [...]
>
> Well, I'm going where the water drinks like cherry wine
> I'm going where the water drinks like cherry wine
> 'Cause this Georgia water tastes like turpentine.[40]

37 Steinbeck, *Grapes* 309-10.

38 Kleff 118.

39 The song was later renamed "Blue Yodel."

40 <http://www.cowboylyrics.com/tabs/rodgers-jimmy/t-for-texas-2322.html>, 4 Sept. 2006.

Though California is not mentioned at all, it is quite obvious that the place "where the water drinks like cherry wine" can only be the state on the American west coast.

It is not surprising, after all, that Woody Guthrie also made use of the imagery provided by the promotion campaigns and the media that surrounded him.[41] In his song "Blowing Down This Road Feeling Bad," he sings that

> I'm going where the water tastes like wine
> I'm going where the water tastes like wine
> I'm going where the water tastes like wine,
> I ain't gonna be treated this-a way.[42]

Guthrie's song is an adaptation of the traditional "Goin' down the road feelin' bad," which was well-known to the majority of the Southwestern migrants. On his typescript of the song, which was published in *Songs of Woody Guthrie* in 1941, he wrote: "This is an original version of an old folk song written by W.W. Guthrie, January 1939 KFVD, Los Angeles, California."[43] And indeed, the "old folk song" that was originally called "Lonesome Road Blues" had already circulated in the United States for more than a hundred years, before Guthrie may have picked it up somewhere. In 1923, Henry Whitter was the first to record it with his harmonica and guitar and, according to Jeff Place, "by 1938, nearly forty singers or bands had recorded variants under a wide variety of titles"[44] among

41 Another song which, in the first decades of the 20th century, certainly had a considerable impact on the people's perception of the Golden State and later even became the official state song of California, is "I Love You, California" written by Francis Bernard Silverwood in 1913. It also employs a repertoire of stock phrases and expressions in rendering California, such as "land of honey, fruit and wine" or "Land of Sunshine" (cf. <http://www.netstate.com/states/symb/song/ca_song.htm>, 6 Sept. 2006).

42 Quoted in Kleff 98.

43 Jeff Place, liner notes to "Blowing Down that Old Dusty Road," *Buffalo Skinners: The Asch Recordings*, Vol. 4 (Smithsonian Folkways Recordings: Washington, D.C., 1998) 24. There are many versions of the song – hence the slightly varying titles.

44 Jeff Place, liner notes to "Blowing Down that Old Dusty Road" 25. The Library of Congress collections in the Folklife Center hold a number of recordings from Farm Security Administration Camps in California, on which migrants perform this song. Place points out that "[n]o less than six variants were collected by the W.P.A. California Folk Music Project during the late 1930s" (Jeff Place, liner notes to "Going Down the Road Feeling Bad," *This Land is Your Land: The Asch Recordings*, Vol. 1 [Smithsonian Folkways Recordings: Washington, D.C., 1998] 22). According to one of the project's manuscripts, it has, since 1933, become "the song of migrant families who were tractored out of Texas, dusted out

them Woody Guthrie. By turning the original "Goin'" into "Blowin,'" Guthrie adjusted the lyrics of the standard folk song to the 1930s Dust Bowl disaster in the American Southwest. What is more interesting, however, is the tribute to Rodgers's number one hit, for Guthrie also describes California as a land "where the water tastes like wine."

In another of his songs called "California California," which was sung "over the air waves of KFVD in Los Angeles,"[45] Guthrie makes use of the standard repertoire of metaphors and images of California as well:

> You've all sang your glories
> Of the country back home
> But searching for sunshine
> To California did roam
>
> California California
> Your mountains so high
> Take your golden poppies
> To the land of the sky
> Your wide peaceful ocean
> Your bright colored sand
> Your sunkissed green valleys
> Are the best in this land
>
> If you want to see beauty
> And progress abound
> Just open your sad eyes
> Take a look all around
> Her people are healthy
> All happy and free
> When heaven's on earth
> This is where it will be[46]

of Oklahoma, and flooded out of Arkansas" (quoted in Jeff Place, liner notes to "Going Down the Road Feeling Bad 22). What is even more, it is the song that was allegedly chosen to be sung in John Ford's movie adaptation of Steinbeck's *The Grapes of Wrath*. Moreover, it was Guthrie who suggested this song for the movie, after he had been asked for advice by the movie's producers (cf. Place 1998, liner notes to "Going Down the Road Feeling Bad" 22).

45 WGA, Songs I, Box I, Folder 5. Yet a third example of Guthrie's making use of this imagery is his song "By The Valley So Green & The Ocean So Blue" (1939), in which he sings, most probably referring to the migrants' travels to California, that "[t]hey come from the east, they come from the west, / In search for a place to set down and rest. / 'Tis a rich land of plenty we're marching unto, / By the valley so green and the ocean so blue" (WGA, Notebooks I, Notebook 5, 31).

46 WGA, Songs I, Box 1, Folder 5.

The enumeration of the characteristics of California, with her "mountains so high," her "golden poppies," her "wide peaceful ocean" and her "bright colored sand" evoke an image of a "land of the sky" and a "heaven[] on earth" and very much recalls the "orange crate pastoralism" that was promoted by the media and, as we have seen, adopted by a number of contemporary songs and poems. Besides the song's detailed description of the Golden State, both its beginning and its end are of particular interest. By referring to the second-person plural form "You've all […] [t]o California did roam," the first line suggests that the image of California and, subsequently, the desire to go there, has already permeated into the people's consciousness. Yet, interestingly enough, the last lines, which, most probably, would have the highest memorability, hint at the constructed nature of that image, as the term "sunkissed" immediately reminds us of Sunkist, the company which was predominantly responsible for establishing California's nationwide reputation as a land of wealth and agricultural abundance through a large-scale advertising campaign:

> Your sunkissed green valleys
> Are the best in this land.[47]

Due to the company's leading position in California's agriculture and its large-scale national and international sales of citrus fruits and products, Guthrie's contemporary listeners were certainly well aware of the allusive character of the song's line. Moreover, Guthrie was not the first to play on the word. Already in 1924, Bud de Sylva and Joseph Meyer wrote a song, still popular today called "California, Here I Come," the last four lines of which read: "A sun-kiss'd miss said, 'don't be late,' / That's why I can hardly wait, / Open up that golden gate, / California, Here I Come."[48] Most probably alluding to a Sunkist advertisement, which tried to convince the people of buying the companies' products, advising them not to be too late, as the stocks are constantly decreasing, de Sylva's and Meyer's song, just like Guthrie's "California California," exploits the cultural and symbolic potential of the term.

47 WGA, Songs I, Box 1, Folder 5.

48 Cf. <http://ingeb.org/songs/whenthew.html>, 6 Sept. 2006. The "miss" mentioned in the song could, of course, also be an allusion to another Californian growing company, "Sun-Maid," which usually employed the picture of a young, black-haired girl in their advertising campaigns. As the official website of the company states, in 1924, the Sun-Maid brand became a symbol of the San Joaquin Valley's agricultural economy and culture (cf. <http://www.sun-maid. com/ about/ our_history/1920s.html>, 6 Sept. 2006).

The allusion made in Guthrie's song becomes even more obvious as soon as we consider another version of the song, which appeared in *Woody and Lefty Lou's Favorite Collection of Old Time Hill Country Songs*, the same small booklet in which the lyrics of Guthrie's "Do Re Mi" were published in 1937. There, the chorus of the song reads:

> California! California!
> Your mountains so high
> Take your golden poppies
> To the land of the sky.
> Your wide peaceful ocean
> Your bright colored sand
> Your *sunkist* green valleys
> Are the best in this land.[49]

In order to drive his point home, Guthrie even changed the spelling of the adjective. Now, every reader of his small booklet who was not aware of the allusion when he played the song on the radio, would certainly be able to fathom the strategy of the song. Yet, it is not only the constructed nature of the image of California that is hinted at here. On a more general level, the allusion to the company reminds us of the fact that the "green valleys" of California are not common land anymore, as they have long been partitioned and sold to agricultural industries, which exclusively aimed at a maximization of their profits. The vision of a self-sufficient yeoman life at the frontier, which the majority of migrants had in mind when they traveled west, is questioned, if not deconstructed. Though, at first sight, the concluding lines of the song seem to epitomize the panegyric description of California, the reference to the company's name in the penultimate line implies a certain degree of ironic detachment.[50]

The irony is no longer implicit in Woody Guthrie's "Do Re Mi." Let us once again consider the chorus of the song:

> If you ain't got the do re mi, folks,
> If you ain't got the do re mi,
> Why, you better go back to beautiful Texas,
> Oklahoma, Kansas, Georgia, Tennessee,
> California is a garden of Eden,
> A paradise to live in or see.
> But, believe it or not,

49 Smithsonian, RRFAC, *Woody Guthrie Papers*, Box 2, Folder 4, emphasis added.

50 Thus, in contrast to Jackson (71-72), who states that Guthrie's "California! California!" is an exception, as it does not debunk, but perpetuate the conventional image of California as a state of abundance, I argue that the ambivalent potential of the widely disseminated term "sunkist" indeed contained critical implications.

You won't find it so hot,
If you ain't got the do re mi.[51]

Here, the paradisiac image of California is distorted by the police officer's limitation that its wealth might only be accessible to those who are already well-off. "Your number 14.000 for today," he proclaims in the first verse of the song and suggests that those who were attracted by the media's fashioning of sunny California as a state of plenty and abundance had better "hang on" in their home states. And the speaker of the song goes on to give good advice to the migrant workers in the second verse:

If you want to buy you a home or a farm
That can't do nobody harm,
Or take your vacation by the mountains or sea.
Don't swap your old cow for a car,
You better stay right where you are,
You'd better take this little tip from me.
'Cause I look through the want ads every day
But the headlines on the papers always say:

If you ain't got the do re mi, folks,
If you ain't got the do re mi,[…][52]

In one of his manuscripts, Woody Guthrie contextualizes the second verse of his "Do Re Mi," stating that "[t]he California newspapers and magazines print purty pictures and purty descriptions of the Land of Sunshine and Paradise that is California" in order to "bring folks out here to tour the country and drop off a few midwestern dollars."[53] As long as they do not stay in the state, those "folks" are welcomed guests who, as the song has it, "take [their] vacation by the mountains or sea" or "buy a home or a farm." Yet the advertisements also attracted farm owners and agricultural workers from the Southwest, whose hopes were destroyed as soon as they reached the border of the Golden State. Thus, 'Californian Dream' and nightmare were closely entwined: "Come to California for a glorious vacation. Advise anyone not to come seeking employment, lest he be disappointed; but for tourists, the attractions are unlimited," warned an advertisement for sunny California.[54]

The penultimate line of the second verse of Guthrie's song once again hints at quite another kind of "want ads" that, as explained above, were

[51] Leventhal and Guthrie 82-83.
[52] Leventhal and Guthrie 85.
[53] WGA, Songs I, Box 1, Folder 7.
[54] Gregory 22.

supposed to attract migrant workers to California in order to create an oversupply of labor and, subsequently, a decrease in wages. It is easy to imagine that these contradictory messages caused confusion and skepticism among the migrants. Consider, for example, the following poem by Flora Robertson entitled "Why we come to California," which, like Guthrie's "Do Re Mi" and his "California California," captures the mix of hopes and doubts that was stirred by the commercial media:

> California, California
> Here I come too.
> With a coffee pot and skillet,
> And I'm coming to you.
> Nothing's left in Oklahoma,
> For us to eat or do.
> And if apples, nuts and oranges,
> And Santy Claus is real,
> Come on to California,
> Eat and eat till your full.[55]

In his analysis of the poem, James N. Gregory argues that by setting up an unfulfillable condition – "if [...] Santy Claus is real" – the speaker of the poem calls the 'Californian Dream' of "apples," "nuts" and "oranges" and the possibility of "eat[ing] and eat[ing] till your full" into question.[56] Thus, the illusionary character of the wishes and hopes of the migrants is revealed: California, as the poem implies, is by no means a state of abundance for everyone, but a false tale, a mere construction of the media – a notion which is also manifest in Guthrie's songs.

Yet, besides this thematic correspondence, it is the compositional analogy between Robertson's poem and Guthrie's song "California California" which catches one's eye. The poem's first line and the song's title as well as the first line of its second verse make use of a 'double invocation' of California, which is, throughout the poem and the song, addressed in the second-person singular "you" or "your" respectively. These thematic and formal correlations between Guthrie's song and the poem not only suggest that the ambivalent attitude towards the alleged 'Californian Dream' was widely circulating; they also give substance to the claim that Guthrie's songs were indeed strongly tied to their cultural 'con-texts.'

Another textual trace which, again quite implicitly, deconstructs the belief that the Golden State is a place of prosperity is to be found in

55 Quoted in Gregory 21.

56 Cf. Gregory 21. Interestingly, the apples, nuts and oranges mentioned in the poem both fit the image of California as a place of agricultural prosperity and the image of a Christmassy plate full of fruits and nuts.

Guthrie's autobiography. Guthrie recollects a short dialogue between two hoboes which he supposedly listened to on one of his nightly rides on the train:

> How's crops in South California?
> Crops – or cops?[57]

That the second hobo understands "cops" instead of "crops" might be no coincidence. As soon as we reconsider the last two lines of the second verse of Guthrie's "Do Re Mi," we might find a clue relating to the hobo's (mis)interpretation of his fellow's words:

> 'Cause I look through the want ads every day
> But the headlines on the papers always say:
>
> If you ain't got the do re mi, folks,
> If you ain't got the do re mi,[58]

It is the media to which the speaker of Guthrie's song dedicates the last line of the second verse. The reference to the "headlines on the papers" suggests that the police officer's behavior, as portrayed in the first verse, was not an act of arbitrariness, but part of a major campaign that aroused public interest in the second half of the 1930s. Interestingly enough, another version of "Do Re Mi" more explicitly hints at the fact that the police officer's reaction to the migrants was indeed part of an official anti-migrant policy. Here, the last two lines read:

> 'Cause the governor on the radio today
> Climbed up to the microbephone [sic] and he did say:
>
> If you ain't got the do re mi, folks,
> If you ain't got the do re mi,[59]

Let us have a look at one of those "headlines on the papers" and the respective article. The following is taken from the *Los Angeles Herald Express* of February, 4th, 1936:

> While a tumultuous row was raging in city council over Police Chief James E. Davis' 'expeditionary force' of policemen to halt the indigents over California's far-flung borders, the lid was successfully clamped on the Arizona-California line today. The spectacular row in the council broke out when Councilman P.

57 Guthrie, *Bound for Glory* 215.
58 Leventhal and Guthrie 85.
59 Smithsonian, RRFAC, *Woody Guthrie Papers*, Box 2, Folder 4.

> P. Christensen, consistent critic of Davis, introduced a resolution demanding by whose authority the police chief was sending 136 of his 'coppers' to the State line 'trenches.' At the same time Deputy Chief Homer Cross said the entry ports on the Arizona boundary had been blocked against transients in an effort to halt the 'flood of criminals' and divert the stream of penniless transients. Within 3 more days, Cross estimated, the blockade would be similarly effective on the Oregon and Nevada lines, abutting California territory. [...] At the California capital Deputy Attorney General Jess Hession declared he believed Davis' methods illegal. Governor Frank F. Merriam withheld comment but State Senator Thomas Scollan, who had brought about defeat of an indigent-barring law at the last session of the legislature, characterized the 'expeditionary forces' as 'damnable, absurd, and asinine.'[60]

In 1936, as a reaction to the continuous influx of migrants to California, Los Angeles police chief James E. Davis obviously took matters into his own hands and sent, according to this article, 136 of his 'coppers' to the state line trenches in order to "halt the 'flood of criminals' and divert the stream of penniless transients." Though the article gives no evidence of Governor Frank Merriam "climb[ing] up to the microbephone" and explicitly proclaiming the new immigration policy, he still "with[held] comment," which might well be read as a tacit agreement to Davis's decision. Though others, like State Senator Thomas Scollan, or Davis's opponent, Councilman P.P. Christensen, overtly attacked Davis' "bum blockade," as it was soon called derogatorily, state and city officials did little to interfere despite the clear usurpation of authority. Quite the contrary, some of them even welcomed the new situation. On February, 6th, 1936, the mayor of Los Angeles pointed out that

> It is important to note [...] that Los Angeles is facing a desperate situation if we permit every incoming freight train to bring us a new shipment of unemployed, penniless vagrants, to consume the relief so seriously needed by our needy people and to create a crime menace almost beyond conceivable control.[61]

Only one day later, in another L.A. Times article, the Deputy Chief of the L.A. police department, Cross, tried to put the police's actions on a legal basis and explained why people would not be allowed to enter the state. He pointed out that

60 "Indigents Barred At Arizona Line," *Los Angeles Herald Express* 4 Feb. 1936, <http:// newdeal.feri.org/tolan/tol09.htm#c>, 4 Sept. 2006.

61 "Rule Guard At Border Legal," *Los Angeles Herald Express* 6 Feb. 1936, <http://newdeal.feri.org/ tolan/tol09. htm>, 4 Sept. 2006.

> [t]here is no basis for charges of unconstitutionality in connection with the police department's campaign. We are enforcing Section 587-C and Section 667, Sub-Section 2, of the Penal Code of California. The first section holds it a misdemeanor for anyone to ride railway cars within the State without paying fare. Section 667 holds that anyone wandering about the State without visible means of support is a vagrant and guilty of misdemeanor.[62]

Courtesy of the Ralph Rinzler Folklife Archives and Collections, Smithsonian Institution.

Chief Davis's "bum blockade," which was supposed to protect California against the "unemployed, penniless vagrants" and the subsequent "crime menace" became, at least for the following six weeks, a major concern in the media and, most probably, a source of inspiration for Woody Guthrie, who configured the event in his song "Do Re Mi" – the title and the first line of its chorus reading like a colloquial adaptation of the above-quoted phrase of Section 667 of the Californian immigration law: "without visible means of support." Moreover, Guthrie configured the confrontation with the border police in a sketch,[63] which, by rendering his (alleged) personal experience with one of the officers, contributed to his self-fashioning as one of the Southwestern migrants.

In his *The Grapes of Wrath*, John Steinbeck has an anonymous migrant talk about the "bum blockade" as well. The following passage elaborates on the same argument as Section 667 and the chorus of Guthrie's song:

> This is a free country. Fella can go where he wants. That's what *you* think! Ever hear of the border patrol on the California line? Police from Los Angeles—stopped you bastards, turned you back. Says, if you can't buy no

62 Quoted in "Vagrants Rounded Up In City And County," *Los Angeles Times* 7 Feb. 1936: 3.

63 "Garden of Eden," Smithsonian, RRFAC, *Woody Guthrie Papers,* Box 3, Folder 4.

> real estate we don't want you. Says, got a driver's license? Le's [sic] see it. Tore it up. Says you can't come in without no driver's license.[64]

Though this first anti-migrant campaign was not specifically addressed at the Southwestern "Dust Bowl refugees," whose migration to California would reach its peak only in 1938 /39, it demonstrated the seriousness many Californians attached to the rising migrant problem. Moreover, the series of conservative pamphlets and reports as well as unequivocal cartoons in the newspapers shaped the Californian image of the migrant, which was to last in the minds of the majority of Californians for the rest of the decade. Though the "bum blockade" was abolished one and a half months after Chief Davis had sent his legions to the Californian border, the migrants' image as poor criminals coming to California only in order to "dig into some of the Relief Gold" prevailed.[65]

Cartoon in the *Los Angeles Times*, 5 Feb. 1936.

Moreover, the fact that the Southwestern migrants, once they settled in the San Joaquin valley in the second half of the 1930s, replaced the Mexican and the Chinese workers, who had made up the agricultural labor force ever since the beginning of the 20th century, fostered the rise of the anti-migrant attitude that was soon blended with racist tendencies.[66] The general fear of the home- and penniless led to the establishment of vigilante groups whose members patrolled the highways and railroad in order to enforce Section 587-C of the Penal Code of California, which, as already quoted above, "holds it a misdemeanor for anyone to ride railway cars within the State without paying fare." Cisco Houston, a friend of Guthrie's, recalls his experiences with these "railroad bulls" or "yard bulls," as they were commonly referred to:

64 Steinbeck, *Grapes* 163.
65 Guthrie, *Woody Sez* 27.
66 Cf. chapter 3.4 of this study.

> I can remember being stoned out of a ... well, we didn't get off [the train], but we were stoned. [...] They all had a school for yard bulls and the meaner these guys could be, of course, the better they liked it. They all tried to build reputations and people had heard something about this ... and Woody, he wrote a song, of course.[67]

For those migrants who were, in spite of all obstacles, able to enter the state the 'Californian Dream' soon turned into a horrible nightmare. In a *New York Times Magazine* article from 1939, a migrant from Oklahoma who had just arrived in California ironically comments on the fact that he had indeed been deceived by the idea that California would be paradise. He soon came to realize that "[t]hey told me this was the place o' milk an' honey, but Ah guess the cow's gone dry, and the tumblebugs has got in the beehive."[68]

By having a police officer use quite similar cliché-ridden images of California, such as a "Garden of Eden" and "a paradise to live in," in his rejection of the migrants, Guthrie's song demythologizes the image of California as a state of abundance and plenty and thus participates in a general skepticism towards the 'Californian Dream' and comments on the radically discriminating immigration policy of the Californian administration.

Moreover, the song's ironical stance is underlined by the musical structure of the song. Its biting irony is evoked by the incongruity between its "sincere backbone," to use Guthrie's own words, and its cheerful melody, which, due to the Italian phrase "do re mi" rather reminds us of an *opera buffa* than a rendering of one of the bleakest chapters in American history. The tune of "Do Re Mi" deliberately appropriates a song composed by Benjamin Hapgood Burt in 1908, which is called "Hang Out the Front Door Key." In the 1930s, it was performed and recorded by the Blue Sky Boys, whose tunes Woody Guthrie used in a number of songs. The Blue Sky Boys became extremely popular during the era of mandolin and guitar brother duets, which reached its peak in the 1930s. Earl and Bill Bolick, the two members of the Blue Sky Boys, started their career as Good Coffee Boys in 1935. Only one year later, being just sixteen and eighteen years of age respectively, they first

67 Cisco Houston, interview with Lee Hays, 10 Jan. 1961. Smithsonian, RRFAC, *Woody Guthrie Papers*. The song of Guthrie's that Houston alludes to is "East Texas Red," which deals with one of the most prominent railroad bulls in the late 1930s.

68 Quoted in Charles L. Todd, "The 'Okies' Search For A New Frontier," *New York Times Magazine* 27 Aug. 1939: 10, <http://memory.loc.gov/afc/afcts/ images/nyt001/0002.tif>, 6 Sept 2006.

recorded for RCA Victor. Over the next four years, the Blue Sky Boys made nearly 100 recordings for RCA that made them one of the more popular brother duos of the period. Here is an excerpt of the lyrics of their "Hang Out the Front Door Key":

> Percy Wilson Gay left his wife one day
> Then she'd always says 'be home on time'
> Don't have me a-waitin' here when dinner time comes near
> Be here when we set down to dine [...]
>
> He called her on the telephone
> This is what he'd sing to her alone
> Hang out the front door key love
> Hang out the front door key
>
> Don't wait up for me love I may be out 'til three
> I'm with a very sick friend love who'd do the same for me
> So leave a light in the fall tonight
> And hang out the front door key.[69]

It is not coincidence that Guthrie took the tune of this song for his "Do Re Mi." First of all, taking a popular melody that most people are already acquainted with seems to be a good strategy not only to catch and hold the listeners' attention, but also to make them hum along, even though they do not know the text.

Moreover, in order to understand how Guthrie's technique of taking a well-known melody intensified the political potential of the song, we have to consider the semantic relationship between his "Do Re Mi" and the Blue Sky Boys' pretext. Let us reconsider the content of "Hang Out the Front Door Key" first: Though Mrs. Gay, as the first verse suggests, has not become tired of asking her husband to come home on time, Percy Wilson Gay, again and again, finds excuses why he always comes home late and leaves his wife waiting with dinner. "Don't wait up for me love," but "[h]ang out the front door key," he suggests to calm down his wife who, as it seems, cannot stand his fad of staying away so long anymore. Thus, in order to get him good and proper, as the song tells us in its second part, she leaves the house without telling him where she would go. She calls him and, like he has done before, puts him off with a flimsy excuse: Eventually, Mr. Gay finds a note she left on the table, which ironically mocks his rhetoric of feeble excuses and his foul suggestion of hanging out the front door key:

69 <http://www.traditionalmusic.co.uk/bluegrasslyrics/Hang_out_the_front_door_key.html>,4 Sept. 2006.

On the table he found a little note
He opened it and this is what it wrote
Hang out the front door key love
Hang out the front door key

Set up awhile for me love just as I have for thee
I'm with a very sick friend love who thinks a lot of me
Your little wife's gonna like night life
So hang out the front door key.[70]

It is interesting that the central element around which the whole plot of the song is constructed, is, as the title already suggests, the front door key of the couple's house. Following from that, the song's ironic rendering of the private debate on entrance, exit and trust might well be regarded as parallel to Guthrie's rendering of the political discourse of entrance to and exit from California and, what is even more, the general mistrust in the Southwestern migrants. Thus, the domestic struggle of husband and wife, whose interests and expectations seem to be incompatible and eventually lead to mutual disappointment in their relationship, seems to fit the political debate on immigration issues rendered in Guthrie's "Do Re Mi." By establishing both a musical as well as a thematical correlation between his song and the popular tune of "Hang Out the Front Door Key," the Okie bard certainly managed to increase the social and political potential of the former, as the contemporary audience, one may assume, was well aware of the 'intermusical' references he made use of.

70 <http://www.traditionalmusic.co.uk/bluegrasslyrics/Hang_out_the_front_door_key.html>, 4 Sept. 2006.

3.4 "Have you seen that vigilante man?": The Fear of Fascism in the Fields of California

Those Southwestern migrants who did not give up on the road or at the Californian border and eventually made it to the alleged 'land of milk and honey' encountered a social and political situation that was far from inviting. Living in provisional camps, which were converted into reasonably adequate accommodation facilities only when the Farm Security Administration took matters in its hands late in the 1930s, the migrants were exploited by the Californian growing companies who offered them jobs at ridiculously low wages. What is even more, the organized growing companies employed vigilante troops that violently enforced discipline and prevented uprisings among the migrant workers.

By configuring instances of vigilante attacks on the migrants, some of Guthrie's songs take a distinct stand on the inhumane strategies the agricultural companies resorted to in order to subjugate their workers. Moreover, they point to the racist tendencies of the disparaging treatment suffered by the migrant workers, who had taken the place of the Chinese, Japanese and Mexican immigrants traditionally employed by the growing large-scale companies ever since the 19th century.

Beginning with an analysis of Guthrie's "Vigilante Man," this chapter explores the compositional and rhetorical features employed in Guthrie's songs to capture the fear of fascism in the fields of California. By correlating his songs to a variety of other textual traces of the cultural archive of the 1930s, this contextualizing reading is to give substance to the claim that the imagery employed in Guthrie's renderings of vigilante attacks on the migrants circulated widely among the Californian conservatives, and was shaped both by fascist ideology and rhetorics prominent in the 1930s in Europe and the United States. The second half of this chapter, centering on Guthrie's "Rancho Grande Vigilante," reveals that Guthrie utilized this imagery not only in order to render the migrant workers' fear and sufferings, but also in order to articulate and encourage resistance against the vigilantes and to provide "unionism" as an option for improving their conditions.

* * * * *

On December, 8th, 1939, the readers of the *Voice of the Agricultural Worker*, a newspaper that was published in one of the migrant camps put up by the Farm Security Administration, stumbled across the following joke:

> A tourist and his small son were travelling in California through the cotton belt. The son upon seeing a cotton picker stand up asked his father what it was. His father replied, 'That's a cotton picker, son.' The son boy [sic] after some thought said, 'Daddy, them things look almost like people when they stand on their hind legs, don't they?'[1]

Apparently, the tourist's son comes to his strange conclusion because he does not know better. Yet, most probably, it is not the naivety and ignorance of the boy that made people laugh and think about this joke. Rather it derives its potential from the fact that the analogy drawn by the tourist's son represents a common attitude of rural Californians in the second half of the 1930s – the mere fact that it is a joke, which, one may argue, only works properly if it takes up and deals with attitudes and notions which have already disseminated widely, gives substance to this claim. Let us have a look at Woody Guthrie's song "Vigilante Man,"[2] a contextualizing analysis of which might give us a clue as to the joke's punch line. Here are the first two verses of his song:

> Have you seen that Vigilante man?
> Have you seen that Vigilante man?
> Have you seen that Vigilante man?
> I've been hearing his name all over the land.
>
> Well, what is a Vigilante man?
> Tell me what is a Vigilante man?
> Has he got a club in his hand?
> Was that a Vigilante man?[3]

It was. Vigilantes were groups of men paid by company officials to intimidate workers who were attempting to organize themselves into unions. In order to combat the accelerating drive for unionization in the early

1 Quoted in Stein 64.

2 According to the OED, a vigilante is a member of a vigilance committee, "a self-appointed committee for the maintenance of justice and order in an imperfectly organized community" (<http://dictionary.oed.com/cgi/entry/50277463?query_type=word&queryword=vigilant&first=1&max_to_show=10&single=1&sort_type=alpha>, 4 Sept. 2006). The respective adjective "vigilant" is derived from the Latin word "vigilare" ("to keep awake") and means "wakeful and watchful" (<http://dictionary.oed.com/cgi/entry/50277465?query_type=word&queryword=vigilant&first=1&max_to_show=10&single=1&sort_type=alpha>, 4 Sept. 2006).

3 Leventhal and Guthrie 237-38.

1930s, these self-appointed law enforcement troops were employed by the large Californian company owners and growers in order to combat any kind of collective uprising of the workers, who were mistreated and exploited as a cheap labor force in the Californian fields.[4] Any attempt to assert their interests by collective bargaining was thus, sooner rather than later, suppressed by a counter-attack by the powerful Californian Right, spearheaded by the Associated Farmers[5], which, with the blessing of the California Farm Bureau Federation, was founded by a number of the state's most prominent agriculturalists in early 1934. The Associated Farmers' immediate target was the Cannery and Agricultural Workers Industrial Union, which, with a powerful propaganda campaign, had initiated some major strikes among agricultural workers in the early 1930s.[6]

The unorganized migrants, who had begun arriving from the Southwestern states of Texas, Oklahoma, Arkansas and Missouri since the middle of the 1930s, dramatically increased the social tensions in the state and contributed to the growers' fear of unionization. Thus, first and

4 At that time, California's system of agricultural production was highly industrialized. Largely devoted to the production of vegetable, lettuce, fruit of all kinds and melons, this system did thus not only require the expenditure of large amounts of capital, but also great amounts of hand labour, which, from the middle of the 1930s onward, was provided by the influx of Southwestern migrants: "One of the essential elements of industrialized agriculture is the use of great quantities of hand labor hired at certain seasons of the year, paid by the piece or by the hour, and dismissed when no longer required. [...] The labor to meet this demand cannot be found on the farms of California or in the neighboring cities. [...] The roving casual-labor supply which this type of production necessitates has been drawn since the earliest days of Californian agriculture, from successive groups of imported alien labor. Gangs of Chinese laborers gave way to the Japanese, followed by the Filipinos who were ultimately replaced by Mexicans. Today the Mexicans are no longer the principal element in this labor supply which is increasingly composed of native American stock" (United States Congress Senate, Comittee on Education and Labor, 77th Congress, *Violations of Free Speech and Rights of Labor* [Washington, D.C.] 36-37).

5 The Associated Farmer Organization was established in 1934 and included the big growers and 'farm-factory'-owners. According to Charles L. Todd, its intention was "to promote the prompt, orderly and efficient administration of justice," the implementation of which did, most probably, also require vigilante action (Charles L. Todd, "Trampling Out the Vintage," In: *Common Sense* July issue 1939: 7).

6 The most significant strike in the history of agricultural labor in California occurred in late 1933. It was a strike of cotton pickers in the San Joaquin Valley, which was backed by the Cannery and Agricultural Workers' Industrial Union. (cf. United States Congress, *Violations of Free Speech* 210; cf. also Gregory 89).

foremost, they were the ones who had to suffer from vigilante attacks. The speaker of the song, portrayed as a migratory worker himself, outlines one of these attacks in the next two verses of Guthrie's song, emphasizing the collective suffering of the migrants by the introduction of the first-person plural:

> Rainy night down in the engine house,
> Sleeping just as still as a mouse,
> Man come along and chased us out in the rain.
> Was that a Vigilante man?
>
> Stormy days we'd pass the time away,
> Sleeping in some good warm place
> A cop come along and we give him a little race.
> Say, was that a vigilante man?[7]

Apart from epitomizing the vigilantes' merciless policy by depicting an assault on innocent migrants "sleeping just as still as a mouse," the first part of Guthrie's song hints at another terrifying characteristic of vigilantism: The repeated questioning of the song's speaker (in the first three lines of the first verse and in the last lines of verses two to four) implies that nobody seemed to know where and when these vigilante men would actually strike next nor who they really were. And indeed, most often the vigilante men belonged to a secret police force which was dormant "in days of peaceful social exploitation,"[8] as Benjamin Stolberg put it in an article about vigilantism that appeared in the Nation in 1937, and only stirred up the workers in cases of "unlawful assembly, inciting to riot [or] disorderly conduct."[9] Moreover, the vigilante men did not form a homogeneous group, but were recruited from various professional backgrounds and were thus not easy to identify as troublemakers. Whenever they appeared to intimidate the workers, they made sure that nobody would uncover their real identity, as the following excerpt taken from a *Los Angeles Times* article, illustrates. It renders a vigilante intervention in Santa Rosa, California, on August 22nd 1935:

> Amid wild scenes which included gunfire and teargas, a band of nearly 300 self-styled vigilantes tared and feathered two asserted Communists today and beat three others after an all-night raid against agitators. […] Gunfire and tear gas were brought into play when the crowd descended upon the home of Nitzburg [one of the 'agitators'], who lives on a ranch in the Petaluma district.

7 Leventhal and Guthrie 238/240.

8 Benjamin Stolberg, "Vigilantism, 1937," *The Nation* 14 Aug. 1937: 166.

9 Stolberg 168.

> As the crowd, driving automobiles with covered license plates, […] Newspapermen from Santa Rosa who accompanied the band described the scenes as the wildest in Sonoma country's history since three men were lynched several years ago for the slaying of three San Francisco policemen. The crowd shaved the heads of Green and Nitzburg and showered the men wilth [sic] tar and feathers. […] The vigilantes either had their faces masked or blackened and some wore burnt-cork mustaches. Most of them wore old clothes. All of the men seized were forced to kiss the American flag at some time during their captivity.[10]

Besides the "covered license plates" of their automobiles, the "masked" or "blackened" faces and the "burnt-cork mustaches" used by the vigilantes to disguise themselves, it was their "attacking from within," which turned vigilantism into a perfect stealth strategy for the disruption of political opposition. Thus, in his account of right-wing agitation in Californian agriculture in those days, Kevin Starr recalls Robert Hicks and William Harr, then officers in the California National Guard, who "dressed in shabby clothes and foreswore shaving when they attended classes at the school, hoping to resemble a Hollywood version of Bolshevik conspirators."[11] Thus, to return to Guthrie's "Vigilante Man," the repetitive questioning of its speaker suggests his constant fear that these armed – and often hidden – forces might, all of a sudden, turn up and strike again.

That the vigilantes' actions were politically motivated and stirred by an anti-communist attitude is accentuated by the next verses of Guthrie's song, which refer to one of the most famous victims of vigilantism in the 1930s:

> Preacher Casey was just a working man,
> And he said, unite all us working men.
> They killed him in the river some strange man.
> Was that your vigilante man?
>
> Oh, why does a vigilante man
> Oh, why does a vigilante man
> Carry that sawed off shotgun in his hand?
> Would he shoot his brother and sister down?[12]

By mixing the tragedy of Casey, the fictional archetype of political protest and spiritual strength, with alleged authentic experience, Guthrie's

10 "Vigilantes Tar 'Reds.' Three Okies Beaten By Night Raiders' Drive On Communists," *Los Angeles Times* 23 Aug. 1935, 15, addition mine.

11 Kevin Starr, *Endangered Dreams: The Great Depression in California* (New York/Oxford: Oxford UP, 1996) 166.

12 Leventhal and Guthrie 240.

song mediates parts of Steinbeck's novel *The Grapes of Wrath* to his listeners. In the novel, Preacher Casey is portrayed as a missionary who is no longer spreading the Christian gospel, but the socialist ideology among the migratory workers and sharecroppers who are suffering from devastating living and working conditions. Casey tries to convince them that joining the union is a means to overcome economic exploitation. However, he is killed by the handymen of some great land-owning company, the proprietor of which fears that Casey might be successful in his endeavor to organize the migrants. Consider the relevant passage from Steinbeck's novel, in which Casey and Tom Joad, after they tried to escape a vigilante attack, are eventually caught by the thugs at night:

> A sharp call, 'There they are!' Two flashlight beams fell on the men, caught them, blinded them. 'Stand where you are.' The voices came out of the darkness. 'That's him. That shiny bastard. That's him.'
>
> Casey stared blindly at the light. He breathed heavily. 'Listen,' he said. 'You fellas don' know what you're doin'. You're helpin' to starve kids.'
>
> 'Shut up, you red son-of-a-bitch.'
>
> A short heavy man stepped into the light. He carried a new white pick handle.
>
> Casey went on,'You don' know what you're a-doin'.'
>
> The heavy man swung with the pick handle. Casey dodged down into the swing. The heavy club crashed into the side of his head with a dull crunch of bone, and Casey fell sideways out of the light.[13]

Identified as a "red son-of-a-bitch," ex-preacher Casey is attacked and eventually killed by the vigilante troops, whose members were, according to Steinbeck, recruited from the local people who "whipped themselves into a mold of cruelty."[14]

Grotesquely enough, to come back to Guthrie's song, the vigilantes' brutality might even extend to their own relatives, as the question "[w]ould he shoot his brothers or sisters down?" implies, which, as one may argue, may be taken as more than rhetorical. Bryan Garman explains that "[a]s such, a vigilante man was often quite willing to 'shoot his brother or sister down,' to suspend his moral obligations if he could improve his financial situation."[15] Thus, it is not surprising that a passage from the official guidelines to vigilantism, the so-called "ten scab commandments,"[16] sug-

13 Steinbeck, *Grapes* 527.

14 Steinbeck, *Grapes* 386.

15 Garman, *A Race of Singers* 181.

16 Cf. Stolberg. The 'ten scab commandments' were a set of rules that, if followed properly, were supposed to help industrialists to systematically demoralize strikers. These commandments were part of an anti-union agenda named the 'Mohawk Valley Formula,' which first appeared in an article in the *Labor Relations Bulletin*

gests "bring[ing] about the formation of a large armed police force to be built up by utilizing local police, state police if the governor cooperates, vigilantes, and special deputies, the deputies being chosen if possible from other neighborhoods."[17] Such a strategy of recruiting vigilantes was meant to avoid the dilemma of encountering close friends or relatives, which was sensed to be hardly bearable, even for the cruelest thug in town.

Figuratively, the expression "brothers and sisters" might also hint at the fact that the masses of migratory workers traveling to California in the 1930s were American citizens and thus, metaphorically speaking, indeed "brothers and sisters" of the inhabitants of the Golden State.[18] Such a reading, though it might seem far-fetched at first sight, becomes more plausible as soon as we have a look at one of the columns Guthrie wrote for *The People's World*. Entitled "Kids first. Hoboes second. Rich folks last," it deals with, among other issues, a *Los Angeles Times* article retelling the story of "the flood, drouth, an' dust bowlers a comin' to Calif. [sic] in their rickety, rundown handful of belongin's, an' their children."[19] Guthrie critically comments on the article's insinuating bias, which was

> not to make you feel in your heart a genuine sorrow for your brothers and sisters of our American Race that's got to live in such places, but to try to make you believe that these Underprivileged people are designing in their hearts to 'Dig some Easy Gold' – off you Taxpayers.[20]

of the National Associations of Manufacturers soon after the Remington Rand strike at Ilion, New York, in 1934. The formula that had been designed by company president James Rand indicated in detail the steps to be taken in a campaign of national strike-breaking.

17 Quoted in Stolberg 168.

18 The assumption that the phrase 'brothers and sisters' does not only refer to direct relatives, but might also be understood in a more general sense is substantiated by the fact that Guthrie used this phrase in a figurative way more than once (cf., for example, "My brothers and my sisters are stranded on this road" in his "I Ain't Got No Home" [Leventhal and Guthrie 138]). In his song "Boomtown Bill" (Kleff 40), Guthrie sings about his "union brethren and sistren." Garman points out that "[b]y using such class-conscious language, Guthrie identifies [the migrants'] plight as a social rather than an individual problem" (Garman, *A Race of Singers* 180). What is even more, the expression fuses the socialist ideology with a religious diction, a concoction that is elaborated on in more detail in chapter 3.6 of this study.

19 Guthrie, *Woody Sez* 27.

20 Guthrie, *Woody Sez* 28-29.

Guthrie's comment, which underlines the figurative reading of "brothers and sisters," does not only reveal the author's conservative stance, as he argues that the migrants' intention was to "Dig some Easy Gold," i.e., to put their names on the relief lists. It also hints at a more general anti-migrant attitude, the reconstruction of which helps to contextualize the next verse of Guthrie's "Vigilante Man":

> I rambled around from town to town
> I rambled around from town to town
> And they herded us around like a wild herd of cattle
> Was that your vigilante men?[21]

As the verse reveals, the anti-migrant prejudices were not only based on political stigmatization, but also carried strong racist overtones, as the victimized migrants are compared to "a wild herd of cattle." This notion of the Southwesterners as animal-like, undomesticated creatures developed predominantly among rural Californians who were, according to John Steinbeck, "terrified for their property" for they "saw the flare of want in the eyes of the migrants. They said, 'these goddamned Okies are dirty and ignorant. They're degenerate, sexual maniacs. These goddamned Okies are thieves. They'll steal anything. They've got no sense of property rights.'"[22] One must be extremely careful in taking Steinbeck's observations as objective renderings of the migrants' image among the Californians of those days. The prejudices, however, did exist, as a letter by Mrs. Effie Ball Magurn addressed to President Franklin D. Roosevelt reveals:

> A Federal migratory camp is being established adjacent to my property at Porterville, Tulare Country, California.
> Knowing the character of migrants from my experience in dealing with, I object to these hordes of degenerates being located at my very door.
>
> These 'share croppers' are not a noble people looking for a home and seeking an education for their children. They are unprincipled degenerates looking for something for nothing.
> The fact that they are leaving their native land unfit for human habitation is not surprising. Their ignorance and maliciousness in caring for trees, crops, vines, and the land is such that California will be ruined if farming is left to them.

21 Leventhal and Guthrie 240.
22 Steinbeck, *Grapes* 386.

> Please do not put these vile people at my door to depreciate my property and to loot my ranch.[23]

These "vile people," these "hordes of degenerates," as the migrants are most derogatorily referred to in the letter, settled down either on the ditch banks of the Californian fields or, if they were lucky enough, in one of the Federal migratory camps put up by the Farm Security Administration. A considerable number of Californians regarded them as not only being devoid of any moral integrity, but also characterized them as "shiftless and lazy and irresponsible and ha[ving] too many children."[24] Like Mrs. Magurn, many Californians feared that the migrants would eventually spoil the Californian fields due to their "ignorance and maliciousness in caring for trees, crops, vines and the land." Apart from these alleged flaws in character, the migrants' malnourished physique and their deplorable settlements among the ditch banks contributed to a stereotypical image of the Southwesterner as a kind of primitive subspecies of the white American, which, in turn, worsened the migrants' opportunities in the job market.

Another feature which added to the Californians' perception of the migrants as an inferior group of people was their slightly nasal drawl typical of their Southwestern accent. Thus, the few migrant children who got a chance to attend a Californian school were, as Gregory has it,

> told in no uncertain terms that their way of speaking was improper, even defective. Many educators felt that next to cleanliness, it was most important to teach the migrant children proper English, and that meant disposing of the Southwestern accent.[25]

Woody Guthrie, as one may add, was well aware of the distinctive potential of the Southwestern speech patterns, which shaped the image of the migrants in the Californian public, and used them purposefully when he was singing his songs on the radio or in the migrant camps. As he could switch the Southwestern accent on and off, he deliberately employed it as a performative strategy both to identify with his migrant audience and to create a feeling of collective identity among the migrants.

Interestingly enough, the characterization of the Southwestern migrants as uncivilized and barbarous was not unique to the 1930s, but had

23 Quoted in Stein 61.

24 Carey McWilliams, quoted in Studs Terkel, ed., *Hard Times: An Oral History of the Great Depression* (New York: The New Press, 2000) 243.

25 Gregory 130.

been prevalent in the American consciousness ever since the middle of the 19th century. In those days, during the continuous process of the westward expansion of the agrarian frontier, the Great Plains had been considered "the Great American Desert," which, as Henry N. Smith explains, was not suitable for any kind of agriculture and thus uninhabitable by Anglo-Americans.[26] Smith argues that it was generally believed that "[a]lthough regions too dry for farming [such as the Great Plains] could be inhabitated by migratory tribesmen following their flocks and herds, such peoples were considered uncivilized. They could not be integrated with American society and were therefore perpetual outlaws."[27] Compared to the "Bedouins of the Arabian desert [or] the Tartars of Asiatic steppes,"[28] the farmers who attempted to cultivate the allegedly infertile and arid regions in the American Southwest "would become nomadic brigants, a menace to settled agricultural communities farther to the East."[29] In 1836, Washington Irving speculated on the development of the people living on the Plains in his *Astoria, or Anecdotes of an Enterprise beyond the Rocky Mountains*:

> On the plains, beyond the limits of possible civilization, may spring up new and mongrel races, like new formations in geology, the amalgamation of the 'debris' and 'abrasions' of former races, civilized and savage; the remains of broken and almost extinguished tribes; the descendants of wandering hunters and trappers; of fugitives from the Spanish and American frontiers; of adventurers and desperadoes of every class and country yearly elected from the bosom of society into the wilderness.[30]

Likewise, an anonymous writer pointed out in the *Hunt's Merchants' Magazine* in 1851 that the Great Plains were to be overrun by "[a] mixture of races, creeds, habits and customs, fusing into one people, and contending for the supremacy of language and tradition."[31]

There is reason to believe that this depiction of the people on the Plains as "mongrel races," as half-civilized nomadic tribes scraping their living on the drought-stricken fields, still influenced the Californians' perception of the Southwestern migrants in the second half of the 1930s. Facing the thousands of down-trodden and emaciated migrants arriving in their run-down jalopies, the myth of the Great American Desert and, accord-

26 Cf. Smith 175.
27 Smith 176, addition mine.
28 Smith 177.
29 Smith 177.
30 Quoted in Smith 177
31 Quoted in Smith 178.

ingly, the image of its inhabitants as uncivilized, if not criminal half-castes springing from the "'debris' and 'abrasions' of former races," must have been, at least to a certain extent, stirred up again in the minds of the Californians.

Additionally, the stigmatization of the Southwestern migrants in the Golden State was possibly reinforced by the fact that social stratification, particularly in rural California, had always been strongly characterized by racial issues. Ever since the establishment of large-scale agricultural enterprises in the 1870s, field workers had been recruited from racial minority groups like the Chinese, the Filipinos and the Mexicans. Now, with the enormous influx of thousands of Southwestern families staying and working in the Californian fields, the system of social stratification that had developed around race and field labor was forced to accommodate itself to the new situation. Consequently, Walter J. Stein argues:

> Despite their whiteness, the Okies rapidly became identified in the minds of rural Californians as field workers. Field workers had always been viewed as racial inferiors in the social order. In spite of their white skins, the Okies inherited the racial prejudice that Californians had hitherto applied to the minority groups.[32]

In an essay published in *Rural Sociology* in 1942, sociologist Stuart M. Jamieson put it in a slightly different way, pointing out that "'Okies,' 'Arkies' and 'Texies' have taken the place of 'Chinks' and 'Dagos' in rural terminology."[33]

That the anti-Okie prejudice did not only exist in "rural terminology," but also affected the living situation of the migrants might best be illustrated by an anecdote remembered by Carey McWilliams in an interview with Studs Terkel. As Commissioner of Immigration and Housing in the administration of California's Governor Culbert L. Olson, McWilliams points out that "[o]nce I went into the foyer of this third-rate motion picture house in Bakersfield and I saw a sign: Negroes and Okies upstairs."[34] Contemporary Dorothy Healey recalls a Californian citizen suggesting that they should not be given bathtubs, as they "won't know how to use them."[35] A more radical solution to the 'Okie problem' was sug-

32 Stein 60.

33 Quoted in Stein 60. In a number of his songs, Guthrie also took a stand on the racist prejudices towards the non-American field workers (cf. Jackson 127ff.)

34 Quoted in Terkel 243.

35 Dorothy Healey, interview with Joe Klein, n.d. (WGA, Accessions 2004, 67.4, Box 1, Folder 12).

gested by some "good citizens of Imperial Valley"[36] who, though half-humorously, suggested "that the 'Okies' be lined up and shot."[37] Thus, one might well argue that Benjamin Stolberg, in his article about vigilantism, in which he refers to the company thugs as "hick Führers,"[38] fails to encompass the extremity, as it was not only Nazi terminology that was "consciously copied by innumerable vigilante adventurers in America."[39] Quite obviously, people had even more in mind. Edward Robbin, Los Angeles Editor of *The People's World* in those days, recollects what he observed during a strike of migratory workers in Salinas, California, in 1936:

> We returned to Los Angeles that night, shakened and sobered by what we had seen. For after talking it over, the three of us agreed that we had witnessed not just a strike situation, but an example of fascist rule in the town of Salinas. A city surrounded by police, city officials, growers, and scab herders with their headquarters in the Jeffery Hotel, violence in the streets and on the picket lines: weren't these the very ingredients of Nazi and fascist rule we had been studying in the European scene?[40]

Of course, one has to be extremely careful in taking such a statement as a reliable reconstruction of the past. Yet, it is interesting that, once again, the analogy between vigilantism and German fascism is drawn. What is even more, the expression "scab herders," which immediately rings with Guthrie's image of being "herded [...] around like a wild herd of cattle," also implies the animal-like nature of the scabs and thus underlines the racist attitude towards the migratory workers.

In 1937, social investigators who visited the San Joaquin Valley, one of California's most intensively cultivated regions, used a similar fascist phrasing as they stated that "white workers [...] were living in the woods like wild animals."[41] Another, similar comparison is drawn by Carey McWilliams in his comprehensive report about the rise of capitalist entrepreneurship in the west coast's agriculture, *Factories in the Fields.*

36 Todd 7.

37 Todd 7.

38 Stolberg 167.

39 Stolberg 167.

40 Edward Robbin, *Woody Guthrie and Me: An Intimate Reminiscence* (Berkeley, California: Lancaster-Miller, 1979) 22.

41 Carey McWilliams, *Factories in the Fields: The Story of Migratory Farm Labor in California* (1939; Berkeley/Los Angeles: U of California P, 2000) 54. Of course, Williams's report is also biased in that it is written from a leftwing perspective. Still, it underlines the prominence of the racist, or even fascist, discourse in those days.

McWilliams recalls an interview with a grower that was recorded after a general strike had broken out on his farm in 1935: As the grower had put up a fence around the workers' camp in order to "keep the lawless element out,"[42] he answered when questioned about this camp that "agitators continually refer to it as a stockade, a cattle corral, or a prison, and its inhabitants as slaves or prisoners."[43] Again, the interviewee's comparison of the fenced camp to "a stockade" or "a cattle coral" rings with the central image in Guthrie's song.

Quite in contrast to their predecessors, the white migrants would soon be suspected of Communist agitation, as Hugh Osborne, representative of the Associated Farmers and Imperial County Supervisor, states in an article published in *Common Sense*:

> The whole proposition is Communist through and through! It stinks of Russia! Our women won't be safe on the streets. We never wanted this camp in here. White men are no good in our business. We like our Mexicans. They don't complain: they live where we put them, and they aren't forever organizing. As for those bulletins which they say we sent out to get those migrants here, they were the work of the Communist Party.[44]

Unlike the Mexicans who, at least according to Mr. Osborne's comment, "aren't forever organizing," the migrant workers from Texas, Oklahoma and Arkansas were said to join their forces in a union. Therefore, the racial prejudice was soon fused with rumors of a Communist conspiracy that might have had its origin in the migrant camps, in which the 'Okies' and 'Arkies' would find food and shelter and which were commonly regarded as hotbeds of Communist agitation. As Carey McWilliams has it, the Associated Farmers' propaganda "identif[ied], [at least] in the popular mind, the 'Red' or 'Communist' with the 'foreigner.'"[45] Thus, whenever there was any kind of attempt to negotiate labor rights or wages, the vigilante committees immediately knew how to cope with such incidents. "At one [migrant] camp," John Steinbeck observed, "it is the custom of deputy sheriffs, who are also employees of a great ranch nearby, to drive by the camp for hours at a time, staring into the tents as though trying to memorize faces."[46] Whenever there seemed to be the slightest

42 Quoted in McWilliams 237.
43 Quoted in McWilliams 237.
44 Quoted in Todd 7.
45 McWilliams 136.
46 John Steinbeck, "Dubious Battle in California," *America and Americans (and Selected Nonfiction)*, ed. Susan Shillinglaw and Jackson J. Benson (New York: Penguin, 2002) 75.

form of political protest, they attacked under the pretense of reinstalling law and order, or, as had been officially declared by the Associated Farmers, to enforce a "moral rearmament" among the migrant workers.[47] Their use of extremely violent measures, such as union busting, scapegoating, lynching and red-baiting with the help of guns, clubs and even tear gas in order to prevent uprisings and to demoralize strikers, soon created the fear of a 'domestic fascism' which was, at least according to leftwing and liberal intellectuals, inspired by the developments in Europe at that time.[48]

Though this menace of domestic fascism put into practice by the militant vigilante men was a nationwide phenomenon, as the last line of the first verse of Guthrie's song – "I been hearin' his name all over the land" – implies, it was particularly prominent in California, where "the mechanism of fascist control ha[d] been carried to further lengths than elsewhere in America."[49] Thus, the Golden State was soon regarded as "that state of the union which ha[d] advanced furthest toward an integrated fascist set-up":[50] Due to its industrially organized agricultural system that was characterized by large-scale, intensive, diversified and mechanized growing and harvesting, large parts of the land belonged to a relatively small number of growers. Already in 1870, when the development of the Californian agricultural system into a huge 'agribusiness' began, "1/500 of the population of California owned one half or more of the available agricultural lands of the State."[51] Consequently, small farmers and migratory sharecroppers soon became typical representatives of the agricultural workforce, as they were flexible enough to meet the growers' demands. Yet, they did not have any standing at all and were soon economically exploited, politically persecuted and characterized as "less than human" by the Associated Farmers.[52] In an article appearing in *The*

47 "Pickett, Steinbeck, And Mr. McWilliams," *People's World* 4 Aug. 1939: 77.

48 At closer inspection, a comparison between this highly organized attempt to undermine any kind of communist agitation and the anti-communist policy which was implemented in fascist Germany at the same time is found to be too far-fetched. Yet, although the use of the term "fascism" in the American context certainly lacked theoretical rigor, it was applied to American society by a broad range of liberals and leftists (cf. Stolberg).

49 McWilliams 9.

50 Carey McWilliams, quoted in Daniel Geary, "Carey McWilliams and Antifascism," *The Journal of American History* 90.3 (2003): n. pag., <http:// www.historycooperative.org/journals/jah/90.3/geary.html>, 7 Sept. 2006.

51 McWilliams 23.

52 Dorothy Healey, interview with Joe Klein, n.d. (WGA, Accessions 2004, 67.4, Box 1, Folder 12).

Nation, Herbert Klein and Carey McWilliams describe the usual way of treating migrants working for the large-scale agribusinesses in the Californian fields:

> The great company farm-factories are watched by armed special deputies and machine-gun equipment has been installed in several establishments. Living in company camps, the workers are made to realize that they can be summarily evicted. The existence in the locality of a sturdy 'stockade' is a visible warning of possible concentration.[53]

By creating an atmosphere of fear, the company owners made sure right from the beginning that there would not be any uprisings among the workers. The threat of being "summarily evicted," which is indeed reminiscent of a fascist set-up, kept them, at least most of the time, calm and peaceful. Moreover, the migrants were discouraged by the extremely bad and highly provisional living conditions they had to cope with. In a quite detailed description of one of the company camps, Klein and McWilliams illustrate the miserable living conditions of the migrant workers, finishing their account with an observation that they were indeed treated like animals:

> About ten miles from Salinas, conveniently removed from the main highway, an enclosure has recently been built. A stout and unbroken wall of planks a dozen feet high forms a rectangular stockade which is divided off into several compartments on the inside, the whole occupying an acre or more. Along one wall are ranged a group of outhouses, the only sign that the structure is intended for humans rather than swine.[54]

Whenever, in spite of all these preventive measures to keep the migrants from organizing, some dissatisfied workers started to complain or even to strike, the self-appointed groups of vigilante men were brought into operation. Let us examine the following depiction of a strike of apricot pickers in the Brentwood district in Contra Costa County in June 1934, in which vigilante thugs and deputy sheriffs took violent action against alleged conspirators:

> Heads were busted, and the usual suspects rounded up. In this instance, 150 strikers were herded by deputies into a cattle corral – like enclosure in the

53 Herbert Klein and Carey McWilliams, "Cold Terror in California," *The Nation* 24 July 1934: 97.

54 Klein and McWilliams 97.

> center of Brentwood. This spectacle of American citizens being herded into a temporary concentration camp had prophetic import.[55]

The "prophetic import" of such an incident is obvious: not only did it evoke associations of the worst kind, as the cattle corral is compared to a "concentration camp" in Nazi Germany; the vision of human beings being chased around like wild animals seemed to have deeply struck the contemporary consciousness. Thus, in another article taken from *The People's World*, the same image was employed by its author Ellen McGrath, who pointed out that "[t]hroughout the harvest season state patrol cars drove through the hop fields and fruit orchards and make short shrift of union men. Pickets were herded into patrol cars and dumped at the county line."[56]

The image was also taken up by Woody Guthrie, who sung that "they herded us around like a wild herd of cattle." Moreover, apart from employing it in his "Vigilante Man," he also used it in an article he wrote for *The People's World* entitled "$30 Wood Help." While describing another vigilante attack, he points out that "they made us all line up in front of th [sic] big limousene, an' walk like a string of convicts out into a cow pasture."[57] Even in his liner notes to "Vigilante Man" Guthrie employs that comparison, which, as we have seen, circulated in the Californian fields in the second half of the 1930s and was charged with racial and political overtones:

> For a long time I heard about the Vigilante man, but didn't never know for sure who he was. One night in Tracy. Cal., up close to Frisco, I found out. About 150 of us found out.
> It was cold and rainy that night. It was the month of March. A car load of them rounded us up and herded us out into a cow pasture. Some of the boys stayed out there in the rain and some of us went back into town.[58]

Taking into consideration that this recollection of a vigilante assault appeared in one of the most prominent anthologies of folk song in order to introduce one of Guthrie's Dust Bowl Ballads, it may be an act of self-fashioning rather than a true autobiographical account. Yet, autobiographical or not, Guthrie's description does not only refer to a single incidence, but, more generally, portrays a tragic facet of migrants' life in California, which, to come back to where we began, is also rendered in

55 Starr, *Endangered Dreams* 164.

56 Ellen McGrath, "State Patrol Chief Herds Last Scab," *People's World* 14 May 1939: 19.

57 WGA, Accessions 2004, 67.4, Box 3, Folder 33, 22.

58 Lomax, Guthrie and Seeger 234.

the joke published in the *Voice of the Agricultural Worker*, which was cited at the beginning of this chapter. The anecdote about the tourist's son, who, observing a cotton picker lifting his body for a short pause to take a breath, cannot but conclude that "them things look almost like people when they stand on there hind legs," is just another textual manifestation disclosing the racist attitude towards the migrant workers in California. Comparing the migrant workers to "a wild herd of cattle," Guthrie's configuration of a vigilante attack in his "Vigilante Man" takes part in the contemporary discourse in that it resorts to a quite similar imagery, which, as the correlation of his song with a number of contemporary texts has shown, was indeed both widely disseminated and ideologically charged.

However, in spite of the fact that the Southwestern migrants were discriminated against and terrorized by violent vigilante groups backed by a powerful agricultural organization, the situation, at least according to Guthrie, was not hopeless. The solution to the vigilante problem is already hinted at in his "Vigilante Man." Let us, once again, consider Guthrie's rendering of the attack on the innocent migrants sleeping in the engine house:

> Rainy night down in the engine house,
> Sleeping just as still as a mouse.
> Man come along and he chased us out in the rain.
> Was that a vigilante man?
>
> Stormy days we'd pass the time away
> Sleeping in some good warm place
> A cop come along and we give him a little race,
> Say, was that a vigilante man?[59]

It is the last two lines of this passage that deserve particular attention, as they, at least implicitly, no longer configure the migrants as helpless and passive victims. As the ambiguous expression "we give him a little race" indicates, it might well be the migrants, who, unified and empowered, have taken action against the vigilante man in order to defend themselves. Thus, the migrants' acting in concert is suggested to bear the potential to overcome the repression and to transform the collective suffering into collective action. Another, yet unpublished song of Guthrie's called "The Rancho Grande Vigilante" renders the idea of actively opposing the allegedly powerful vigilantes more explicitly:

[59] Leventhal and Guthrie 237-38/240.

Out on the Rancho Grande
There was a Vigi-lante [sic][60]
And with a sawed off shot gun
He made his self right handy,
… He made his self right hand--y.
He was a pistol packin' papa,
He was a win-chester popper,
He was a tear gas bomb dropper,
And so we just had to stop 'im.

Chorus:
I like to roam out yonder
Out where the Oakies wander
And hog-tie Vigilantes
Out on the rancho grande …
… Out on the rancho gran-de.
I like my Straw-berry roany
'Cause he's a good Union Pony,
He's a high steppin' Pacer,
And he's a real Union Racer.

I like the Rancho Grande,
I like it fine and dandy
I'm ridin' and a ropin'-
Bull doggin' Vigi-lantees,
… Bull doggin' Vigi--lanteees.
I like the C.I.O. dear-ly
I like the big round up year-ly
I get a Vigi-lante
Each mornin' bright and ear-ly, [Chorus].

My hoss is some single-footer,
Yes, he's a real deputy cutter,
He's a champion fox trotter,
He's a Vigi-lante spotter.
… A Vigi-lante spot-terrrr.
Now when the sun hits the valley,
Or when at sun down I sally,
I keep my eye peeled varmits,
And my gun for Vigi-lanteees. [Chorus][61]

Obviously, this song sheds light upon the relationship between the migrants and the vigilantes, which differs from that outlined in Guthrie's "Vigilante Man." Though, in the first verse, the vigilante is still described

60 The various hyphenations, which are also to be found in the manuscript version of the song, are, most probably, supposed to indicate word stress and length.

61 WGA, Songs I, Box 3, Folder 23.

as a heavily armed guy people would certainly be afraid of, the song takes a surprising turn, which is already hinted at by a change of perspective in the last line of the first verse. After enumerating the characteristics of the vigilante man, repeatedly referring to the personal pronoun "He" at the beginning of the verse's lines, the focus shifts to the migrants, who, instead of running away and hiding where the vigilante might not find them, decide to take matters into their own hands. Suddenly, as the chorus of the song implies, it is the migrants' turn, who now "hog-tie Vigilantes / Out on the rancho Grande."

Interestingly enough, the term "hog-tie,"[62] which evokes the image of a hunter having tied up his prey on a stick to carry it home, is clearly reminiscent of the imagery that Guthrie resorted to in his "Vigilante Man," in which the migrants were compared to a "wild herd of cattle" being chased by merciless vigilantes. Yet, here, it is not the migratory workers, who are treated like animals, but the vigilantes themselves. The song's second verse gives substance to this analogy:

> I like the Rancho Grande,
> I like it fine and dandy
> I'm ridin' and a ropin' –
> Bull doggin' Vigi-lantees,
> … Bull doggin' Vigi-lanteees.
> I like the C.I.O. dear-ly
> I like the big round up year-ly
> I get a Vigi-lante
> Each mornin' bright and ear-ly.

By fashioning himself as a cowboy, "ridin' and a ropin' / Bull doggin' Vigi-lantees," the speaker of the song deliberately inverts the relationship between hunter and hunted as outlined in Guthrie's "Vigilante Man." Now, it is he who is chasing the henchmen of the landowners with unconcealed pleasure. Moreover, as the last line of the verse suggests, he does so on a quite regular basis, as if it were a leisure time activity.

That Guthrie's mode of emplotment very much resembles the typical scenario of a cowboy chasing his cattle across the prairie, is no coincidence, as he looked to a well-known country song called "El Rancho Grande" as a model for his song. Originally published in Spanish as "Alla en El Rancho Grande" in 1927, it was translated into English and

62 The term "hog-tie" is also used for a cowboy/rodeo practice of tying hands then feet together to render the hog – or person – immobile.

republished by Bartley Costello and Silvano R. Ramos in 1936.[63] Eventually, it was country singer Gene Autry who popularized the song and turned it into one of *the* traditional American cowboy ballads. Autry started his career with a short program as 'Oklahoma's Yodeling Cowboy' on the local radio station KVOO in Tulsa, Oklahoma, in 1929. After having signed a record contract with Columbia Records, he performed on the "National Barn Dance" for radio station WLS in Chicago. Finally, in 1934, Autry first appeared on television screens nationwide as a musical entertainer and actor, thereby increasing the popularity he had already gained. Among his 635 recordings, which sold more than 100 million copies, happened to be a version of Costello's and Ramos's "El Rancho Grande." Here is an excerpt of the lyrics of the song as translated by Bartley Costello:

> Give me my ranch and my cattle
> Far from the great city's rattle
> Give me a big herd to battle
> For I just love herding cattle.
>
> I love to roam out yonder
> Out where the Buffalo wander
> Free as the Eagle flying
> I'm roping and a-tying
> I'm roping and a-tying. [...]
>
> Give me the wide open spaces
> That's just where I know my place is
> I love the Ro-de-o dearly
> And the Big Round-up yearly.[64]

The song outlines the standard patterns and ingredients of a cowboy's life: the "wide open spaces," in which he roams "free as the Eagle flying," embody the American ideas of the frontier and the individual pursuit of

63 John Lomax and Alan Lomax, eds., *American Ballads and Folk Songs* (New York: Macmillan, 1964) 361.

64 <http://www.cowboylyrics.com/tabs/cowboy/el-rancho-grande-6894.html>, 7 Sept 2006. An adaptation of the song is also found in *Woody and Lefty Lou's Favorite Collection of Old Time Hill Country Songs*. Here, the expression "wild herd of cattle" is used almost verbatim: "I love to roam out yonder, / Out where the buffalo wander, / To see the eagle flyin' / And hear the breezes sighin', / And hear the breezes sighin-n-n-n. / I love my bronc and my saddle, / I love those *wild herds of cattle* / I love my ranch on the prairie, / I love the gun that I carry. / [...] / Giev [sic] me a big herd of cattle, / Far from the great city's rattle, / Give me a big herd to battle, / For I just love herding cattle" (cf. Smithsonian, RRFAC, *Woody Guthrie Papers*, Box 2, Folder 4, emphases added).

happiness. "Far from the great city's rattle" the cowboy is leading a life close to nature, which is reminiscent of the Jeffersonian ideal of the American yeoman. His life and his work revolve around his cattle, which also takes a dominant position in the song. The cowboy's love for "herding cattle" – a phrase that immediately brings us back to Guthrie's "Vigilante Man," where it is employed as a metaphor for the inhumane treatment of the migrants – is outlined in the first verse already.

Read against this foil of one of the most popular contemporary cowboy songs, the potential of Guthrie's "The Rancho Grande Vigilante" increases significantly. By rewriting the lyrics, and by using the tune of a song that was certainly known to the majority of the Southwestern migrants, Guthrie did not only manage to catch and hold his audience's attention; he also provided his listeners with an already established framework of associations. Thus, the analogy drawn in his "The Rancho Grande Vigilante," in which the migrants are depicted as cowboys chasing vigilantes "out on the Rancho Grande," is, to a large extent, substantiated by the recipients' knowledge of Ramos's and Costello's cowboy ballad, which was, according to Guthrie, "a favorite to lots of people right today, and will continue to be for a long time, because a song that is simple, easy to remember and hum and whistle, is the kind that goes on and on, never getting old."[65]

However, quite in contrast to the cowboy, who, though he "love[s] herding cattle" and "the Rodeo dearly," would never think of killing his cattle, which is the basis of his existence, the migrants do not seem to be content with rounding up the vigilantes. Lines like "I get a Vigilante / Each mornin' bright and early," or, even more explicitly, "I keep my eye peeled varmits / And my gun for Vigi-lantees" suggest that they, as soon as they catch the vigilantes, take revenge for the violent assaults they had to suffer. Though Guthrie's song takes up the basic pattern of the cowboy ballad, its romanticizing tone, idealizing a life at the frontier and close to nature, is thus replaced by an aggressive mood that reflects the growing tensions between agricultural laborers and landowners in California in the second half of the 1930s.

Finally, one might well wonder why Guthrie wrote two songs dealing with the phenomenon of vigilantism which are so different in their mode of emplotment and, what is more interesting, in their characterization of the relationship between vigilantes and migratory workers. Whereas his "Vigilante Man" exposes the inhumane treatment of the migratory sharecroppers as a "wild herd of cattle," the tables seem to be turned in his "The Rancho Grande Vigilante," which, though it draws on very similar

[65] Cf. Smithsonian, RRFAC, *Woody Guthrie Papers*, Box 2, Folder 4.

imagery, portrays the migrants as the herders and the hunters of vigilantes. In this song, they are no longer victimized; instead, it seems to be their turn, as they react to the vigilante threat in a playfully aggressive and remarkably self-confident manner.

A possible clue to this fairly surprising change of perspective is given in Guthrie's "The Rancho Grande Vigilante" itself. As expressions like "Union Pony," "Union Racer," or lines like "I like the C.I.O. dearly" in the first three verses of the song imply, the speaker's grown self-confidence and his commanding handling of the vigilante threat seem to be a result of his new identity as a member of a worker's union. Only as such is he able to defend himself against the vigilantes, and, what is even more, to eventually become more powerful than the violent thugs in the fields and in the labor camps. The collective action of the migrants already hinted at by the use of the first-person plural in the last line of the first verse is thus emphasized by the vocabulary of organized labor employed throughout the song.

To conclude, both Guthrie's "Vigilante Man" and his "The Rancho Grande Vigilante" take a stand on the contemporary racist, or even fascist, discourse in California, employing imagery which was widely circulating in the second half of the 1930s and was used both by the anti-migrant lobby and by representatives of liberal or leftwing circles. Whereas Guthrie's "Vigilante Man" articulates the migrants' fear and alleged powerlessness, his "The Rancho Grande Vigilante" offers a more optimistic scenario, in which the vigilante threat is done away with through the power of unionization. By utilizing a traditional cowboy song as a pretext for his "The Rancho Grande Vigilante" and by appropriating the ideologically charged "herding"-image so prominent in the contemporary discourse, the song suggests an inversion of the existing relationship between field workers and vigilantes and propagates collective action as the ideal way to overcome the menace of fascism in the fields of California.

3.5 "Hamburgers in the hereafter": Debunking the Politics of Pentecostalism

> Some of the preachers that promise you hamburgers in the hereafter get on my nerves; what I'd really like to do part of the time is to give 'em a hunk of blackberry pie right in the face (Woody Guthrie)[1]

Under the pressure of their almost unbearable situation in the alleged 'Sunkist State,' a considerable number of the migrants from the American Southwest sought relief in religion as a last resort. As their expectations of a paradisiac existence in California had been destroyed, they looked for compensation and found it in the promises of a heavenly hereafter made by various fundamentalist denominations.

Though Woody Guthrie's socialization in the American Southwest was certainly affected by fundamentalist ideas and ideals, he soon developed a critical attitude towards these denominations, which, according to him, took the migrants' minds off the actual causes and causers of their miserable living conditions by propagating an ethics of suffering. In a number of his songs he distances himself from the concept of an otherworldly paradise, and, at the same time, promotes unionism as a reliable innerworldly solution to the social and economic problems faced by the Southwestern migrants in the second half of the Great Depression.

After outlining the intriguing psychodynamics and the underlying social and cultural conditions which made many migrants turn towards Pentecostalism after their arrival in California, the following chapter first focuses on some of Guthrie's rewritings of traditional religious songs which, rather uncritically, articulated an ethics of suffering. Both in order to shed light on the various rhetorical and compositional features Guthrie employed to debunk the politics of Pentecostalism in his more critical songs, and to situate them in the tradition of political songwriting, the following part of this chapter is concerned with the bard of the Industrial Workers of the World (I.W.W.), Joe Hill. An analysis of his oeuvre is worth a detour, as Hill's songs considerably shaped Guthrie's politically motivated rewritings of traditional religious hymns, which are dealt with after the digression on Hill. Moreover, this chapter attempts to show that the renaissance of Joe Hill and his songs in the 1930s, which was also fostered by Woody Guthrie, was due to the socio-cultural developments of the time.

1 Lomax, Guthrie and Seeger 88.

* * * * *

Back home in Oklahoma, Arkansas, Kansas and Missouri, fundamentalist Protestantism had played an important role in the life of the Southwestern migrants. The majority of them adhered to Southern Baptist or Southern Methodist denominations, which were characterized by their strong emotional appeal. "Services," as James Gregory observes, "were conducted in a fervent, revivalistic style that emphasized the search for personal salvation while allowing for a good deal of enthusiastic group participation."[2] Oftentimes, the regular worshipping of God was accompanied by singing and powerful sermons, which had a strong emotional appeal, virtually sweeping away the church audience.

In California, everything was different. The migrants were unwelcome guests on the predominantly Northern Methodist and Northern Baptist territory, with the major congregations strongly deviating from the religious standards they had been used to back in the Southwest. The services were unemotional and cold in comparison to those in the Southwest, and the communal experience of ecstatic singing the migrants had enjoyed in the churches of their home states did not at all belong to the repertoire of the Californian religious practices. In short, the churches on the American west coast offered 'brain' religion to people who were used to religion appealing to the 'heart.'

In this religious *diaspora*, many Southwestern migrants turned to the more radical denominations of evangelical Protestantism, which seemed to offer at least provisional spiritual compensation. Most important among this variety of religious groupings were those organizations which belonged to the Holiness and Pentecostal movement, such as the Assemblies of God, Church of the Nazarene, Pentecostal Holiness, and a number of Churches of God and Full-Gospel assemblies, which, in the second half of the 1930s, became a spiritual refuge for the majority of the migrants from the Southwestern states.

Though this large-scale conversion to Pentecostalism was not only caused by the Dust Bowl migration, the migrants became the major target group of this off-shoot of radical Protestantism, not only due to their need for an adequate form of religious worship, but also because of their poor social conditions, which was a reason for most of the established Californian congregations not to accept the newcomers. Thus, the migrants had to resort to Pentecostalism, as "there were few other religious

2 Gregory 197. For the reconstruction of the cultural significance of religion for the migrants both in the Southwest and in California, I predominantly referred to Gregory's illuminating account of Okie culture in California.

institutions where poor Southwesterners felt comfortable and welcome, where they knew they could go without being ashamed of their clothes or accents, where they could socialize with 'home folks.'"[3] The Pentecostal movement became a gathering place for the disinherited, for those who had already lost their faith in the world and now adhered to a predominantly escapist attitude. "The typical Pentecostal believer," as Robert M. Anderson puts it,

> found himself in straitened cirumstances, and relegated to a social position lower than his forebears. [...] Economically, socially, culturally, and even physically displaced and deprived, the convert to Pentecostalism often found in this new-old version of Christianity an ideological and emotional affinity to his religious heritage, broadly conceived.[4]

No wonder that the traumatized, dislocated and marginalized migrants were ideal recruits for a movement that "expressed and dignified [their] marginality"[5] and provided them with a feeling of acceptance in a community of kindred spirits.

Moreover, Pentecostalism also provided the migrants with the standards of religious practice they were familiar with: The revivalistic style of the services, the singing and the dancing, the excitement and the active participation of the crowd persuaded many migrants to convert to Pentecostalism. Music played an important role, and instead of the traditional and more conservative organ and piano tunes, the Pentecostal services often included euphoric religious hymns and gospels. One of the most prominent religious hymns was called "No Disappointment in Heaven," which also belonged to Woody Guthrie's repertoire:

> There's no disappointment in heaven,
> No weariness, sorrow, or pain;
> No hearts that are bleeding and broken,
> No song with a minor refrain.
> The clouds of our earthly horizon
> Will never appear in the sky,
> And all will be sunshine and gladness,
> With never a sob nor a sigh.
>
> I'm bound for that beautiful city
> That the Lord has prepared for his own,
> Where all the redeemed of the ages

3 Gregory 203.

4 Robert M. Anderson, *Vision of the Disinherited: The Making of American Pentecostalism* (New York/Oxford: Oxford UP, 1979) 136.

5 Anderson 136.

Sing Glory around the white throne.
Sometimes I grow homesick for heaven,
And the glories I there shall behold!
What a great day 'twill be when my Saviour I see
In that beautiful city of Old.[6]

Heaven, as the verses suggest, is a place where men will be released from all the burdens they have to carry on earth. There will be "no weariness, sorrow, or pain"; instead, all will be "sunshine and gladness," which makes the speaker of the song feel "homesick for heaven," as he cannot wait to leave all his earthly toil and trouble behind. What has been pictured in metaphorical terms in the first two verses, becomes tangible in the next two verses, which enumerate the untroubled blessings of a heavenly existence:

We'll never pay rent for our mansions
The taxes will never come due;
Our garments will never grow threadbare,
But always be fadeless and new.
We'll never be hungry or thirsty
Nor languish in poverty there,
For all the rich bounties of heaven
His sanctified children will share.

There'll never be crape on the doorknob,
No funeral train in the sky;
No graves on the hillsides of glory,
For there we shall nevermore die.
The old will be young there forever
Transformed in a moment of time;
Immortal we'll stand in His likeness,
The stars and the sun to out-shine![7]

Following the verses' argument, life in the hereafter will be characterized by two features: First, there will be no material restrictions, as no one has to starve or suffer from poverty. Second, there will be no physical restrictions, as heavenly existence is eternal; those who enter the "beautiful city" in the sky "shall nevermore die."

The song clearly outlines the concept of faith as propagated by Pentecostalism: A rejection of the existing world with all its social inequalities, paired with a strong conviction that there will be a better and eternal life after death, without any of the hardship they suffered in this world.

6 WGA, Notebooks I, Notebook 4, 82.
7 WGA, Notebooks I, Notebook 4, 82.

This prospect of an otherworldly existence is understood to have helped many of the working poor to endure the social misconditions they were generally exposed to. Likewise, Anderson argues that

> [b]ecause of their position on the margins of the social order and their inadequate access to means for ameliorating their conditions of existence, many of the working poor have responded to their situation in ways that have been labeled anti-social, escapist, and unrealistic. In fact, they are at once protests against their alienated, relatively impoverished social position and attempts to alter it or, at least, temporarily ease its painful effects. Among these responses are crime, delinquency, violence, heavy drinking, drug addiction, gambling, prostitution, sexual promiscuity, and extremely other-wordly religion. Moral and ethical judgements of the difference between the last of these – religion – and the others should not be allowed to obscure its functional equivalence.[8]

Anderson clearly outlines the function of "extremely other-worldly religion" as a means of the poor to both silently protest against the miserable living conditions they have to suffer from and as an attempt to "temporarily ease its painful effects."

That a song rendering the ethics of suffering as promoted by Pentecostalism was also sung by Woody Guthrie might come as a surprise, as Guthrie is generally said to have been rather critical of any religious denomination. However, he actually sang a number of songs that promised a rewarding existence in a heavenly hereafter and, most probably, he did so because such songs appealed to his migrant audience. In his annotations to another religious song, called "Ain't A Gonna Grieve," Guthrie even admits that he "made up this song to have something to sing when I got jobs around at churches of all the different faiths."[9]

Yet, though he certainly had a considerable repertoire of religious hymns and gospels, the Okie bard indeed tended to be skeptical of the escapist attitude propagated in these songs, as his annotations to his version of "No Disappointment in Heaven" reveal. For him, it seems, the crux of the matter was not the expectation of an otherworldly paradise promoted in the song. Rather he understood the song as providing "some good suggestions for Political Platforms. [...] Their [the politicians'] goal has to be like this: That Kingdom Come, That Will be Done, down here on earth so it'll be just like Heaven!"[10] With this remark, Guthrie added a political dimension to the song, turning it into an implicit criticism of those politicians who, according to Guthrie, always proclaim that "such

8 Anderson 227.

9 WGA, Songs I, Box I, Folder 1.

10 WGA, Notebooks I, Notebook 4, 82.

stuff as this aint supposed to be thought about doen here."[11] Another of Guthrie's religious hymns which, in a very similar way, propagates the conviction that there will be a better world after death, is his "Riding on that Salvation Train," written in 1939, when Guthrie was working for the Californian radio station KFVD:

I'm a ridin' on that Salvation Train
I'm a ridin' on that Salvation Train
It's that same old train that brought me to this world
It's soon a goin' to carry me away.

O' my brother you caint ride but one
O' sister you caint ride but one
O' you caint ride but one thru that armageddon
O' chilluns you caint ride but one. [...]

O' brother you caint ride four
O' sister you caint ride four
O' you caint ride four and get to the golden shore
O' chilluns you caint ride four.

O' brother you caint ride five
O' sister you caint ride five
O' you caint ride five and get eternal life
O'chilluns you caint ride five.[12]

Once again, the promises of a "golden shore" and an "eternal life" are at the centre of the song. The image of a train that both brings human beings to this world and carries them away again underlines the escapist notion of wordly existence merely as a stage to be passed through. Yet, it is not the lyrics of the song which deserve particular attention here. Rather it is Guthrie's annotation, which does not only hint at his skepticism towards such an otherworldly faith once again, but also points to one of the major influences on Guthrie's songwriting. At the bottom of the manuscript page of "Riding on that Salvation Train," Guthrie, self-critically evaluating his song, wrote: "Little too much pie in the sky to be good."[13] This short annotation contains a line from a song written by a famous political songwriter, whose (life and) oeuvre shall get, in a concise excursus, particular consideration here, as both his ideological convictions and his techniques of songwriting, concerning both musical and textual composition, had a significant impact on Woody Guthrie and certainly help to

[11] WGA, Notebooks I, Notebook 4, 82.
[12] WGA, Notebooks I, Notebook 4, 146.
[13] WGA, Notebooks I, Notebook 4, 146.

explain the latter's critical attitude towards religion, uttered in the above annotations and, as we shall see later, more explicitly in a number of his songs.

* * * * *

Joseph Haeglund or Joe Hill, as he called himself in the country of his choice, arrived in the United States in 1902 at the age of 20. After having spent his childhood in Jevla, Westerjutland, where he received a common school education and learned the first bits and pieces of the English language at the Y.M.C.A. in his hometown, he worked as a seaman on freighters plying between Gothenburg and England. He took various jobs in New York, before he once again ended up as a maritime worker on a freight steamer to Hawaii, where he got in contact with American migratory workers and learned about their hardship and toil. Soon after, he became a committed member of the radical workers' union Industrial Workers of the World (I.W.W.), the foundation of which was the result of a fusion of the Socialist Labor Party, the Western Federation of Miners, and the American Labor Union in 1905. Being the first union "in which workingmen and women of all skill levels, colors, and ethnicities could unite,"[14] the I.W.W. opposed the elite craft unionism of the American Federation of Labor and steadily attracted new members, at least in the first years after its foundation.[15]

Singing was a major part of the I.W.W. culture and it was mainly employed to promote its ideology. Apart from newspapers, pamphlets and cartoons, it was songs in particular which "were frequently heard in the fields and in the jungle camps under the railroad bridges"[16] and which were used to spread the I.W.W.'s political message. Joe Hill eventually became the most prominent bard of the radical organization, contributing to its singing culture, as Ralph Chaplin, the number two singer of the I.W.W., recalls in his autobiography:

> He could play almost any kind of musical instrument and delighted in improvising satirical parodies of well-known songs. [...] Joe Hill could never under-

[14] Garman, *A Race of Singers* 92.

[15] One must add that the total membership of the I.W.W. never exceeded 150.000 workers at any time. Yet, in the first decade of its existence, the "Wobblies," as the members of the I.W.W. were called, were very successful in organizing strikes and campaigns against exploitation by the newly established corporate capitalism (cf. Garman, *A Race of Singers* 92).

[16] McWilliams 157.

> stand why his parodies became so popular. He was greatly surprised to find himself in the limelight and his roughneck songs famous through the world.[17]

In the poor economic situation of the 1910s, Hill's "satirical parodies of well-known songs" quickly reached a large audience of workers in all economic sectors. Expressing the laborers' discontent with their low wages and bad working conditions and promoting the idea that it was not the ballot box, but direct action which would change the social structure, his tunes eventually became an ideological threat to the ruling elites. Hill transposed "the historic mission of the working class to do away with capitalism"[18] into songs, which propagated a revolution of the established social hierarchy and a redistribution of power into the hands of the working class.

In 1914, however, Joe Hill's political conviction found a more radical expression than in his songs. He was accused of killing the Salt Lake City grower J.G. Morrison, after having confronted him and his two sons in his shop with an accomplice. Though there was little evidence that Hill actually committed the murder, he was convicted and eventually, in spite of a number of letters of protest, even from such well-known personalities as the Swedish consul and American President Wilson, sentenced to death after a spectacularly short trial. Not surprisingly, the conviction and final execution of Hill was suspected to be the result of a conspiracy by the company owners, who wanted to get rid of a powerful enemy, a suspicion which made him and the ideas he promoted even more influential than they had been before.

Interestingly enough, it was Hill himself who contributed to his being fashioned as a martyr sacrificing his life for the labor movement: Though all the other details appertaining to the Morrison case indicated that Hill was innocent, he did not rely on any kind of judicial support. Rather, he dismissed the attorneys who were supposed to exonerate him, which would have actually been no difficult endeavor, as there were witnesses enough describing Morrison's assailants as being several inches smaller than Hill's six feet. Moreover, to add even more dramatic potential to his imminent death, Hill wrote several letters to his most intimate friends which contributed highly to his self-fashioning as a kind of socialist messiah. Here is one he wrote to 'Big Bill' Haywood, one of the leading figures in the I.W.W.:

17 Quoted in Greenway, *American Folksongs* 191.

18 "Preamble to the I.W.W. constitution," *The Little Red Song Book: Songs to Fan the Flames of Discontent*, I.W.W. (Columbia, South Carolina: Harbinger Publications: 1995) n. p.

> Goodbye, Bill: I die like a true rebel. Don't waste any time mourning – organize! It is a hundred miles from here to Wyoming. Could you arrange to have my body hauled to the state line to be buried? I don't want to be found dead in Utah. Joe Hill.[19]

Assuring himself and the reader of the letter that he would die a "true rebel['s]" death, Joe Hill did not forget, even in the last hours of his life, what he had been propagating ever since he had become an adherent of the I.W.W.'s ideology. The simple appeal to stop mourning his death and to organize did not only nip any kind of sentimental notion in the bud; it also put emphasis on his sacrificing his life for the socialist mission. Even on the day of his execution on November, 15th, 1914, Joe Hill did not give up his self-fashioning. Shortly before the guns were fired by the execution squad, he screamed "Yes, aim! Let her go! Fire!" at the executioners, as if he wanted to make sure that his death would really be regarded as that of a true martyr.[20]

Both the notion of a capitalist conspiracy, which was made responsible for his death, and his self-fashioning as a socialist martyr assured Hill a prominent place in the collective memory of the American Left. In the *International Socialist Review* of December 1915, Ralph Chaplin, Hill's singing comrade, remembered the funeral procession and recalled the slogans which were written on the sleeves of participants:

> Thousands in the procession wore I.W.W. pennants on their sleeves or red ribbons worded, 'Joe Hill, murdered by the authorities of the state of Utah, November the 19th, 1915' or 'Joe Hill, martyr to a great cause,' 'Don't mourn, organize, Joe Hill.'[21]

In December 1916, one year later, James Larkin commented upon Hill's life and death in an article for the *International Socialist Review*, once again fostering the image of Hill as a new messiah:

> Joseph Hillstrom, one of the Ishmaelites of the industrial world, was to hand and they 'shot him to death' because he was a rebel, one of the disinherited, because he was the voice of the inarticulate downtrodden; they crucified him on their cross of gold, spilled his blood on the altar of their God – Profit. Therefore, Comrades, over the great heart of Joe Hill, now stilled in death, let us take up his burden, rededicate ourselves to the cause that knows no failure, and for which Joseph Hillstrom cheerfully gave his all, his valuable life.[22]

19 Quoted in Greenway, *American Folksongs* 195.

20 Cf. Greenway, *American Folksongs* 195.

21 <http://www.spartacus.schoolnet.co.uk/USAhillJ.htm>, 18 Sept. 2006.

22 <http://www.spartacus.schoolnet.co.uk/USAhillJ.htm>, 18 Sept. 2006.

Larkin's words sound like a sermon praising Christ, who sacrificed himself for the sake of the generations of Christians to come and thus ensured his spiritual continuance among his followers. Joe Hill, as the voice of the utterly powerless, also gave his life for the fulfillment of a mission, and Larkin's article admonishes his adherents to "take up his burden" and carry on with what he, whom the capitalists "crucified [...] on their cross of gold," had begun.

However, it was not only the (self-)fashioning of Joe Hill that turned him into a socialist messiah. It was also his songs, which disseminated a message that was a true alternative to the established Christian gospel. And indeed, during their first attempts to propagate their revolutionary political aims in song, the I.W.W. and its most prominent bard had to face a powerful opponent in the streets of the working-class districts in Chicago and elsewhere: The revolutionary ideas that Joe Hill and other singers of the I.W.W. preached from the soapbox conflicted with the principles of religious complacency spread by the Salvation Army, whose brass bands swarmed in the cities in the first decades of the 20th century in order to calm the dissatisfied workers by promising a rewarding life after death. Consider the following song by Johnson Ottman and E.O. Excell, which was part of the standard repertoire of any Salvation Army band:

> When upon life's billows you are tempest tossed,
> When you are discouraged, thinking all is lost,
> Count your many blessings, name them one by one,
> And it will surprise you what the Lord hath done.
>
> Are you ever burdened with a load of care?
> Does the cross seem heavy you are called to bear?
> Count your many blessings, every doubt will fly,
> And you will keep singing as the days go by. […]
>
> When you look at others with their lands and gold,
> Think that Christ has promised you His wealth untold;
> Count your many blessings. Wealth can never buy
> Your reward in heaven, nor your home on high.[23]

The song most probably appealed to many members of the working class in the streets of the big industrial cities immediately, as the first lines of each verse metaphorically render the various dimensions of their hardships: The majority of workers fell victim to rapidly changing labor market conditions, thus living a "tempest tossed" life indeed, always facing

23 <http://ingeb.org/spiritua/whenupon.html>, 14 Sept. 2006.

the risk of losing all at once. Moreover, the better part of the employees had to work under very bad conditions – hence the rhetorical question at the beginning of the second verse, which points to the workers' feeling of carrying "a load of care" which seemed to be too heavy time and again. Finally, the sense of injustice grew even stronger and added to the frustration of the poor, as a small minority of company owners was able to accumulate "lands and gold," as indicated at the beginning of the last verse of the song. Yet, the speaker does not stop here, but offers a solution to the disaster: He advises his audience to "count [their] many blessings" and to forget the miserable conditions they suffer from. Eventually, there will be a reward in heaven, which is, as the speaker promises, more than worldly "wealth can buy."

The prospects of a heavenly reward after death are also propagated by another Salvation Army classic called "In the Sweet Bye and Bye":

> There's a land that is fairer than day,
> And by faith we can see it afar;
> For the Father waits over the way
> To prepare us a dwelling place there.
>
> In the sweet bye and bye
> We shall meet on that beautiful shore;
> In the sweet bye and bye
> We shall meet on that beautiful shore.
>
> We shall sing on that beautiful shore
> The melodious songs of the blest,
> And our spirits shall sorrow no more
> Not a sigh for the blessing of rest.
>
> To our bountiful father above
> We will offer our tribute of praise;
> For the glorious gift of His love
> And the blessings that hallow our days.[24]

Once again, the "home on high" is promised to be every good Christian's reward after death. It is described as "a land that is fairer than day," a "dwelling place," which, as the second line of the song suggests, the devout believer may already see from "afar." The heavenly prospectus pointed to in the song is reason enough to be grateful to the Almighty and to forget all the toil and trouble here on earth, since "on that beautiful shore [...] our spirits shall sorrow no more." Interestingly enough, the devastating conditions that were, at least metaphorically, hinted at in the

24 <http://www.mudcat.org/@displaysong.cfm?SongID=3029>, 14 Sept. 2006.

previously discussed "Count your blessings, count them," are not even mentioned here, thus emphasizing the insignificance of this life in comparison to heavenly redemption.

Joe Hill was a radical critic of this 'ethics of suffering' and never tired of discrediting it as a means to calm down the dissatisfied working class and, what is worse, to legitimize the exploitation of their labor force. Following the tradition of Jack Walsh, a professional orator of the Socialist Party in those days, who had organized the first I.W.W. brass band in order to oppose the "street-corner evangelism"[25] of the Salvation Army, Hill largely contributed to the success of the union's street singing with his catchy parodies of the Army's hymns. Using the same tunes, he turned their propagation of an apology of suffering topsy-turvy. Joe Hill's most famous song, "The Preacher and the Slave," which he first performed at an I.W.W. meeting in Portland, Oregon, in 1910, is a mock-version of the Salvation Army song quoted above. Moreover, it is this song that Guthrie referred to with the annotation to his "Riding on that Salvation Train," pointing out that there is "too much pie in the sky [in the song] to be good." Let us examine the first verse and the first chorus of Hill's "The Preacher and the Slave":

> Long-haired preachers come out ev'ry night,
> Try to tell you what's wrong and what's right;
> But when asked how 'bout something to eat,
> They will answer with voices so sweet:
>
> You will eat, bye and bye,
> In that glorious land above the sky.
> Work and pray, live on hay,
> You'll get pie in the sky when you die.[26]

Hill unmasks the street Evangelists' tactics of spreading their gospel by accusing them of not satisfying the people's actual needs, but lulling them with promises of a heavenly paradise, which would await them on the condition that they worked, prayed, and lived "on hay," thus leading an ascetic life. The catchy phrase "pie in the sky when you die" does not only sum up the idea of an ethics of suffering in a single line, but, due to its triple rhyme and its profane choice of words, ridicules the cliché-ridden imagery of its Salvation Army model. Hill goes even one step further, as he accuses the preachers of the Army of instrumentalizing

25 Greenway, *American Folksongs* 175.
26 *The Little Red Song Book* 49.

their religious slogans for economic reasons. Consider the second verse of his song:

> And the starvation army they play,
> And they sing and they clap and they pray,
> Till they get all your coin on the drum;
> Then they tell you when you're on the bum:[27]

The most prominent charity organization of the times is denounced as a "starvation army," which is accused of exploiting those who believe in its slogans of salvation. Collecting money from their adherents on the pretext of spending it on charitable endeavors, they invested it in the growth of their own organization instead. Ironically, the poor, deprived of their last cent, were then comforted with the promises of a heavenly hereafter as they were out begging for alms.

Though Hill's polemics against the Salvation Army, denouncing it as a mere economic enterprise, is certainly over the top, his central argument can also be found in other contemporary texts. Already in 1906, one Professor Huxley, who was quoted in an article appearing in *The Central Christian Advocate*, observed the Salvation Army's metamorphosis from an institution of charity into an economic enterprise:

> Who is to say that the Salvation Army in the year 1920 shall not be a replica of what the Franciscan order had become in 1260? [The Franciscans] within thirty years of the death of St. Francis became one of the most powerful, wealthy and worldly corporations in Christendom.[28]

In his paper quoted in the *Advocate*, Huxley continues to elaborate on the development of the Salvation Army. Comparing it to the Woman's Christian Temperance Union and the Young Man's Christian Association, he asserts that the Salvation Army was "founded as a soul-saving device," but, "possibly in consonance with the Samaritan drift of our generation [has] relegated the evangelistic phase to a secondary place,"[29] as it was, according to Huxley's findings, laying more and more emphasis on "investing capital in philanthropic energies."[30] Though the aim of the Salvation Army to "redeem […] slums, pauperism and iniquity"[31] was probably not yet out of sight, capitalist terminology seemed to be ad-

27 *The Little Red Song Book* 49.

28 Quoted in "Apparent Decadence of the Salvation Army," *Literary Digest* 17 Feb. 1906: 761.

29 Quoted in "Apparent Decadence" 761

30 Quoted in "Apparent Decadence" 761.

31 Quoted in "Apparent Decadence" 761.

equate, at least for Huxley, to describe the complex organization of the Army, which resembled a private enterprise that constantly collected money from its devotees in order to reinvest it in large-scale infrastructural facilities. Thus, it is not surprising that a number of people in need felt betrayed by the Army's practices, which did not live up to its role as a charity organization that was originally supposed to satisfy the basic needs of those at the bottom of the social spectrum. In his song "The Preacher and the Slave," however, Joe Hill does not stop at criticizing the Salvation Army's politics. He also suggests an alternative way out of the poor's disastrous situation, as he goes on:

> Workingfolk of all countries, unite,
> Side by side we for freedom will fight.
> When the world and its wealth we have gained
> To the grafters we'll sing this refrain:
>
> You will eat, bye and bye,
> When you've learned how to cook and to fry;
> Chop some wood, 'twill do you good,
> And you'll eat in the sweet bye and bye.[32]

The only chance to overcome their devastating living and working conditions is, according to Hill, to unite in order to fight for a better life. Yet, this better life is not a heavenly existence after death, as propagated in the Salvation Army hymn "In the Sweet Bye and Bye." It is rather the "world and its wealth" that are at stake now and that are, as the song suggests, easily attainable after uniting. The last chorus, then, addresses those who are held responsible for the labor force's plight, the "grafters", who will not be able to exploit their workers any longer, as they have gathered strength and independence through unionization. Due to their newly-acquired collective power, the workers do not keep silent anymore, but raise their voices to ridicule their former bosses who are now forced to learn "how to cook and fry" and to "chop some wood" themselves. Thus, Hill's song demythologizes the "pie in the sky" and replaces it with the prospect of 'wordly wealth' that may be easily gained as soon as the working poor take responsibility for their own lives and organize in a union.

Joe Hill's songs, which obviously subverted the theology of the Salvation Army by proposing a kind of socialist salvation, attracted many people to the I.W.W., at least in the first years of its existence. The Salvation Army desperately tried to hold its devotees, but many working and

[32] *The Little Red Song Book* 49.

unemployed people regarded it as a rather hypocritical endeavor. Though no less a person than Lenin, in his essay on "Socialism and Religion," assumes that religious movements find a perfect breeding ground among the poor classes, as "[i]mpotence of the exploited classes in their struggle against the exploiters just as inevitably gives rise to the belief in a better life after death as impotence of the savage in his battle with nature gives rise to belief in gods, devils, miracles, and the like,"[33] there is reason to believe that the relative success of Hill's parodies is partly due to an anti-religious notion of many working-class people who, owing to their devastating living conditions and their increasing understanding of the fatal dynamics of laisser-faire capitalism, could no longer believe in what they were promised. This 'religious recession' was observed by Paul Lafargue, who commented upon the "Causes of Irreligion in the Proletariat" in an article for the Socialist Weekly *Neue Zeit*. The *Literary Digest* of February, 17th, 1906, summed up his argument that

> [w]orkingmen [...] know no providence excepting their power to work, and their daily wage. While the capitalist can see Providence in the favouring circumstances which have furthered his prosperity, there is none to be discerned [...] in the lot of one who is born to work for a wage, who lives and dies a wage-earner.[34]

Joe Hill (and other I.W.W. singers) stirred these doubts in the theology of predestination and providence, denouncing it as a mere myth and replacing it with the I.W.W.'s socialist ideology, according to which the workers should take responsibility for their own lives and emancipate themselves from the indoctrination of religious movements like the Salvation Army, which were regarded as instruments of the established capitalist system. With the power of the sung word, the I.W.W. bard established an ideological and musical subculture, whose repercussions were long-lasting. Both through his (self-)fashioning as a martyr for the labor movement and through his propagating the socialist gospel as a true alternative to the Christian faith in his songs, Joe Hill more than any other spokesman of the I.W.W. became a prominent figure in the evolution of the political protest song, whose impact on future generations of song writers, among them Woody Guthrie, must not be underestimated.

* * * * *

33 Marxist Internet Archive: <http://www.marxists.org/archive/lenin/works/1905/ dec /03.tgz>, 14 Sept. 2006.

34 "Causes of Irreligion in the Proletariat," *Literary Digest* 17 Feb. 1906: 246.

In the aftermath of the great stock market crash of 1929, which, at least for the majority of leftwing intellectuals, had proven the failure of the capitalist system, the renaissance of the labor movement, which was strengthened by Roosevelt's New Deal policy, in particular by his National Industrial Recovery Act of 1934, contributed to a revival of the cult of the I.W.W. and its most famous bard, Joe Hill. It is thus not surprising that Alfred Hayes wrote a poem in appreciation of the 'Wobbly' singer in the early 1930s, which was turned into a song by Earl Robinson six years later, when the union movement had gained momentum again.[35] Woody Guthrie also became aware of the radical songwriter when he acquired an edition of the worker's anthology of protest songs, the *Little Red Songbook*, which was first published as a four-song collection by Mac McClintock in 1908 and has grown in popularity ever since then, still available in its 36th edition today.

Though Guthrie's interest in the 'Wobbly bible' grew only when he joined the Almanac singers in 1940[36], a lot of Guthrie's earlier songs tip their hat to Joe Hill. Admittedly, Guthrie was not as radical and outspoken as Hill had been in his song-writing, yet he owed him a lot, not only as far as his general political orientation was concerned, but also with respect to the technique of songwriting and composition. Guthrie carried on the I.W.W. bard's tradition of parodying popular Christian hymns that were sung in the Californian churches, in the fields, and in the poor districts of the industrialized cities. Comparing the I.W.W.'s songs to sermons held to spread a political gospel, thereby already hinting at their subversive stance, he evaluated the 'sung manifesto' of Joe Hill and other socialist bards as follows:

> The I.W.W. folks sprung up amongst the migratory workers, fruit, farm and harvest workers. They rode the rods and walked the ties, and spread their gospel every where. They got to be called the I Won't Work folks. [...] They

35 Hayes's poem had a significant impact on Hill's image as a martyr of the labor movement and has been appropriated by a number of musicians ever since the first sung version appeared in 1936. Its first and, most probably, best-known stanza reads: "I dreamed I saw Joe Hill last night, / Alive as you or me. / Says I, 'But Joe, you're ten years dead.' 'I never died,' said he. / 'I never died,' said he" (quoted in Hampton 60).

36 The Almanacs' collection of workers' songs titled *Talking Union* was composed and recorded, as it is said in the liner notes, "in the tradition of Joe Hill" (quoted in Garman, *A Race of Singers* 93). In the fall of 1941, Elizabeth Gurley Flynn, a prominent Wobbly and a close friend of Hill's, visited the band and gave them a collection of Hill's papers, which were read by the members of the band, in particular Guthrie, who, as his bandmate Lee Hays once recalled, "perused [them] quite thoroughly" (quoted in Garman, *A Race of Singers* 94).

> rambled everywhere and sang and worked and made speeches. Their song was worth about an even dozen sermons.[37]

It is probably not by chance that Joe Hill's mock-versions of religious songs strongly affected Woody Guthrie's songwriting in the late 1930s. In California, Guthrie experienced a climate of social tensions which, on the one hand, made many people turn to the Pentecostalist religion as a last resort; on the other hand, the misconditions among the migratory workers in the Californian fields stirred drives for unionization and fostered the political conviction to set something against the gospel of earthly suffering and heavenly reward as propagated by Pentecostalism. And Guthrie set something against it, as he did not believe in the transcendent idea of a world beyond death; rather he promoted political action as the one and only means to overcome the devastating situation of the working class. In his liner notes to Lomax's *Hard-Hitting Songs for Hard-Hit people*, he unmistakably points out that

> [s]ome of the preachers that promise you hamburgers in the hereafter get on my nerves; what I'd really like to do part of the time is to give 'em a hunk of blackberry pie right in the face.[38]

Like Joe Hill, Woody Guthrie was convinced that the only way to improve the condition of the working class was "to blast away in [the riches'] face[s] with politics, votes, petitions, letters, union speeches and meeting halls running full blast."[39] Though he was neither a member of the Communist Party nor a convinced adherent of its ideologies, its general idea of the necessity to overcome capitalism in order to liberate the working class from exploitation seemed convincing to him.[40] In one of his col-

37 Lomax, Guthrie and Seeger 87.

38 Lomax, Guthrie and Seeger 88.

39 Lomax, Guthrie and Seeger 87.

40 It was in 1938, when he was already performing his show on Los Angeles's KFVD, that he got into contact with Ed Robbin, then Los Angeles editor for *The People's World.* In early 1939, Robbin invited Guthrie to sing at a union meeting that was sponsored by the Communist party and was held to celebrate the freedom of Tom Mooney, a radical agitator who had, after having spent twenty-two years in jail, been pardoned and released from prison. Robbin also introduced Guthrie to the actor Will Geer, who eventually accompanied Guthrie on his tours through the Californian migrant camps. Being active partisans of the Communist movement, both of them recognized Guthrie's enormous potential and were soon convinced that his catchy tunes and straightforward lyrics would function as a weapon in their struggle both against the capitalist system and against the distribution of a religious ideology promoting an ethics of suffering,

umns for the socialist magazine *The People's World* he points out that "the preachers raise cane about a lot of things, but they seldom (about like me) approach the problem of the day, its handling, or its solution, its cause, its starting place, its present condition, or probable outcome,"[41] once again putting emphasis on the necessity of direct intervention. In a striking reminiscence of Joe Hill's call to teach the people "how to cook and to fry" as a means of emancipating themselves from oppression, Guthrie recollects:

> Preachers can go hungry if they think it helps, but I know when I was drivin' a tractor on Bill Phillips' Farm down in Jericho, Texas, well, I needed groceries right that minute and I says to myself: 'What good does it do to grease a Tractor after the cussed thing has wore out and fell apart?' Same way with a hard workin' man, you give him groceries to take care of his stomach and his soul will take care of itself. If your soul is eternal, it won't git lost, and if it's everlasting, it won't git hungry ... Groceries now is what I believe in.[42]

Guthrie also gave vent to his rage and anger in a number of his songs which, not only as far as their thematical basis is concerned, but also with respect to their composition technique, are very similar to Joe Hill's. Yet, before we come to Guthrie's sung criticism of the ethics of suffering spread by Californian Pentecostalism, let us first have a look at one of the most prominent religious hymns of the time, called "This world is not my home," which had been made popular by the Carter Family and was well-known throughout the country. Examine the first verse and the chorus of the song:

> This world is not my home, I'm just passing through
> My treasures are laid up somewhere beyond the blue
> The angels beckon me from Heaven's open door
> And I can't feel at home in this world anymore
>
> O Lord you know I have no friend like you
> If Heaven's not my home then Lord what will I do?
> The angels beckon me from Heaven's open door
> And I can't feel at home in this world anymore[43]

The speaker of the song clearly states that he is just "passing through"; thus this world is but an intermediate stop on the way to a better world

which, in the times of the Great Depression, more than ever before, seemed to be the appropriate means to calm the starving poor (cf. Cray 138ff.).

41 Guthrie, *Woody Sez* 149-50.

42 Lomax, Guthrie and Seeger 88.

43 <http://arnet.pair.com/RedEllis/lyr/worldnotmyhome.htm>, 14 Sept. 2006.

"somewhere beyond the blue." The song, which enjoyed a great popularity in the 1930s, was part of Guthrie's repertoire. However, he was well aware of its deluding potential, as a footnote on the manuscript of his slightly different version of the song reveals, which cynically debunks the ethics of suffering promoted in the religious traditional: "Good question: If heaven's not my home O Lord what would I do? Where is heaven? Whats [sic] look like? Anybody rich? Lots of folks poor? Anybody out of a job? Heavens okay but lets have it right here on earth like Jesus said."[44] Consequently, Guthrie took the song's tune and turned his version into a sociocritical statement:

> I ain't got no home, I'm just a roaming 'round,
> Just a wandering worker, I go from town to town.
> The police make it hard wherever I may go,
> And I ain't got no home in this world anymore.
>
> My brothers and my sisters are stranded on this road,
> It's a hot, dusty road that a million feet have trod.
> Rich man took my home and drove me from my door,
> And I ain't got no home in this world anymore.
>
> Was a farming on the shares and always I was poor,
> My crops I laid into the banker's store.
> My wife took down and died upon the cabin floor,
> And I ain't got no home in this world anymore.
>
> Now as I look around, it's very plain to see
> This world is such a great and funny place to be,
> The gambling man is rich, the working man is poor,
> And I ain't got no home in this world anymore.[45]

Like the speaker of the religious pretext, the speaker of Guthrie's song laments the fact that he does not have a "home in this world anymore." Yet, in contrast to the traditional hymn, in which the image of the speaker's "passing through" is employed allegorically to symbolize the vanity and transitoriness of his life, the corresponding expression "a roaming 'round" in Guthrie's rewriting quite literally refers to the Southwestern migrants, who, dislocated and uprooted, indeed had no "home in this world anymore." The beckoning angels are replaced by the less hospitable police, the rich and the gambling men, who do not at all welcome the migrants, but cannot wait to either arrest or exploit them in the Californian fields. Guthrie's parody thus strips off the spiritual dimension of the

44 WGA, Notebooks I, Notebook 4, 157.
45 WGA, Songs I, Box 1, Folder 1.

religious model, but keeps its imagery, which turns out to be apt to render the miserable situation of the "wandering worker[s]," who are constantly looking for a new place to go.

Moreover, instead of regarding himself as someone "passing through" who, without any kind of critical stance, accepts the misconditions in this world as God-given, the speaker of Guthrie's song blames the capitalist system that leaves nothing for the working man. At the same time, as the first verse implies, the "rich men" and the "bankers," who instrumentalized the executive authorities, i.e., the police, to safeguard the established order and to prevent any kind of protest or uprising, are held responsible for the migrants' plight. The religious pretext, which, as noted earlier, had a wide distribution and whose tune was certainly known to the majority of Guthrie's potential listeners, thus provided the Dust Bowl balladeer with a frame of reference that helped him to reveal the hypocritical attitude of the religious institutions and, at the same time, to spread his political ideas. By resorting to a popular tune and by adding a new message to it, which contradicted the implications of the original song, Guthrie deliberately enhanced the semantic surplus of his song.

This technique of songwriting, it is true, can be observed in a number of the Dust Bowl balladeer's songs. Yet, there are at least three reasons why Guthrie's mock-versions of religious hymns and traditionals stand out: First, there are no other songs of Guthrie's in which this technique of palimpsest-like rewritings of the traditional texts or songs respectively has been so distinctly and so systematically employed. Second, and following from this, the almost diametrical contrast between the ideas promoted in the religious pretext and the ideology outlined in Guthrie's parodies made, as one may well argue, the appropriation of the traditional melodies extraordinarily efficient, as Guthrie's songs conjured up a framework of associations which the Southwestern migrants were extremely susceptible to, but which was, as soon as his rewritten lyrics set in, abruptly called into question. Finally, and in general, these mock versions of religious traditionals indeed reveal the strong impact of Joe Hill's songwriting on Guthrie's.

Yet, with his parodies of religious hymns, Guthrie not only criticizes the ethics of suffering as propagated by the Pentecostal institutions in California; he also offers, very much in Hill's tradition, an alternative to this otherworldly salvation: For him, unionization, as a form of applied socialism, was the appropriate means to overcome the toil and the discrimination of the working class. In order to advocate unionism in song, Guthrie frequently resorted to the form and the prevalent imagery of a religious pretext in order to substitute its metaphysical consolation for the belief in the unions' power to improve conditions for the working people. His song "Farmer-Labor Train," for example, propagates the power of the union to unify workers from different parts of the country, from different economic sectors and with different ethnicities and, in so doing, to eventually replace those who have caused their miserable economic situation:

> From the high Canadian Rockies to that land of Mexico
> The city and the country, wherever you may go,
> Through the wild and windy weather, the sun, the sleet and rain,
> Comes a-whistling thru the county, this Farmer-Labor-Train.
>
> Listen to the jungle, the rumble and the roar,
> She's a-rolling thru New England to the West Pacific Shore;
> It's a long time we been waiting, now she's whistling round the bend,
> Now we'll ride into the White House on that Farmer-Labor Train.
>
> There's lumberjacks, and teamsters, and sailors from the sea,
> And there's farming boys from Texas and the hills of Tennessee;
> There's miners from Kentucky, and there's fishermen from Maine,
> Every worker in the country rides that Farmer-Labor-Train.
>
> There's warehouse boys and truckers, and guys that skin the cats,
> The men that run the steel mills, the furnace and the blasts
> Through the smoky factory cities, o'er the hot and dusty plains,
> And the cushions they are crowded on this Farmer-Labor-Train. [...]
>
> There are folks of every color, and they're sitting side by side,
> From the swamps of Louisiana and across the Great Divide;
> From the wheat fields and the orchards and the lowing cattle range,
> And they're rolling on to victory on this Farmer-Labor-Train.[46]

The song enumerates all regions, branches, and sectors which have been affected by the union movement – among them the Southwestern "farming boys from Texas and the hills of Tennessee." In doing so, one may well assume, it attempts to portray unionism as an almost omnipresent phenomenon which is "rolling on to victory."

After having dealt with the various passengers of the train in such a meticulous manner, the song once again names its destination, which is already hinted at in the chorus: the "Farmer-Labor-Train" is heading towards Washington, where, as the last verse of the song has it, "the crooked politicians [...] knew their time had come, / 'Cause the union men and women put the gamblers on the run." The union, the song suggests, is

[46] WGA, Songs I, Box 1, Folder 9.

able to do away with both the political and the economic plight people have been suffering from for so long.

The image of the train employed in the song underlines the dynamics of unionism as a movement both powerful and unstoppable. Yet, it is not only the train's unbridled drive that turns it into an image apt to map the union movement. The 'train'-image is also used in a number of religious hymns to describe the course of an individual's life from birth to death and to an otherwordly existence, as in the song "Riding on that Salvation Train." Here are the lyrics of the song's first verse once again, in which the image of a train underlines the transitoriness of life and reminds us that we are merely "passing through" it, before we enter the heavenly realm, where we are compensated for our sufferings:

> I'm a ridin' on that Salvation Train
> I'm a ridin' on that Salvation Train
> It's that same old train that brought me to this world
> It's soon a goin' to carry me away.[47]

In contrast, the train in Guthrie's song has a clear-cut and identifiable destination within reach, both in geographical terms and in terms of political feasibility. Similar to his "I Ain't Got No Home," the song replaces the notion of religious escapism with the propagation of political action. In order to enhance its potential and to underline the substitutionary character of unionism as a means for worldly salvation, Guthrie employed a metaphor well established in religious folklore and frequently used in songs, e.g. in a religious hymn called "Life's Railroad to Heaven," which makes use of the image of a train to put emphasis on life's transitoriness and places great hopes in a "blissful shore" awaiting the 'true' believer.

> Life is like a Mountain Railroad,
> With an Engineer that's brave.
> You must make the Run successful,
> From the Cradle to the grave.
> Watch the curves, the fills, and tunnels,
> Never falter, never fail.
> Keep your hand upon the Throttle,
> And your eye upon the Rail.
>
> Blessed Saviour, Thou wilt guide us,
> Till we reach that blissful shore,

[47] WGA; Notebooks I, Notebooks 4, 146.

Where the Angels wait to join us
In their Peace forever more.[48]

"From the cradle to the grave," as the song suggests, one has to make sure not to be thrown off track by adhering to a proper Christian conduct; only then will one be able to get to an otherworldly paradise "where the Angels wait to join us." With the "curves, the fills, and tunnels" allegorizing the hurdles and obstacles in life, the journey in the train is, as it were, an industrial variation on the Christian conception of life as a pilgrimage, during which one has to overcome a number of dangers and temptations challenging true faith. It is thus not by chance that the song's last verse, which renders the arrival of the faithful in heaven, concludes with the enthusiastic exclamation "Weary Pilgrim! Welcome Home!"

Guthrie's song about the union train is equally enthusiastic in tone; however, its enthusiasm is based on the conviction that the working people indeed have the chance to overcome their seemingly hopeless situation through their own efforts. Considering the disastrous situation of the working people all over the country, it clearly opposes the notion of an ethics of suffering and promotes an ethics of union-based agitation for radical political, social and economic reforms.[49]

Another song of Guthrie's follows yet a different strategy to promote unionism as a powerful means to overcome the plight of the working people. In its rendering of a vigilante attack on members of the miners' union during a copper strike in Calumet, Michigan, his "Nineteen Thirteen Massacre" evokes a biblical intertext in order to hint at the salvationary function of the union:

Take a trip with me in nineteen thirteen
To Calumet, Michigan, in the copper country.
I'll take you to a place called Italian Hall
And the miners are having their big Christmas ball.

48 WGA, Notebooks I, Notebook 5, 62. The words of this song are usually credited to M.E. Abbey, the music is credited to Charles D. Tillman. Many of these religious songs are to be found in Guthrie's manuscripts. The fact that he wrote biting parodies of such songs must, therefore, not mislead us to assume that Guthrie did not write or perform them himself. Actually, his repertoire of religious hymns and traditionals was overwhelmingly large. After all, in order to write parodies of these songs, Guthrie had to be aware of the traditional imagery, the structure and the tunes and melodies they employed.

49 Another of Guthrie's (later) songs which, more explictly, renders unionism as a substitute for the Christian faith and whose point is already epitomized in its title, is "Union's my Religion" (cf. WGA, Songs I, Box 4, Folder 28).

I'll take you in a door and up a high stairs
Singing and dancing is heard ev'rywheres,
I'll let you shake hands with the people you see
And watch the kids dance 'round the big Christmas tree. [...]

The copper boss thugs stuck their heads in the door,
One of them yelled and he screamed, 'There's a fire.'
A lady she hollered, 'There's no such a thing.
Keep on with your party, there's no such thing.'

A few people rushed and there's only a few,
'It's just the thugs and the scabs fooling you.'
A man grabbed his daughter and he carried her down,
But the thugs held the door and he could not get out.

And then others followed, a hundred or more,
But most everybody remained on the floor.
The gun thugs, they laughed at their murderous joke,
And the children were smothered on the stairs by the door.

Such a terrible sight I never did see;
We carried our children back up to their tree.
The scabs outside still laughed at their spree,
And the children that died there was seventy-three.[50]

As the speaker of the song tells us, company thugs disrupted a Christmas party for the miners' children by shouting "Fire!" and then locked all the doors from the outside. All of a sudden, the peaceful and jolly atmosphere, in which "singing and dancing [was] heard ev'rywheres," turned into a horrible nightmare, as seventy-three children were trampled and smothered in the crush that followed. On January, 10th, 1914, *The Literary Digest* covered the incident rendered in Guthrie's song in an article pointing out that "black even against this gloomy background [of the copper war] stands out the Christmas eve horror of Italian Hall, Calumet, when in the panic resulting from false alarm of fire seventy-five [sic] persons – most of them wives and children of miners – were trampled to death."[51]

50 Leventhal and Guthrie 174ff.

51 "Michigan Press On The Copper War," *Literary Digest* 10 Jan. 1914: 47, addition mine. Relying on another source, Jackson (115) states that the incident did not take place in Calumet, but in the village of Red Jacket. He also points out that the cause for the disaster as rendered in Guthrie's song does not correspond with 'the truth' (cf. Jackson 116). Leaving aside the question of what really happened in Calumet or Red Jacket respectively, what matters is the fact that Guthrie's rendering, which is based on second-hand information, is a drama-

Aside from the striking title of Guthrie's song, the dreadful scenario portrayed in it immediately calls forth the biblical story of the Massacre of the Innocents.[52] Ordering his thugs to lock the workers and their families in their "Italian Hall," though he must have been well aware that such an attack was likely to cause a fatal panic among the workers, which would, in turn, claim its victims' lives, the dreadful conduct of the homicidal company boss echoes the rage of the Biblical manslayer Herod, who ordered his guards to kill every newborn baby in his country, for he was afraid that Jesus Christ might be among them:

> Then Herod, when he saw that he was mocked of the wise men, was exceeding wroth, and sent forth, and slew all the children that were in Bethlehem, and in all the coasts thereof, from two years old and under, according to the time which he had diligently enquired of the wise men.[53]

Just as the king of Israel tried to get rid of the new messiah as he feared the enormous influence the latter might have on the people, the company owner, as Guthrie's ballad implies, tries to eradicate the rising generation of potential rebels and agitators, who might endanger the established societal order. Undoubtedly, the song's portrayal of the human disaster immediately evokes a feeling of utmost indignation among its audience, as it not only shows the inconsiderate cruelty of the company thugs, but also stresses the seemingly desperate and hopeless situation of the workers.

However, the song may well be sensed to carry some optimistic potential, as soon as the implications of its biblical intertext are taken into consideration. Just as Christianity, though frequently subdued by powerful opponents, emerged as the dominant religion of the western hemisphere, the working class will, as the song implies, eventually triumph over its unscrupulous oppressors. Thus, in spite of the horror it portrays, Guthrie's song heralds a great time to come for the working class by giving substance to the notion that unionism, or Socialism as its ideolog-

tization deliberately distorting, highlighting or leaving out certain issues for its own purposes.

52 Actually, Woody Guthrie probably learned about the massacre from Ella Reeve 'Mother' Bloor, one of the most popular representatives of the radical movement in the 1930s. Guthrie met her in Los Angeles (cf. Woody Guthrie, "Woody Guthrie Album," [WGA, Manuscripts II, Box 1, Folder 35]) and also read her autobiography called *We Are Many* (cf. Cray 287), in which Bloor dedicated a whole chapter to the events in Calumet, which was titled "Massacre of the Innocents" and thus, even more directly than the title of Guthrie's song, hints at the relevant biblical passage.

53 *The Bible*, ed. Caroll and Prickett, Matthew, 2, 16.

ical framework, will, in the near future, develop strategies for the oppressed, the exploited and the humiliated of today.[54]

Both the critical attitude towards religion and the promotion of unionism as a reliable alternative to religious consolation found, to be sure, expression mainly in the songs Guthrie wrote after he got in contact with a number of leftwing intellectuals in New York City at the beginning of the 1940s – his "Nineteen Thirteen Massacre," for example, was first written in 1940. Yet, it was the plight of the Dust Bowl migrants and their being palmed off by "hamburgers in the hereafter" by the Californian Pentecostalists, which was critically commented upon in Guthrie's songs already at the end of the 1930s. Very much in the tradition of Joe Hill's songs, Guthrie used religious hymns to debunk the ethics of suffering the Pentecostals propagated to relieve the distressed and dislocated migrants.

However, as the analysis of his religio-critical songs has shown, Guthrie's songs not only resorted to the rhythmical and melodic structures of religious traditionals, but, at times, also appropriated conventional religious images to render the disastrous conditions of the workers. Therefore, both by referring to well-known tunes and by drawing upon religious imagery, the songs managed to establish frameworks of associations and expectations among their audience, which was thus emotionally affected and, as one may assume, more susceptible to the songs' attempt to turn the escapist notion of Pentecostalism into the channel of social revolution. Guthrie's "Nineteen Thirteen Massacre," though first written in the early 1940s and thus not directly concerned with the Southwestern migrants, works with yet another intertextual strategy to promote unionism as a true alternative to religion. Its deliberate reference to a biblical pretext adds semantic surplus value to the vigilante assault configured in the song and hints at the eventual triumph of unionism.

Moreover, with its blending of a biblical plot with political implications, Guthrie's "Nineteen Thirteen Massacre" also corroborates the idea that both Socialism and the Christian faith, at least in its purest sense, share a certain radical vision and promote radical aims. This amalgamation of Socialism and religion, according to which unionism is no longer

54 The potential of unionism to overcome the plight of the working people is, to be sure, heralded in a number of Guthrie's songs, which shall not be discussed here in detail. His song "Union Maid" (cf. Leventhal and Guthrie 233ff.), to name one of his most popular, implicitly hints at the emancipatory power of the union, not only in terms of the struggle between the working people and the entrepreneurs, but also with respect to the relationship between the genders. Another song which points to the power of the union is Guthrie's "Rancho Grande Vigilante," which is dicussed in detail in chapter 3.4 of this study. For an analysis of a larger selection of Guthrie's union songs cf. Jackson 204ff.

regarded as merely a wordly substitute for, but rather a transformation of fundamental Christian values, into practical politics, could already be observed in the analysis of Guthrie's outlaw song "The Unwelcome Guest," which referred to the Acts of the Apostles as the yardstick for moral behavior.[55] Yet, the belief that the basic ideas of socialism were indeed considered to share common ground with the fundamental Christian concept of collective solidarity manifested itself even more noticeably in Woody Guthrie's rewriting(s) of the life of Jesus Christ.

55 Cf. chapter 3.2 of this study.

3.6 "A hard working man, and brave": (Re)Fashioning Jesus Christ as the Archetypal Socialist

> It aint just once in a while that I think about this man, it's mighty scarce I think of anything else. But he said his self that it was mighty risky business to walk up before the police, or the judge, or the Congress, or the president, and say for the rich folks to give the poor folks money and lands and houses and farms back to them. Mighty unpopular thing. Being right is just the opposite of being popular. (Woody Guthrie)[1]

Undoubtedly, the deluding effects of an ethics of suffering promoted by various fundamentalist denominations, among them Californian Pentecostalism, were constantly warned about by the socialist movement, which aimed at an improvement of actual living and working conditions. Yet, already in the second half of the 19th century, socialist intellectuals discovered the radical potential of the Christian faith and its 'manifesto,' the New Testament. In the so-called 'social gospel movement,' basic Christian ideas and concepts were politicized and employed for socialist purposes.

The economic and political mess of the Great Depression seemed to foster a resurrection of this synthesis of religious and political radicalism, which also found expression in a number of Guthrie's songs. With his sung fashionings of Jesus Christ primarily as a carpenter's son, Guthrie contributed to the revival of the social gospel by deliberately appropriating the figure of Jesus Christ as the archetypal socialist.

Challenging historian Brad D. Lookingbill's claim that Guthrie's politicized renderings of the life of Jesus Christ result from his personal conversion to socialism at the end of the 1930s, this chapter argues that the integration of Christian concepts with socialist ideology characterized a specific form of 'grass-roots' socialism prominent on the Southwestern Plains. What is more, Guthrie's sung fashionings of Jesus Christ as a cultural and political icon follow a distinct literary tradition already emerging at the beginning of the 20th century. Thus, though Guthrie might well have become political only late in the 1930s, his songs are tied to larger cultural patterns, the reconstruction of which will give insight into the wide circulation of the imagery he resorts to. In order to examine his songs' social and cultural potential, this chapter also con-

1 Manuscript of "A Hard-Working Man Was Jesus" (WGA, Notebooks I, Notebook 4, p. 180).

siders the musical intertexts Guthrie makes use of in the process of shaping his image of Jesus Christ.

* * * * *

In his essay "Dusty Apocalypse and Socialist Salvation: A Study of Woody Guthrie's Dust Bowl Imagery," Brad Lookingbill examines, as the subtitle of his contribution already suggests, the various images Guthrie employs in his songs in order to render the experience of the Dust Bowl and the subsequent migration of hundreds of thousands of Southwesterners to California. Moreover, his essay is concerned with the increasingly overt political implications of Guthrie's songs after his acquaintance with leftwing radicalism in the late 1930s. Lookingbill's detailed investigation focuses on the relationship between Guthrie's imagery and religious fundamentalism as rooted in the culture of the Great Plains. He points out that Guthrie's songs not only fashion the physical struggle of the uprooted and dislocated farmers, but also "portray the spiritual migration from a dusty apocalypse to a socialist salvation [and thus] offer historians a valuable tool for an intellectual understanding of how the trials of dust and depression affected individuals."[2]

Confronted with the plight of the migrants and the social misconditions in California, Guthrie, as Lookingbill argues, also undertook such a 'spiritual migration' and 'converted' to socialism because it promised hope in times of economic uncertainty. For Guthrie, "the prophetic certitude offered by socialism appealed to his diverse tastes far more than church-based religion,"[3] which he was brought up with. Though Guthrie, as a child of the fundamentalist Southwest, could not get rid of his religious heritage, he began to use his music in order to articulate social criticism and, in so doing, "integrated his spiritualism with a politically and socially conscious view that encompassed his own life experiences, but the fundamentalist influence remained."[4]

The synthesis of Guthrie's spiritualism with a new kind of political radicalism was also rendered in his songs, in which, as Lookingbill argues, "[i]n character with the fundamentalist culture, Guthrie used religious symbols to identify his efforts to spread the socialist gospel."[5] As an example, Lookingbill draws on one of the songs by the Dust Bowl troubadour, called "Jesus Christ," which, according to his conversion

2 Lookingbill, "Dusty Apocalypse" 397, addition mine.
3 Lookingbill, "Dusty Apocalypse" 403.
4 Lookingbill, "Dusty Apocalypse" 403.
5 Lookingbill, "Dusty Apocalypse" 404.

thesis, epitomizes the mixture of Guthrie's religious upbringing and his political radicalization. He argues that "[Guthrie] proletarianized the life of Jesus in a ballad, claiming the 'bankers and the preachers, they nailed him on the cross.'"[6] Let us have a closer look at Guthrie's song in order to both recapitulate and critically examine Lookingbill's reading. Here are the lyrics as written down by Guthrie on March 5th, 1940:

> Jesus Christ was a Man that traveled thru the land
> And a hard working man, and brave,
> He said to the rich, give your goods to the poor,
> And they laid Jesus Christ in his grave
>
> Yes Jesus was a man, a carpenter by hand,
> His followers true and brave,
> One dirty coward called Judas Iscariot
> He has laid poor Jesus in his grave.
>
> He went to the preacher, he went to the sheriff,
> And he told them all the same.
> Sell all of your jewelry and give it to the poor,
> But they laid Jesus Christ in his grave.
>
> When Jesus come [sic] to town the working folks around
> Believed what he did say,
> But the bankers and the preachers they nailed him on the cross
> And they laid Jesus Christ in his grave.
>
> The poor working people followed him around
> And sang and shouted gay,
> But the cops and soldiers nailed him in the air
> And they laid Jesus Christ in his grave.
>
> The people held their breath when they heard about his death
> And everybody wondered why –
> It was the rich landlord and the soldiers that they hired
> To nail Jesus Christ in the sky.
>
> This song it was written in New York City
> Of Rich Man, preacher, and slave –
> If Jesus was to preach as he preached in Galilee
> They would lay poor Jesus in his grave.[7]

Indeed, the figure of Jesus Christ is refashioned in Guthrie's song in that his general affiliation with the working class is highlighted: Not only did

6 Lookingbill, "Dusty Apocalypse" 404, addition mine.
7 WGA, Songs I, Box 2, Folder 14.

he descend from a carpenter; he is also a hard-working man himself, standing up for the interests of the poor and oppressed. His enemies, who eventually manage to lay him in his grave, can clearly be identified as representatives of the political and economic institutions which were, according to the socialist ideology, responsible for the suppression and the exploitation of the working poor in the Great Depression: the bankers, who, with a merciless interest rate policy, ripped off those for whom a bank loan seemed the only way out; the preachers, who allowed themselves to be instrumentalized by the economic and political leaders to propagate an ethics of suffering, thus sanctioning the social misconditions by putting off the people with the promise of a rewarding existence in a heavenly hereafter; the cops and the soldiers as henchmen of political and economic leaders instructed to prevent any kind of uprising or drives for unionization among the workers; and, finally, the rich landlord, who made migrant agricultural workers slave away on the Californian fields. Particularly by mentioning the landlords as those who "laid Jesus Christ in his grave," the Savior's fate is brought into line with that of the migrants in the 1930s, who also felt victimized by the large-scale agricultural businesses in California.

In his notes to the song, the Okie balladeer pointed out that "this ballad about the life of Jesus Christ shows you that he was nothing more than a union man, a carpenter, really what you would call in our day and time, a union organizer."[8] Thus, the story of Jesus Christ as outlined in Guthrie's ballad may indeed be characterized as a 'proletarianized' account of the Savior's life, which helped promote the socialist gospel. However, one may well doubt whether the synthesis of the religious icon 'Jesus Christ' and socialist ideology in the song is really a result of Guthrie's conversion to socialism as argued by Lookingbill. Though "[t]he interpretation of a socialist Guthrie birthed amid the humanitarian crisis of the Dust Bowl has always had a strong appeal,"[9] Jeff Morgan critically observes, "[t]o assume that the Dust Bowl exodus dramatically changed Guthrie as a creative force is to ignore the cultural and private realities that shaped him,"[10] let alone, as one may be tempted to add, the problem(s) of biographical readings in general. Yet, Morgan's reference to the "cultural [...] realities that shaped him" and – what seems to be even more significant in a contextualizing approach towards Guthrie's oeuvre – his songs, seems to be a trail worth picking up in order to fathom the social energy of Guthrie's song about the Savior, a trail which leads us to

8 WGA, Manuscripts II, Box 1, Folder 35.
9 Morgan 2.
10 Morgan 2.

a variety of literary and non-literary texts also taking part in shaping the image of Jesus Christ, thus constituting the intertextual framework which Guthrie's song(s) can be correlated with.

In 1922, Upton Sinclair published a novel entitled *They Call Me Carpenter*, in which he interpreted the life and teachings of Jesus Christ. In his book, Jesus Christ returns to modern times and describes the treatment which he has to face. In a chapter called "Christ visits western city," the novel's protagonist is giving a speech to a working-class audience. Here is the announcement of his speech by President Brown of the Western City Labor Council:

> The next speaker is a stranger to most of you, and he is also a stranger to me. I do not know what his doctrine is, and I assume no responsibility for it. But he is a man who has proven his friendship for labour, not by words, but by very unusual deeds. He is a man of remarkable personality, and we have asked him to make what suggestions he can as to our problems. I have pleasure in introducing Mr. Carpenter.[11]

And, being a spokesman for the toiling poor, Mr. Carpenter indeed makes some suggestions that, clothed in a polemic call against capitalist exploitation, should help his audience to overcome their predicaments. Employing the rhetorical strategy of a union leader, he manages to stir up the crowd with a set of provocative questions in his speech:

> 'You are the representatives of organized labour. I do not know your organization, therefore I ask: For what are you united? Is it to follow in the footsteps of your masters, and bind others as they have bound you?'
>
> He waited for an answer, and the Chairman, upon whom his gaze was fixed, cried, 'No!' Others also cried, 'No!' and the audience took it up with fervour. Carpenter turned to them. 'Then I say to you: Break down in your hearts and in the hearts of your fellows the worship of those base things which mastership has brought into the world. If a man pile up food while others starve is not this evil? If a woman deck herself with clothing to her own discomfort, is not this folly? And if it brings folly, how shall it be admired by you, to whom it brings starvation and despair? [...]'
>
> 'A tree is known by the fruit it gives; and the masters are known by the lives they give to their servants. They are known by misery and unemployment, by plague and famine, by wars, and the slaughter of people. Let judgement be pronounced upon them.'[12]

11 Upton Sinclair, *An Upton Sinclair Anthology*, ed. by I.O. Evans (Newcastle-on-Tyne: Northumberland Press, 1934) 200.

12 Sinclair 204.

It is easy to imagine that the "masters," whom the speaker accuses of being responsible for the misery and the unemployment of their "servants," do not approve of his subversive ideas. Thus, not surprisingly, Sinclair comes to the conclusion that Jesus Christ, or Mr. Carpenter respectively, would be no more welcomed by contemporary America than he was by the people of Jerusalem of 30 A.D. Strikingly enough, the scenario outlined in the novel bears a strong resemblance to the coda of Guthrie's ballad on Jesus Christ, which argues along similar lines, as it speculates on how Jesus Christ would be treated in New York City in 1940:

> This song it was written in New York City
> Of Rich Man, preacher, and slave –
> If Jesus was to preach as he preached in Galilee
> They would lay poor Jesus in his grave.[13]

Yet, it is not only Sinclair's novel that deals with the figure of Jesus Christ, who is fashioned, like in Guthrie's song, as a member of the working class. In his 1934 study *Contemporary American Literature and Religion*, Halford E. Luccock observed that, from the beginning of the 20th century onwards, all kinds of socio-critical poetry had been characterized by "its religious spirit and often its religious content, particularly its employment of the figure of Jesus."[14] He goes on arguing that

> [w]hen we examine this poetry from the viewpoint of its relationship to religion, the theme of Jesus becomes all the more significant. The emergence of Jesus as theme and motive is apparent not only in so-called religious poetry but in poetry unqualified by any adjective. Since 1910 there has been a new resurrection of Jesus from the tomb of convention and tradition.[15]

Luccock adds that this resurrection "cannot be regarded as a resurgence of interest in creedal [sic] Christianity; it is rather interest in Jesus as a personality, a source of inspiration, a refuge to which the poet turns under the shock of the present scene or situation."[16] And indeed, it is easy to imagine that it was the shock of the present social inequalities and the sufferings of hundreds of thousands of economically and politically underprivileged families that made Guthrie employ the personality of Jesus in his song as well.

13 WGA, Songs I, Box 2, Folder 14.
14 Halford E. Luccock, *Contemporary American Literature and Religion* (Chicago: Willett, Clark & Company, 1934) 224.
15 Luccock 224-25.
16 Luccock 225.

Before we come back to the Dust Bowl balladeer, however, let us have a look at the configuration of Christ as a working man in the contemporary religious poetry hinted at by Luccock: Elizabeth Waddell's poem "Crusaders," for instance, which was written and published in the 1910s,[17] clearly propagates a rethinking of the figure of Jesus Christ as a representative of the poor and oppressed:

Crusaders

They have taken the tomb of our Comrade Christ,
Infidel hordes that believe not in man.
Stable and stall for his birth sufficed
But this tomb is built on a kingly plan.

They have hanged him round with pomp and parade,
They have buried him deep under steel and stone,
But we come leading the great crusade
To give our Comrade back to his own.[18]

In contrast to those "infidel hordes" who have always "hanged him round with pomp and parade" and thus seemed to deny his origin as son of a craftsman, the poem declares that the time has come "to give our Comrade back to his own," i.e., to rediscover his working-class origin. Interestingly enough, the epithet "Comrade" for Jesus, does not only fit to the notion of a crusade utilized in the poem; it also bears socialist connotations[19] and thus puts forward the idea of a politicized Jesus Christ.

The same term is also employed as a denominator for the Savior in Sarah N. Cleghorn's "Comrade Jesus," written in 1915, in which Jesus Christ is not only fashioned as a member of the working class, but as a political activist and spokesman for the poor polemicizing against the rich:

Comrade Jesus

Thanks to Saint Matthew, who had been
At mass-meetings in Palestine,

17 The exact date of the poem's composition is not known. Yet, it was quoted as a motto in Upton Sinclair's *The Profits of Religion* first published in 1918.

18 Quoted in Luccock 225.

19 The entries on the term "comrade" in the OED substantiate both the military and the socialist connotation pointing out that the term is used to denote "a fellow soldier" and may also be employed "by socialists and communists as a prefix to the surname, to avoid such titles as 'Mr.' Hence, a (fellow-) socialist or communist" (<http://dictionary.oed.com/cgi/findword?query_type=word&query word=comrade>, 4 Oct. 2006).

We know whose side was spoken for
When Comrade Jesus had the floor.

'Where sore they toiled and hard they lie,
Among the great unwashed dwell I –
The tramp, the convict, I am he;
Cold-shoulder him, cold-shoulder me.'

By Dives' door, with thoughtful eye,
He did tomorrow prophesy:
'The kingdom's gate is low and small;
The rich can scarce wedge through at all.'

Ah, let no local him refuse!
Comrade Jesus hath paid his dues.
Whatever other he debarred,
Comrade Jesus hath his red card.[20]

At a "mass-meeting" – a term which also belongs to the standard repertoire of socialist terminology – he appears as a speaker calling himself "the tramp" and "the convict," thus identifying himself with those at the bottom of society. His affiliation with the working class and his devotion to the interests of the exploited and suppressed is ultimately emphasized by his obtaining the "red card," indicating his membership in the I.W.W.

The rethinking and refashioning of Jesus Christ as representative of the lower strata of society is also put forward in a poem by Verne Bright, which first appeared in *The Christian Century* of May 6th, 1931, which, strikingly enough, bears a similar title as Cleghorn's poem. Like Waddell's "Crusaders," the first stanza of his "Comrade Christ" is an accusation of those who have neglected Christ's original social background, as they "have hid our God in a golden sepulcher" and "have made our Christ a sniveling pampered priest":

Comrade Christ

Give us Jesus Christ, the Carpenter.
What to us is your white-liveried God?
O men of the anvil, of the loom, the sod,
They have hid our God in a golden sepulcher;
They have made our Christ a sniveling pampered priest,
A paltry giver of fine bread and wine –
Our Christ is a God of Men, as men divine,
Holding in brotherhood the lost and the least.[21]

20 Quoted in Luccock 227.

The imperative in the first line of the stanza suggests that such a fashioning of Jesus Christ as a "sniveling pampered priest" does not mean anything to the masses of working people. Rather it is his being a carpenter that, as the line implies, is his most significant feature. "What to us is your white-liveried God?" the speaker of the poem then asks in a rhetorical manner and underlines the uselessness of the conventional image of Christ for the "men of the anvil, of the loom" and "the sod." Against this image, the second stanza of Bright's poem refashions the Savior by emphasizing his unbroken solidarity with the working folks:

He toils in the desert place by our side;
He delves with us beneath the granite hill;
He weeps above our brothers who have died;
He dreams with us in the darkness hot and still;
No surpliced shriver of the sins of men –
Christ, the Carpenter, has come again.[22]

In Woody Guthrie's song "A Hard-Working Man Was Jesus," the figure of Jesus Christ is rendered along similar lines. As the title of the song already suggests, he is portrayed as a representative of the working class, heralding a brighter future for the poor:

A hard working man was Jesus
A hard working man was he –
He said that the poor would win this world,
And then what a heaven 'twould be![23]

Instead of a paradisiac hereafter, the song suggests the idea of a heavenly existence on earth, which shall be gained as soon as the poor, presumably guided by Jesus Christ, "win this world" for themselves.[24]

The Savior's solidarity with the working people also forms the basis of the argument in Guthrie's song "Christ For President," which even goes one step further, as it not only fashions Jesus as a representative and caretaker of the working people, but imagines him, due to his affiliation

21 Quoted in Luccock 228.
22 Quoted in Luccock 228.
23 WGA, Notebooks I, Notebook 4, 180.
24 Alluding to the sermon on the mount (*The Bible*, ed. Caroll and Prickett, Matthew, 5, 5: "Blessed are the meek: for they shall inherit the earth."), the verse cited also emphasizes the idea to turn the existing world into a heaven instead of waiting for a heavenly hereafter as suggested e.g. by the Pentecostal denomination (cf. chapter 3.5 of this study).

to the working people, as the ideal candidate for the highest political office in the country:

> Let's have Christ our president.
> Let us him for the king.
> Cast your vote for the carpenter
> That you call the Nazarene.
> The only way you can ever beat
> These crooked poli[ti]cian men
> Is to run the money changers out of the temple
> And to put the carpenter in.
>
> O it's Jesus Christ our president
> God above our king
> With a job and a pension for young and old
> We will make hallelujah ring!
>
> Every year we waste enough
> To feed the ones who starve.
> We build our civilization up
> And we shoot it down with wars.
> But with the carpenter on the seat
> Away up in the capital town
> The U.S.A. would be on the way
> Pros-perity bound![25]

In order to eventually "beat the crooked poli[ti]cian men" who are currently governing the country, the song's first verse suggests "run[ing] the money changers out of the temple," which is, to be sure, not only another allusion to the Bible, but also a direct reference to President Roosevelt's inauguration address of March 4th, 1933, in which he proclaimed that "the money changers have fled from their high seats in the temple of our civilization."[26]

Replacing the corrupt politicians in the highest office of the state, Jesus Christ, "the carpenter," takes matters into his own hands and takes care of the American people. Similar to the song cited before, Christ is portrayed as the bringer of a heaven on earth, who will take care of the poor by implementing concrete political measures, such as "a job and a pension for young and old," thus turning the United States into a country which is "prosperity bound." Moreover, Christ as President will, as the song suggests, stop the wars, which, time and again, have shattered American civilization.

25 WGA, Notebooks I, Notebook 5, 105.
26 Quoted in Nate 36.

Considering that, according to Halford E. Luccock, this image of Jesus Christ as a representative of the working class has been used in a considerable number of poems "finding first appearance in magazines and newspapers,"[27] and taking into account the relatively wide distribution of this image due to its occurrence in these media, Guthrie's songs on Jesus Christ appear in a new light: Both his fashioning of the Savior as a member of the working class hunted down by the capitalists in his "Jesus Christ" and his promoting him as the ideal candidate for presidency can well be regarded as part of a tradition of rethinking and rewriting the figure of Jesus Christ as political icon, which experienced a renaissance at the beginning of the 20th century. "Since 1910," as Luccock observes, "there has been a new resurrection of Jesus from the tomb of convention and tradition. It has been another chapter in the long history of the rediscovery of Jesus."[28] And Guthrie contributed to this resurrection with his songs.

However, the fusion of religious symbols with political ideology is not only featured in literary texts. Rather this synthesis of basic Christian values and political ideology in literature represents a tendency that already arose in the second half of the 19th century and strongly characterized the socialist discourse of the time, which also employed religious imagery in order to spread what is generally referred to as the 'social gospel.'[29] According to this social gospel, the Christian faith and the socialist ideol-

27 Luccock 228.

28 Luccock 225.

29 In his analysis of Upton Sinclair's *The Jungle*, Alfred Hornung points out that his writings "reconnect with the ideas of the social gospel movement at the end of the 19th century with which Sinclair identified from early on" (Alfred Hornung, "Literary Conventions and the Political Unconscious in Upton Sinclair's Work," *Upton Sinclair: Literature and Social Reform*, ed. Dieter Herms [Frankfurt: Peter Lang, 1990] 30) For more detailed investigations into the social gospel movement cf. Burbank; cf. also Charles H. Hopkins, *The Rise of the Social Gospel in American Protestantism, 1865-1915* (New Haven, Connecticut: Yale UP, 1940) and Lawrence Goodwyn, *The Populist Movement in America* (New York: Oxford UP, 1978). The English equivalent to the American 'social gospel movement' was 'Christian Socialism,' a movement which arose even earlier "as a reaction against the hostility of the 18th century Established Church towards the discussion of social questions" (Cross and Livingstone 279) and which was strongest in the late 1840s and 1850s. The most famous and influential Christian Socialist was Thomas Cooper, author of the epic poem *The Purgatory of Suicides*. Cooper's career had a powerful impact on another leading spirit of Christian Socialism, the Anglican divine, social reformer and novelist Charles Kingsley, whose most famous novel, *Alton Locke*, drew upon Cooper as a model for its protagonist (cf. Charles E. Raven, *Christian Socialism 1848-1854* [London: Macmillan, 1920] 167).

ogy were not regarded as mutually exclusive, but as complementary concepts, as we learn from an article appearing in the journal *The Christian Work and Evangelist* in New York in 1910, which deals with the alleged controversy between Christianity and socialism:

> Our socialist friends are quite mistaken in accusing the Church as a whole of hypocrisy because its leaders do not attempt the amelioration of the economic condition by Socialist measure. We believe that there is hardly a clergyman in this land who would not become a Socialist to-morrow could he see plainly that it would bring in the kingdom of good-will, happiness, and justice.[30]

As this quotation implies, the Christian religion was indeed regarded as compatible with the ideals and ideas of the Socialist movement, above all the amelioration of the social and economic circumstances of a class or classes. Yet, as the article continues, the author points out that the various established religious institutions seem to have deviated from their original intentions. His conclusion follows promptly: "Were [the church] really Christian," he argues, it "would insist that business be so reorganized that […] men would not have to live with poverty only a day off if work fails or sickness comes."[31] The compatibility of socialist ideology with basic Christian ideals in their purest and non-corrupted sense is also emphasized in Walter Rauschenbusch's study *Christianity and the Social Crisis* published in 1907. As one of the most prominent representatives of the social gospel movement, Rauschenbusch argues that

> just as the Protestant principle of religious liberty and the democratic principle of political liberty rose to victory by an alliance with the middle class which was then rising to power, so the New Christian principle of brotherly association must ally itself with the working class if both are to conquer.[32]

J.E.C. Welldon, in *The Nineteenth Century And After*, argues along similar lines, when he points out that the "Church of Jesus Christ and the Party of Labour […] [w]ithin certain limits [...] pursue the same ends [and] aspire to the same ideals."[33] In his article, Welldon goes on to elaborate on the compatibility of the Christian religion and the ideology of the labor movement by referring to the Bible. In the fourth chapter of the Acts of the Apostles, he claims to find sufficient proof for his thesis.

30 Quoted in "Where Christianity Negatives Itself," *Literary Digest* 31 Dec. 1910: 1238.

31 Quoted in "Where Christianity" 1238.

32 Quoted in J.E.C. Welldon, "The Church and the Labour Party," *The Nineteenth Century And After. A Monthly Review* (London: Spottiswoode & Co., 1913) 949.

33 Welldon 946.

Indeed, the relevant passage reads like the description of a socialist society:

> And the multitude of them that believed were of one heart and of one soul: neither said any of them that ought of the things which he possessed was his own; but they had all things in common.[34]

Concluding that "it seems to be indisputable that the Church and the Labour Party occupy a large space of moral and social ground in common,"[35] Welldon again questions the incompatibility of Christian faith with the political agenda of socialism. Going even further, he strongly promotes the idea that each depends on the other, as "[t]he idealistic movement alone would be a soul without a body [and] the economic class movement alone would be a body without a soul."[36] As regards Christianity's "Divine Founder," Jesus Christ, Welldon points out that he was but "a carpenter's son [who] lived a life of deep poverty, not having where to lay his head," being a "friend of publicans and sinners."[37]

Particularly in the Oklahoman countryside, Woody Guthrie's home state and, back then, "a lingering hotbed of socialism, still glowing from the fires of the populist revolt of the late nineteenth century,"[38] the rhetorics of the socialist movement, which regained immensely in popularity during the Great Depression due to the alleged failure of the capitalist economic system, was characterized by religious imagery of the same type. As Garin Burbank observes, "much of the local Socialist expression in Oklahoma was literally saturated with the arresting imagery of the area's many Protestantisms."[39] Differentiating between the 'imported orthodoxy' of socialism, which was rather secular and concerned itself particularly with industrial and political questions, and an indigenous variation, which appealed to the rural Southwesterners due to its synthesizing of neo-populist ideas with the standards of religious integrity, Burbank suggests that it was the latter which was "tougher than the more well-known urban middle-class version because the country people

34 *The Bible*, ed. Caroll and Prickett, Acts of the Apostels, 4, 32. Interestingly enough, Woody Guthrie's outlaw song "The Unwelcome Guest" also refers to the Acts, thereby already implying a correspondence between basic Christian values and the Socialist ideology (cf. chapter 3.2 of this study).

35 Welldon 952.

36 Welldon 949.

37 Welldon 945.

38 Morgan 2.

39 Burbank 15.

could not permit themselves the luxury of a faith in gradual persuasion."[40]

Moreover, it was this local or regional variant of socialism which developed both its own idiom, which was characterized by the use of religious imagery, and its own narrative, according to which the poor people, who were God's own, should adhere to socialism, as it was understood as the only means of salvation. Let us consider the following call for socialist revolt, which appeared in the socialist paper *Sword of Truth* in Sentinel, Southwestern Oklahoma, on May 13th, 1913:

> Permeate our souls with divine discontent and righteous rebellion. Strengthen within us the spirit of revolt; and may we continue to favor that which is fair and to rise in anger against the wrong, until the Great Revolution shall come to free men and women from their fetters and enable them to be good and kind and noble and human!
>
> O Lord, hasten the day![41]

The text employs typical features of 'prayer language,' such as the frequent use of imperatives, the paratactic syntax, the rather old-fashioned lexical and grammatical forms, e.g. "fair" or "may we", the polysyndetic enumeration of adjectives at the end, and, above all, the invocation of the Lord. Thus, by resorting to the conventions of a religious 'genre' in order to convey political ideas, this 'political prayer' clearly illustrates the synthesis of socialist ideas and basic Christian values inherent in the local version of socialism found in early 20th century Oklahoma. Likewise, Andrew Spratt, in an issue of the *Ellis County Socialist*, prayed for "the Kingdom [to] come, on earth."[42] Yet, he pointed out that "while men are underpaid, while women are overworked[,] while children grow up in squalor, while exploiting and social injustice remain, the Kingdom of Heaven can never come on earth and never will."[43] Thus, only a socialist revolution, as it is implied by Spratt's account, might improve the existing social misconditions.

Taking the basic Christian concept of solidarity as an essential ingredient of socialist ideology, Oklahoman socialists thus propagated the 'gospel of applied Christianity.' They suggested that cooperation and solidarity as fundamental Christian values should be realized and, at the same time, emphasized that people should stop theorizing, which would only result in disappointment. Consequently, instant action against the rul-

40 Burbank 16.
41 Quoted in Burbank 20.
42 Quoted in Burbank 21.
43 Quoted in Burbank 21.

ing classes was promoted and, most strikingly, the imagery of these 'roll calls' bears a strong resemblance to that resorted to in the poems discussed earlier. "Now, comrades, get on the firing line. Keep your eyes on the enemy, trust in the Lord, and keep your powder dry"[44] announced a letter writer to the *Oklahoma Pioneer*, underlining the warlike character of the socialists' struggle.

Finally, it is not surprising that the representatives of Oklahoman grassroots socialism, just like J.E.C. Welldon in his article for *The Nineteenth Century and After*, began to feature the most prominent preacher of Christianity as one of their leaders, Jesus Christ. In 1912, a letter appeared in the *Oklahoma Pioneer* characterizing the Reverend of the Oklahoman town Marlow as "a worthy, clean, and deserving brother and a staunch teacher in economics, Marxism and Christian, [and in] the Socialism of both Marx and Jesus Christ."[45] The comparison of one of the intellectual godfathers of socialism with the spiritual icon of Christian faith contributed to a refashioning of the figure of Jesus Christ as an anticapitalist, working-class hero, who would guide the suffering people through their pain and misery. Thus, according to the account of an Oklahoman socialist, preachers like minister W.L. Thurman showed "beyond the shadow of a doubt that Christ did not bring the Gospel to grafters, interest, profit, and rent takers, but to the working-class; that Christ's church was a working-class church and that grafters were not eligible for membership in it."[46]

Just like these preachers, who were quite often said to be removed from their offices for spreading such subversive ideas, Jesus Christ had been hunted down by the ruling elites. Here is an account of the tragic story of Jesus as presented in the *New Century* of November 22nd, 1911, on the occasion of the dismissal of a socialist preacher in the town of Bohoshe, Oklahoma:

> [I]n our own state of Oklahoma the sordid tragedy of 2000 years ago is reenacted. The elements entering into the case are the same. A man dares speak for the oppressed. The result is the same, failing in their efforts to curb the man, the ruling class have crushed him.[47]

Such an analogy between the dismissal of an Oklahoman preacher and the fate of Jesus Christ brings us back both to Upton Sinclair's novel and, of course, to the last verse of Guthrie's ballad about Jesus Christ, in

44 Quoted in Burbank 24.
45 Quoted in Burbank 23.
46 Quoted in Burbank 25.
47 Quoted in Burbank 24.

which he draws a similar analogy, concluding that "[i]f Jesus was to preach as he preached in Galilee / They would lay poor Jesus in his grave."

Long after the social gospel movement had reached its zenith at the beginning of the 20th century, Guthrie's song integrates religious and political ideas. And there is good reason to believe that it was the social and economic plight of the Depression years which stirred this revival of a concept which had long characterized the cultural realities that, in turn, shaped Guthrie and his songs. The Great Depression seemed to work as the chief catalyst of the radical turn towards a 'new' or 'second' social gospel, which found expression in Woody Guthrie's song about Jesus Christ. Due to high unemployment rates, worsening social conditions and a fascist threat both from abroad and within,[48] the idea of the compatibility of leftwing politics and Christianity received increasing attention again, as the following excerpt from an essay by I.F. Stone published in *The Nation* on October 2nd, 1937, shows:

> [I]t must be confessed that Christianity is inevitably Marxist. A religion based upon the Gospels cannot avoid being a vehicle for ideas which neither fascist nor reactionary can tolerate. For every fifty ministers content to soothe well-fed congregations, there will be at least one who is obsessed with the thought of a child who was born in a stable. He will remember one who preferred fishermen and common folk to Pharisees, who was singularly tactless in his references to the rich, and who was never destined to officiate in a cathedral. This is the type of fellow who listens to workers, share-croppers, and Negroes. He makes trouble.[49]

Most strikingly, Stone's description of the majority of ministers being "content to soothe well-fed congregations" very much echoes the idea of "infidel hordes" that have "hanged [Jesus Christ] round with pomp and parade" as expressed in Elizabeth's Waddell's poem "The Crusaders" cited above. Just like Stone, who remains optimistic, as he is sure that there are still preachers who "thought of a child who was born in a stable" and thus have not forgotten Jesus Christ's social background, Waddell also referred to the "[s]table and stall" which "for his birth sufficed," thereby indicating that the son of God, from the day he entered the world, was a representative of the poor.

Moreover, similar to Welldon's description, Jesus Christ is characterized as a working man, one of the "common folk," always listening to

48 For a detailed analysis of the 'fascist threat from within,' cf. chapter 3.4 of this study.

49 I.F. Stone, "The Romans Would Understand," *The Nation* 2 Oct. 1937: 345.

the people's laments and, as the last sentence of Stone's account suggests, taking matters into his hands in case these people are unjustly treated. By choosing "workers, sharecroppers, and Negroes" as examples of those who depend on Christ's support, Stone appropriates the story of Jesus for the context of the Great Depression. At the end of the article, however, Stone comes up with a generalizing conclusion, observing that that "[f]rom Lollard to Leveler, common men have drawn radical conclusions from their Bibles,"[50] and lays emphasis on the fact that the adherents of Christianity, in the early days, were regarded as a group of rebellious agitators and thus "fed [...] to lions long before the Communist Manifesto."[51] Claude Williams, then a fundamentalist preacher, also put emphasis on the democratic appeal of Christian religion and criticizes those "others" that distort its original ideals with "alien words," as he pointed out that

> I used the Bible as a workingman's book. [...] I had the Son of Man as a carpenter. [...] These people like John the Baptist are our people and speak our word, but they are kidnapped by the others and alien words put in their mouth to make us find what they want to find.[52]

Of course, such statements must not lead to the assumption that the revival of the social gospel in the Great Depression had the same scope and significance as it had had at the end of the 19th century. As James

50 Stone: 345.

51 Stone: 345. Stone's argument, which was, more often than not, also employed by other contemporary socialists to illustrate the compatibility of basic Christian values and Socialist principles, had already been outlined in a highly polemic manner by Friedrich Nietzsche. In his *Zur Genealogie der Moral* (1887), Nietzsche denounces the moral concept promoted by the gospel as a "Sklaven-Moral," which is, by definition, a rejection of the established moral codes and standards (cf. Friedrich Nietzsche, *Zur Genealogie der Moral: Eine Streitschrift, Friedrich Nietzsche. Werke in drei Bänden*, Band II, ed. Karl Schlechta [München: Carl Hanser Verlag, 1969] 782ff.). In his *Der Antichrist* (1895), Nietzsche further elaborates his point and argues that Christianity sided with the weak and the low people ("Das Christentum hat die Partei alles Schwachen, Niedrigen, Mißratnen genommen" [Friedrich Nietzsche. *Der Antichrist: Fluch auf das Christentum, Friedrich Nietzsche. Werke in drei Bänden*, Band II, ed. Schlechta 1167]). Accordingly, Jesus Christ is characterized as an anarchist and a political criminal, who is eventually punished for his crimes with crucifixion ("Dieser heilige Anarchist, der das niedere Volk, die Ausgestoßnen und 'Sünder', die Tschandala innerhalb des Judentums zum Widerspruch gegen die herrschende Ordnung aufrief [...] war ein politischer Verbrecher. [...] Dies brachte ihn ans Kreuz" [Nietzsche, *Der Antichrist* 1189]).

52 Quoted in Terkel 330-31.

Gregory points out, the idea of a "resonance between the promises of Socialism and chiliastic Christianity"[53] had lost its general appeal. The connection between political and religious radicalism had thus been dissolved to a considerable degree when the Depression hit the country in the 1930s. Gregory observes that particularly "among the ministers and religious-minded migrants who came to California one finds only scattered examples of sympathy for radicalism."[54]

However, though the social gospel might have lost its wide-spread appeal, its rhetorics and its imagery or, as Burbank had it, its own idiom was still referred to, not only in political pamphlets or newspaper articles of sorts, but also in literary texts. In John Steinbeck's *The Grapes of Wrath*, the character of the ex-preacher John Casey is portrayed along the lines of a typical representative of the social gospel, who tries to convince the suffering migrants to unite in order to overcome their plight. The figure of the ex-preacher Casey is also taken up in Guthrie's re-writing of Steinbeck's novel, called "Tom Joad," in which Casey is presented as a political activist who does not immerse himself in spiritual contemplation, but takes arms against the injustices his contemporaries have to suffer from. In his song, Guthrie renders a conversation between the ex-preacher and Tom Joad. His words clearly identify him as an adherent of the social gospel:

> 'I preached for the Lord a mighty long time,
> Preached about the rich and the poor
> Us workin' folks is all get together
> 'Cause we ain't got a chance anymore,
> We ain't got a chance anymore.'[55]

Probably due to the popularity of Steinbeck's *The Grapes of Wrath*, Guthrie decided to render the life and deeds of the novel's major characters in a number of his songs, one of them being his "Vigilante Man," which also fashions John Casey as a 'socialist messiah' and gives a brief account of his tragic fate:

> Preacher Casey was just a workin' man,
> And he said, 'Unite all you working men.'
> Killed him in the river some strange man.
> Was that a vigilante man?[56]

53 Gregory 162.
54 Gregory 162.
55 Leventhal and Guthrie 231.

Following from this, both Guthrie's fashionings of Jesus Christ and his sung adaptations of Steinbeck's character John Casey articulated the belief in the compatibility of basic Christian values and socialist ideology and thus participated in the revival of the social gospel in the Great Depression.

That the potential of Guthrie's songs to communicate such ideas was, at least in some instances, enhanced by their musical pretexts, might best be illustrated by reconsidering his song "Jesus Christ," in which, as we have seen, Jesus Christ is persecuted and victimized by the rich men, the bankers, and the landlords, who eventually "lay [him] in his grave." This characterization of Christ as an unjustly blamed and sentenced outlaw is emphasized as soon as we take into account that Guthrie's song deliberately appropriated both the tune and the storyline of the ballad on Jesse James, the most famous outlaw in the American Southwest.[57] In his song collection *Cowboy Songs and Other Frontier Ballads*, John Lomax lists four versions of the sung story of the popular outlaw and, strikingly enough, Guthrie's emplotment of his ballad on Jesus Christ reveals that he must have been aware of at least two of them. Examine the first verse of the following version of "Jesse James," which, according to Lomax's annotations, was originally sung in the eastern Tennessee Mountains:

> Jesse James was a man who traveled through the land,
> Stealin' an' robbin' wuz 'is trade;
> But a dirty little coward by the name of Robert Howard
> Laid Jesse James in 'is grave.[58]

Here is the first verse of another version of the outlaw story that came from the eastern Kentucky Mountains:

> Oh! Jesse was the man, he traveled through the land,
> For money Jesse never suffered pain;
> Jesse and his brother Frank, they robbed the Chicago bank
> And stopped the Danville train.[59]

The resemblances to Guthrie's first verse of his song about Christ are striking. Here it is again:

[56] Leventhal and Guthrie 240. For a detailed analysis of Guthrie's "Vigilante Man" cf. chapter 3.4 of this study.

[57] Cf. also Jackson 199. For a more detailed reading of Guthrie's own version of the story of Jesse James cf. chapter 3.2 of this study.

[58] Lomax, *Cowboy Songs* 155.

[59] Lomax, *Cowboy Songs* 156.

> Jesus Christ was a Man that traveled thru the land
> And a hard working man, and brave,
> He said to the rich, give your goods to the poor,
> And they laid Jesus Christ in his grave.

It is James's traveling "through the land" which Guthrie adopted in his ballad on Jesus Christ in order to provide his migrant audience with a figure to identify with, since they, just like Jesus Christ, were "not having where to lay [their] head[s]" either.[60] In contrast to Guthrie's song on Jesus Christ, however, in which the son of God is fashioned as "a hard working man, and brave," the above versions of Jesse James do not portray the outlaw in consistently positive terms, but render him as a professional criminal, whose "trade" was "robbin' an' stealin'." In order not to spoil the overall image of the figure of Christ, Guthrie, as one might argue, deliberately used some lines from yet a third version of the life and death of Jesse James, which can also be found in the Lomax collection. In this version, the first verse reads:

> Jesse James was a boy that downed many a man,
> He held up the Danville train,
> He robbed from the rich and he gave to the poor,
> He'd a hand and a heart and a brain.[61]

Though Jesse James's "down[ing] many a man" and his "[holding] up the Danville train" clearly expose him as a criminal, the third line hints at the outlaw's moral superiority to the "rich"; suddenly, his criminal deeds become acts of charity by the man with "a hand and a heart and a brain." Likewise, Jesus Christ's moral integrity is highlighted by a similar line stating that "[h]e said to the rich, give your goods to the poor."

The second verse of Guthrie's song, which might serve as another example of Guthrie's combining various elements of the sung story of Jesse James, is modeled after the chorus of the song about the famous outlaw. Here it is once again:

> Yes Jesus was a man, a carpenter by hand,
> His followers true and brave,
> One dirty coward called Judas Iscariot
> He has laid poor Jesus in his grave.[62]

60 Welldon 945.
61 Lomax, *Cowboy Songs* 157.
62 WGA, Songs I, Box 2, Folder 14.

Guthrie's verse bears a strong resemblance to a variation of the Jesse James-chorus as given in the Lomax collection:

> Poor Jesse had a wife to mourn for his life,
> Three children, they were brave;
> But that dirty little coward that shot Mr. Howard
> Has laid poor Jesse in his grave.[63]

In Guthrie's "Jesus Christ," the mourning wife of James is replaced by a reference to Jesus' profession; the brave children of Jesse James who, after he had been killed, were able to cope with the awful situation, are replaced by true and brave followers; finally, the murderer of James is replaced by the traitor Judas Iscariot, who is blamed for the death of Christ.

Following from these musical and thematic analogies between Guthrie's "Jesus Christ" and various sung versions of the story of Jesse James and considering Guthrie's general way of songwriting, it is plausible to assume that he deliberately chose specific elements of the James-story in his fashioning of the son of God. Thus, both the collage-like combination of characteristics of Jesse James in Guthrie's fashioning of Jesus Christ and the appropriation of the tune of one of the most popular outlaw ballads in the American Southwest strongly call forth the image of Jesus Christ as a morally superior outlaw, who has been mistreated and eventually killed by the establishment due to his commitment to the poor. Moreover, Guthrie's song positions Christ in the long tradition of outlaws the Southwesterners were so fond of. "Being right is just the opposite of being popular,"[64] Guthrie observed in one of his notebooks, and this, as his song implies, is true for both Jesse James and Jesus Christ.

With his song, Guthrie certainly contributed to the resurrection of the social gospel during the Great Depression by "proletarianizing" the life of Jesus Christ, as Lookingbill put it. Moreover, he contributed to the creation of a political and cultural icon, which his listeners could identify with and appropriate as a leading figure in their struggle against the ruling classes. However, this fashioning of Christ as a representative of the working class cannot simply be explained by Guthrie's conversion to socialism at the end of the 1930s, when he became affiliated with the political left in California. Rather, his song is part of a tradition of socialist rhetorics which integrated political and religious ideas in order to establish what was called the social gospel.

[63] Lomax, *Cowboy Songs* 154.
[64] WGA, Notebooks I, Notebook 4, 180.

This gospel, which did not replace but augmented the Christian one, began to influence the political discourse at the end of the 19th century and achieved particular prominence in the Oklahoman countryside, where Woody Guthrie must have already become familiar with it in his childhood: As he grew up in a cultural surrounding that was interspersed with socialist elements, one might be tempted to assume that these cultural patterns, which came to life again during the Depression, shaped Guthrie's song(s) about Jesus Christ, which, in turn, contributed to the revival of the social gospel.

Though Lookingbill's thesis of a socialist conversion certainly helps to describe the growing political concern of Guthrie's songs at the end of the 1930s, it fails to acknowledge that the particular combination and integration of the political and the religious were both part of a particular literary tradition and deeply engrained in the contemporary cultural knowledge, which manifested itself in a certain repertoire of images that were revitalized in the Depression years, when the economic and social dilemma contributed to a partial re-establishment of the social gospel. Within this cultural framework, Guthrie's song about Jesus Christ obtains a significant political potential and, owing to its emplotment and musical realization along the lines and tunes of the most popular outlaw ballad in the American Southwest, possesses a remarkable emotional and aesthetic appeal which added to its social energy.

3.7 "All this world's a poker game": Questioning Laisser-Faire Capitalism and Promoting New Deal Politics

The economic plight of the 1930s, which uncovered the fatal defects of laisser-faire capitalism, cried out for an alternative political program apt to help the national economy recover from the recession. President Franklin D. Roosevelt proposed the implementation of a package of numerous interventionist measures to handle the economic disaster. His 'New Deal,' however, which was based on new theories of the market, was not at all a surefire success and soon met with both enthusiastic approval and harsh criticism. So it does not come as a surprise that Roosevelt's controversially discussed plan of action was also taken up in some of Guthrie's songs, which take a stand on the politics and policies of the New Deal and, at the same time, criticize laisser-faire capitalism, which had dominated the American economy before the Depression.

After briefly outlining the scope of Roosevelt's political agenda, this chapter explores both the cultural origin and the social and political functions of the metaphorical frames employed in two of Guthrie's sung renderings of the political controversy concerning the New Deal. By correlating the songs both to a number of contemporary political texts and to letters to the President or to his wife, the following analysis attempts to make evident that the imagery Guthrie used was part of a particular New Deal rhetoric, which was widely disseminated and with which the implementation of Roosevelt's plan of action was marketed. Guthrie employed these metaphoric frames to reduce the complexity of the political discourse and, in so doing, to provide his listeners with a 'licensing narrative' which helped to make sense of the political and economic turmoil in the Great Depression.

* * * * *

In his acceptance speech shortly after his election in 1933, the new President of the United States, Franklin Delano Roosevelt, announced a 'New Deal,' which was to lead the country and its citizens out of the recession that had hit the economy after the stock market crashed in 1929. And indeed, in the immediate aftermath of his election, Roosevelt began to implement a program of federal relief for the unemployed, whose number had risen to about 15 million in the winter of 1932-33. Though direct relief was something that most Americans, including the President, did not regard as an adequate means to overcome the economic plight, the foundation of the Federal Emergency Relief Administration (FERA), which provided grants to support the welfare infrastructure in the various states, seemed the only way out in early 1933. The Agricultural Adjustment Act (AAA), which was also implemented in 1933, was supposed to solve the problem of chronic overproduction in the agricultural sector. A variety of other programs and institutions followed, including the Public Works Administration (PWA), which was instructed to create public service jobs for the unemployed in order to get them off the relief rolls.

In 1933-34, the partially ineffective and too expensive PWA was supported by the Civil Works Administration (CWA) and, in 1935, Roosevelt eventually turned even more to the political and economic left in his 'second New Deal' by implementing policies that disregarded the interests of the wealthy and favored those who were propagating social justice, redistribution of property and equal opportunities: In 1935, the National Labor Relations Act, or Wagner Act, was implemented, which guaranteed the right to organize a union. In the same year, the government passed the Social Security Act, an extensive program which provided financial support for old age-pensioners as well as for the unemployed and the disabled. It was the first step towards a federal system of social security in the United States.

From 1935 onwards, the newly founded Works Progress Administration (WPA), a large-scale job agency, tried to take care of the unemployed and, though it could not really relieve the tense economic situation, helped millions of workers to survive the hardships of the Depression. Since the AAA of 1933 certainly helped the large landowners, but had not taken care of the small farmers and sharecroppers, the Resettlement Administration (RA) was founded in 1935 and, two years later, after the reelection of Roosevelt in 1936, turned into the Farm Security Administration (FSA), which was responsible for the prevention of further top-soil erosion, for the foundation of agricultural cooperatives and the resettlement of smaller farmers, the majority of which came from the drought-stricken territories in the American Southwest, into more fertile regions of the United States.

Though the New Deal did not, to be sure, remain uncriticized, and though Roosevelt often promised more than he could deliver in the end, his plan of action was, for a vast majority of the American poor, indeed the last way out. "In the eyes of many Depression victims," as Robert S. McElvaine has it, "Franklin Delano Roosevelt could do no wrong; he represented hope in the midst of despair."[1] The controversially debated

1 Robert S. McElvaine, ed., *Down and Out in the Great Depression: Letters from the Forgotten Man* (Chapel Hill: U of North Carolina P, 1983) 14.

political program of the American President is also dealt with in one of Woody Guthrie's songs, called "I'm Looking for that New Deal Now," which, quite optimistically, articulates hope for a new beginning:

> All this world's a Poker Game
> The way it's played is a dog-gone Shame;
> I'm a Lookin' for that New Deal now.
> All of the Bankers, I believe,
> Has got a Good Hand up their Sleeve;
> I'm a Lookin' for that New Deal now.
>
> When the Cards was dealt around,
> Wall Street drawed the Aces down.
> I'm a Lookin' for that New Deal now.
> When them Cards was shuffled up,
> The working folks, they lost the Pot.
> I'm a Lookin' for that New Deal now.[2]

The speaker of the song follows the metaphorical implication of the term "New Deal," taken from the semantic field of card games, and compares the world to a "Poker Game." He points out right from the beginning that the "way it's played is a dog-gone Shame," as some of the card players involved in the game are not acting according to its rules. The first group of cheating players are the bankers, who have some extra cards hidden in their sleeves which they pull out whenever necessary. The other cheat is Wall Street, which is, in the second verse of the song, accused of "draw-[ing] the Aces down." Those who apparently lose the game are the "working folks" at the bottom of society, as they fall for the swindle of their cunning fellow gamblers representing the economic elites.

Guthrie's song points to the fraud of the economically powerful and their exploitation of the working class, thereby criticizing the economic system of laisser-faire capitalism, which will, as the double repetition of the song's title within each verse emphasizes, only be overcome by Roosevelt's New Deal. Moreover, the exposure of the immoral behavior of the representatives of the economic bloc, hinted at by the metaphor of cheating, implicitly characterizes the New Deal as a political program which aims at both an economic and a moral recovery of a society which had stepped into the pitfall of moral laisser-faire, as it had been deluded by the material prosperity of the 1920s and had forgotten the traditional values of social justice and solidarity.

As an investigation into the textual archive of the Great Depression will show in the course of this chapter, the imagery of gambling used in

2 WGA, Notebooks I, Notebook 5, 69.

Guthrie's song to identify and denounce those responsible for the economic (and moral) decay was quite common among the working poor during the 1930s.[3] For a majority, the capitalist system was indeed a mere gamble, in which the bankers and stock market dealers seemed to be the winners, while a huge number of people suffered from unemployment and poverty.[4] However, let us turn to Roosevelt first, who emphasizes the moral aims of his plan of action in the following excerpt from his inaugural speech on March 4th, 1933, in which he alludes to the biblical episode on the Cleansing of the Temple[5] in order to announce his program:

> The money changers have fled from their high seats in the temple of our civilization. We may now restore that temple to the ancient truths. The measure of the restoration lies in the extent to which we apply social values more noble than mere monetary profit.[6]

3 In my examination of the working people's attitudes and dispositions towards the New Deal, I will predominantly rely on letters written to Franklin Roosevelt or his wife, Eleanor Roosevelt, during the great slump of the 1930s. This choice is basically due to two aspects: First, there is a large amount of letters still available, many of them written by members of the working class. During the New Deal years, as Robert McElvaine (5-6) has it, "both the volume of mail reaching the White House and the high percentage of it coming from the poor were unprecedented. This was not only attributable simply to the Depression. President Roosevelt gave many people a feeling that he was their personal friend and protector, that they could tell him things in confidence." Thus, "[i]n the week following FDR's inauguration, 450,000 letters poured into the White House. For years the average remained at 5,000 to 8,000 communications each day" (6). Second, the analysis of letters seems to be promising in that, to follow McElvaine again, it is "one of the few means available to obtain […] immediate testimony. […] The words of men, women, and children as they described their problems to persons they believed to be concerned afford a better feeling of what life was like for Depression victims than does any other available source" (5).

4 The banks, to be sure, suffered heavily from the economic crisis as well and were often far from being profitable institutions. As John M. Keynes, whose theory of economics strongly influenced Roosevelt's New Deal, pointed out, "over a great part of the world, and not least in the United States, the position of the banks, though partly concealed from the public eye, may be in fact the weakest element in the whole situation" (John M. Keynes, "The Consequences to the Banks of the Collapse of Money Values," *Collected Writings, Vol. IX: Essays in Persuasion*, by John M. Keynes [London/Basingstoke: Macmillan, 1972] 157).

5 *The Bible*, ed. Caroll and Prickett, Mark, 11, 15: "[…] and Jesus went into the temple, and began to cast out them that sold and bought in the temple, and overthrew the tables of the moneychangers, and the seats of them that sold doves."

6 Quoted in Nate 36.

According to Roosevelt, the time of the "money changers," i.e., those who speculated at the stock market, is over for good, and "social values," not "monetary profit" shall become the guiding principle for the future. His statement, just like Guthrie's song, clearly points at those responsible for the crisis and thus certainly appealed to his voters, who believed that the representatives of the capitalist system had betrayed and exploited the working class whenever they could and, due to their never-ending mongering for profits, had eventually caused the system to collapse. Examine, for example, the following letter of complaint written in 1930 and addressed to Colonel Arthur Woods, then chairman of President Hoover's Emergency Committee for Employment, in which the anonymous writer, who signed with "A Laboring Man," pointed out that "[a] working man puts away a little, sticks to his job and the first thing he knows he's got to donate to releive [sic] a situation he did not create. The big moneyed men created it by juggling with the market."[7] According to the dissatisfied worker, it is the businessmen's "juggling with the market," i.e., their risky ways of investing and their speculating on money that had caused the strained economic situation that he is in.

The imagery of juggling or gambling with the market is, at least implicitly, also employed by John Maynard Keynes, whose writings would become the theoretical backbone of Roosevelt's New Deal. In his well-known essay on the "End of Laisser-Faire," Keynes explains why there is such a maldistribution of wealth:

> Many of the greatest economic evils of our time are the fruits of risk, uncertainty, and ignorance. It is because particular individuals, fortunate in situations or in abilities, are able to take advantage of uncertainty and ignorance, and also because for the same reason big business is often a *lottery*, that great inequalities of wealth come about.[8]

"[R]isk, uncertainty and ignorance," which are here given to explain the "greatest economic evils," may also be identified as the three basic ingredients of a gaming situation. Thus, Keynes's characterization of "big business" as a lottery bears a strong resemblance to Guthrie's comparison of the capitalist economic system with a mere gamble.

And, to be sure, the "big moneyed men['s]" playing with the market was commonly believed to involve a lot of half-legal, if not criminal ac-

7 Quoted in McElvaine 44.

8 John M. Keynes, "The End of Laisser-Faire," *Collected Writings, Vol. IX: Essays in Persuasion*, by John Maynard Keynes (London/Basingstoke: Macmillan, 1972) 291, emphasis added.

tivities, as the following excerpt from another letter written to President Hoover on October 30th, 1930, illustrates:

> Oh the People have been so much belied that you cannot believe anything only what you can see. I hope that Wall St will never have the power again to cause such a panic upon the people money tied up hoarded up Is a crime [sic]. I hope the guilty gang will be punished before I die. I say this whole panic was brought on by a dishonest group which I hope will be punished.[9]

More explicitly than in Guthrie's song, Wall Street, representing the spearhead of laisser-faire capitalism, is accused of having brought economic recession to the country in the letter quoted above. The "panic" the anonymous author of the letter writes about refers to the stock market crash in 1929, which marked the beginning of the Depression decade in the United States. Interestingly enough, Wall Street, or rather, those who are investing in and earning their money by trading stocks are portrayed as a "guilty gang" and a "dishonest group," a characterization that is strongly reminiscent of Guthrie's imagery of cheating. In 1935, 'Cyclone' Davis, a Populist, a Texan politician, and, at times, a poet, used a similar image in one of his lyrical renderings of the Great Depression. Also blaming the bankers and Wall Street speculators for the economic plight, he points out that "[t]he Wall Street bandits / In their lust / Have trampled the people / Into the Dust."[10] A year earlier, a letter addressed to the recently elected President Roosevelt also, at least implicitly, points to the criminal wheelings and dealings of the monied classes by posing a question which must have been achingly familiar to the majority of the working poor:

9 Quoted in McElvaine 42.

10 Quoted in Donald W. Whisenhunt, "The Bard in the Depression: Texas Style," *Journal of Popular Culture* 2 (1968): 372. After denouncing the bankers and Wall Street speculators as those who gather wealth while the majority of the people has to starve, Davis's poem also elaborates on those who cannot afford a living and have to become criminals in order to survive: "And the man who robs a country bank / He only robs by retail / These bandits who in millions rank / Rob by slaughter wholesale." Epitomizing the moral decay in a society in which the rich are the 'real' criminals and the poor are but victims of circumstance, these lines echo very clearly the penultimate verse of Guthrie's song "Pretty Boy Floyd," the political implications of which are discussed in detail in chapter 3.2 of this study.

> Dear President Roosevelt:
>
> [...] What I would like to know is this: how can a bank take our money and get by while an old couple have to let their houses go?[11]

As the two letters cited reveal, it was not only the worsening economic situation that troubled the working poor; both their helplessness and their utter despair were also due to their inability to understand and to accept the functioning of a system which allowed a minority to accumulate wealth even in times of utmost hardship, while those who had a regular job were underpaid, or even dismissed, as the Depression worsened. Though Keynes, in his essay already cited above, exculpates the bankers and characterizes them as "honest citizens, [who] feel a proper indignation at the perils of the wicked world in which they live,"[12] many people still believed that they, by cheating and mistreating the poor, became even richer in Depression times. Woody Guthrie's song "Jolly Banker" captured the common belief that the bankers were those who profited from the Great Depression. Though one has to add that this song probably pictures a banker in the rural Southwest, whose fate certainly cannot be compared to a banker in the urban areas on the east coast, its portrayal of the alleged Depression winner is still telling.

> My name is Tom Cranker and I'm a jolly banker,
> I'm a jolly banker, jolly banker am I.
> I safeguard the farmers and widows and orphans,
> Singin' I'm a jolly banker, jolly banker am I.
>
> When dust storms are sailing, and crops they are failing,
> I'm a jolly banker, jolly banker am I.
> I check up your shortage and bring down your mortgage,
> Singin' I'm a jolly banker, jolly banker am I.
>
> When money you're needing, and mouths you are feeding,
> I'm a jolly banker, jolly banker am I.
> I'll plaster your home with a furniture loan,
> I'm a jolly banker, jolly banker am I.
>
> If you show me you need it, I'll let you have credit,
> I'm the jolly banker, jolly banker am I.
> Just bring me back two for the one I lend you,
> I'm the jolly banker, jolly banker am I.[13]

11 Quoted in McElvaine 119.
12 Keynes, "The Consequences to the Banks" 158.
13 Kleff 364.

As the speaker of the song, the banker hypocritically fashions himself as a caretaker of the farmers, who provides them with the money necessary to make their living. In return, however, he expects "two for the one I lend you," thus exploiting the farmers' dilemma. Being one of the 'gambling men,' the banker gets rich at the expense of the rural poor. That he enjoys his fortunate economic situation and does not have a bad conscience at all is underlined by the repetition of his sung declaration that he is a "jolly banker" indeed.

Another song which renders the grotesque situation in which some people were able to accumulate wealth in spite of the general economic recession is Guthrie's "I Ain't Got No Home," which was already discussed earlier. The last verse of the song reads:

> Now I just ramble 'round to see what I can see,
> This wide, wicked world is a funny place to be.
> The gambling man is rich and the working man is poor,
> And I ain't got no home in this world anymore.[14]

It is Guthrie's image of the "wide, wicked world" which, reminiscent of Keynes's phrasing, underlines the incomprehensibility of a system in which "the gambling man is rich and the working man is poor." It is a world turned topsy-turvy, a world in which honest work does not pay off anymore. It is a world, in which, as Pastor Jesse H. Baird put it in a letter to Roosevelt dating October 19th, 1935, "low standards of morality and the gambling spirit are creating havoc throughout the nation."[15] It is indeed, to return to Guthrie's song about the New Deal, a "poker game," whose participants are playing with marked cards. Let us consider the next verses of his "I'm Looking for that New Deal Now," in which Guthrie continues to describe the round of gamblers:

> The Cards was dealt around the Board,
> And Mr. Hoover 'marked the cards.'
> I'm a Lookin' for that New Deal now.
> And Every time the Cards was dealt,
> They bluffed out Mr. Roosevelt,
> I'm a Lookin' for that New Deal now.[16]

It is not only the bankers as the representatives of the capitalist system who are accused of having employed illegal means to achieve their aims. Herbert Hoover, by 1939 ex-president of the United States, is also said to

14 Leventhal and Guthrie 138-39.

15 <http://newdeal.feri.org/clergy/cl1024.htm>, 16 Sept. 2006.

16 WGA, Notebooks I, Notebook 5, 69.

have "marked the cards." Only by doing so was he able to "bluff [...] out Mr. Roosevelt" and to foil his plans for recovering the nation's economy.

Though Herbert Hoover was certainly not a supporter of radical laisser-faire, but of a 'progressive individualism' which basically followed the principles of subsidiarity and equality of opportunity, he became a political scapegoat for many of the American workers in the first years of the Depression and could not convince the voters of his ideas of how to solve the general crisis. Particularly the Democrats, whose drive for election victory in 1933 was stronger than it had ever been before, exploited Hoover's weak position and portrayed him as a tough and heartless politician who would stop at nothing. "Hooverites are hard to be found," an anonymous poet who identified himself as a Democrat wrote in 1932, "[s]ince they brought this depression 'round."[17]

Due to Hoover's general loss of popularity and the worsening economic situation, which required large-scale federal intervention, Franklin D. Roosevelt, his Democratic opponent, won in a landslide in 1932, and, to be sure, "the vote was not really an expression of confidence in Roosevelt himself. Most of all, the large Democratic vote was simply a repudiation of Hoover."[18] However, Roosevelt's New Deal, though heralded in Guthrie's song as a true alternative to the unfair and cheating politics of Hoover, still brought no real change, as it could not cope with an economic plight of such enormous magnitude. In spite of the numerous attempts to improve the unbearable situation with a variety of interventionist programs, a considerable number of people still suffered from unemployment and poverty for reasons they could not understand and blamed those in power for the economic disaster. The following excerpt from a letter to Mr. Harry Hopkins, Relief Administrator in the Roosevelt administration, dating September 21st, 1935, illustrates the general frustration among the people. The writer complains about the deficits of Roosevelt's New Deal:

> Now there is work waiting here for some of our men and you are for them not getting it. How can you answer to these people for that. They demand some consideration. And I am afraid they will soon tire of this delay and take some action themselves. They have been held down long enough through your petty Political Playing. That is all it is. [...] You were put in that position to do a

17 Quoted from Whisenhunt 378. To be sure, there were a number of politically motivated poems about Hoover, which portrayed him as the scapegoat for the Great Depression. As Whisenhunt puts it, "the blame for Hoover," which also manifested itself in contemporary folklore, "became almost universal" in those days (Whisenhunt 377).

18 McElvaine 21.

> real job and now you find you cannot fulfill it, and are playing around to the interests of the most moneyed men and starve the real working people of the country.[19]

It is not so much the fact that the Roosevelt administration, despite all its promises, was not able to bring back prosperity to the country which is of interest here. Rather it is the metaphor of "Political Playing," which the writer of the letter employs to utter his discontent and which immediately brings us back to the imagery of gambling used in Guthrie's song. It is not only the businessmen who "juggle with the market," but also the leading politicians who, as the letter implies, play with their mandates and their responsibility for their voters. Yet, quite in contrast to the cynical letter of complaint which criticizes Roosevelt's politics, Guthrie's song clearly takes a stand: Here, Hoover is depicted as the cheater. Roosevelt takes part in the game as he has no choice, but – being the honest man that he is – he plays according to the rules. Let us have a look at the next verse of Guthrie's song:

> Franklin D. he drawed a Hand,
> But he couldn't beat them Bankin' Men,
> I'm a Lookin' for that New Deal now.
> Mr. Randolph Hearst he filled his purse,
> For the Workin' Man, times got worse,
> I'm a Lookin' for that New Deal now.[20]

The first two lines of the verse give an explanation as to why Roosevelt's political initiatives could not unfold their impact immediately: The implementation of his politics of intervention was retarded by the too powerful bankers, whom "Franklin D. [...] couldn't beat," for, one may be invited to add, they cheated him. Thus, these lines refute such critical remarks as uttered in the letter cited above and exonerate Roosevelt from being responsible for the sluggish recovery of the economy by "playing around to the interests of the most moneyed men," as the letter put it. Quite on the contrary, Roosevelt's political actions are undermined by these "most moneyed men" and he has no real chance of beating them.

In order to better understand the rhetorical strategy of Guthrie's song, which tries to exonerate Roosevelt and blames the economic bloc for the retardation of the New Deal, one must also consider the date of the song's composition. As a look at the respective typescript page reveals, Guthrie wrote down the song on May 6th, 1939, and we may well assume that he

[19] Quoted in McElvaine 180-81.
[20] WGA, Notebooks I, Notebook 5, 69.

must have composed it shortly before that. In 1939, Roosevelt's New Deal had not only lost its public appeal, but also its power to overcome the plight of the Depression. This decline in popularity already began in 1936, when more and more critical voices uttered their doubts about Roosevelt's plan of action. Here is an excerpt from a letter to Eleanor Roosevelt written on January 24th, 1936, which explicitly refers to the promise the President had made in his inaugural address, which still seemed to be unfulfilled:

> When Pres. Roosevelt gave his promise to drive 'The Money Changers from the Temple' listeners had great hope that at last the common people of the nation would have a hearing but so far he seems zealously to be watching over the interests of financiers and capitalists and the common people are allowed to view a mirage with wonderful promises which disappear on approach.[21]

Besides those critics of Roosevelt and his New Deal who expressed their disappointment of the high hopes they had entertained when he had taken office, some other, more radical voices considered his interventionist policies contradictory to traditional American values and took them as forebodings of a totalitarian regime. On June 26th, 1936, an article written by Mark Sullivan and published in the *Herald Tribune* stated that

> [t]he New Deal is the American variation of the new order that has been set up in three great European countries and some smaller ones. The term 'New Deal' is the American equivalent of the term 'Fascism' in Italy, the term 'Nazi' in Germany, and the term 'Soviet' in Russia.[22]

As radical as such comparisons might have sounded, there is reason to believe that they still had an effect on public opinion, which, in the long run, became skeptical of Roosevelt's New Deal. One of the leading media magnates who had a say in the editorial boards of a number of prestigious newspapers and, due to his conservative attitude, deliberately contributed to the negative depiction of the Roosevelt administration and thus to their loss of popularity, was William Randolph Hearst. Little wonder that he is among the 'card players' in Guthrie's song. Here are the relevant lines again:

21 Quoted in McElvaine 195-96.
22 Quoted in Nate 75.

Mr. Randolph Hearst he filled his purse,
For the Workin' Man, times got worse,
I'm a Lookin' for that New Deal now.[23]

According to the song, Hearst belongs to those who profited from the economic recession and, through his oppositional media campaign, indirectly retarded the implementation of Roosevelt's plan of action. As a consequence, "for the Workin' Man, times got worse," although the President did his best to improve the overall situation.

Criticism of the New Deal grew stronger and stronger in the following years. Eventually, in 1937/38, a second dramatic recession hit the country, and the American people's faith in the President's interventionist program was severely shaken. Consequently, after the Congressional Elections in 1938, Roosevelt had to face a strengthened opposition and could no longer fully implement his New Deal policies. His project Federal One, for example, which was meant to support cultural activities and included the Federal Theatre Project, the Federal Writers' Project, the Federal Art Project and the Federal Music Project, was harshly criticized by the conservative opposition and accused of providing a hotbed for communist agitation. Eventually, in the summer of 1939, the Federal Theatre Project was dissolved, and the other three were restructured on state-level. Again, it was the media machinery of William Randolph Hearst which considerably contributed to the denunciation and eventual failure of these programs.[24] What is even more, about nine million people still suffered from unemployment at the end of the decade and it was not Roosevelt's New Deal, but the Second World War and the growing demand for war machinery which eventually brought back full employment and prosperity to the country.

Taking into consideration both the New Deal's loss of public appeal and its modest success until 1939, Guthrie's song almost reads like a plea for the rehabilitation of the Democratic President and his political plan of action, the failures of which could no longer be denied at that point. However, it is not only Roosevelt who is exonerated, but also his Californian ally, Governor Culbert L. Olson, as the next verse of the song reveals:

Governor Olson drawed some cards,
And the Big Land Companies cleaned the Board;
I'm a Lookin' for that New Deal now.
Mr. Olson, I expect,

23 WGA, Notebooks I, Notebook 5, 69.
24 Cf. Nate 123.

> Will have to call for a Brand New Deck.
> I'm a Lookin' for that New Deal now.[25]

Just like President Roosevelt, the Californian Governor, who was a strong supporter of the New Deal, is cheated by the representatives of the economic bloc. Yet, it is no longer the bankers and the Wall Street gang, but the "Big Land Companies" that control the game and do not let Olson make a coup. He, in whom many of the Californian poor, including the majority of the Southwestern migrants, placed their hopes, "will have to call for a Brand New Deck" to eventually be able to defeat the cheaters and implement the New Deal for California.

With Olson, Guthrie introduces another betrayed and cheated character, who was, not only as governor of California, a lot closer to his potential listeners than the President – Roosevelt did not even seem to be aware of the migrants' situation in California until the very end of the 1930s.[26] Shortly after his election, Olson stated that he would bring about a New Deal for California to handle its specific social and economic problems. He promised to seek recompense for the refugees from the drought regions in the Southwest and thus instantly gained popularity among those who took shelter in the numerous migrant camps in the 'Golden State.'

Olson's election victory in 1938, which marked a change in Californian politics, as the Democratic Party took over after forty years of Republican administration, was largely based on two factors: First, the Democrat faced a very weak opponent, Frank F. Merriam, who was neither popular nor regarded competent enough to solve California's problems. And second, Olson, who was said to be rather ineloquent and not very charismatic, refurbished his image with the help of an effective P.R. campaign. As Robert E. Burke points out in his study on Olson's legislature as governor of California, one of "[t]he key figures [in this campaign] in southern California [was] J. Franke Burke, radio station owner and commentator, who was chairman of the campaign committee."[27]

25 WGA, Notebooks I, Notebook 5, 69.

26 Some critics argue that it was Steinbeck's novel *The Grapes of Wrath* which eventually directed the President's attention to the miserable fate of the Dust Bowl migrants. To be sure, this was only in 1939, about five years after the first storms had hit the Southwestern Plains.

27 Robert E. Burke, *Olson's New Deal for California* (Berkeley, California: U of California P, 1953) 17; cf. also Cray126.

It was J. Franke Burke who, in 1937, contracted Woody Guthrie as an entertainer on his radio station KFVD in Los Angeles.[28] Soon, Burke was to discover Guthrie as an extraordinarily gifted songwriter and (political) commentator,[29] and, most certainly, the Dust Bowl balladeer's job at KFVD also consisted of promoting Olson, who "place[d] [his] chief reliance upon the radio for reaching the people."[30] Thus, the explicitly propagandistic character of Guthrie's "I'm Looking for that New Deal Now" might well be explained by his being employed by Burke's radio station, which was part of the promotion machinery of the Californian governor. In his liner notes to a slightly different version of the song lyrics, published in *Hard-Hitting Songs for Hard-Hit People*, Guthrie, referring to Burke, even claimed that "he had a friend out there in California that was head foreman of Radio Station KFVD and he was a good Liberal Thinker. I know, 'cause I've heard him think. I use to listen to his speeches and then set [sic] down and have a song about 'em."[31]

Yet, Guthrie's song does not stop at promoting Roosevelt's and Olson's New Deal, pointing to the two politicians' responsibility to overcome both their cheating opponents and the economic plight in the country. The "Workin' Folks," as the next verse of the song implies, have to do their own part to contribute to the eventual success of the New Deal:

> The Workin' Folks gotta all pitch in,
> And Play Together if they hope to win.
> I'm a Lookin' for that New Deal now.
> You gotta play 'Ball' with F.D.R.
> An' Mr. Olson, your Govenor.
> I'm a Lookin' for that New Deal now.[32]

28 Cf. Klein 90. Guthrie's first radio program, "The Oklahoma and Woody Show," which he performed with his partner Maxine Crissman, was aired on 19 July 1937.

29 Cf. Klein 114, addition mine: "Actually, Burke had bigger plans for Woody in the spring of 1938. He wanted to send him and Lefty Lo on a statewide tour for Culbert Olson in a sleek, chrome bus along wih a comedian who impersonated Franklin Roosevelt." Moreover, as Cray points out, "Burke had started a weekly newspaper, the Light. The eight-page paper doubled as Olson's campaign sheet and a platform for Burke's causes: group health plans, unions, and an end to exploitation of farm laborers. Since Guthrie was going off the air, Burke suggested that the songwriter might be interested in working on a series of stories covering the plight of the Okies in California. Guthrie, with nothing better to do, agreed" (127).

30 Burke, *Olson's New Deal* 27.

31 Lomax, Guthrie and Seeger 206.

32 WGA, Notebooks I, Notebook 5, 69.

Maintaining the image of a game, the verse not only suggests that the workers should "Play Together," but also advises them to form a team with Roosevelt and Olson to oppose the cheating politicians, bankers and land owners. "You gotta play 'Ball' with F.D.R. / An' Mr Olson, your Governor" thus works as a direct address to the songs' listeners to convince them of the workability of the New Deal and to support their belief in a program whose shortcomings were no longer deniable at that time. Whereas the constant repetition of the line "I'm a Lookin' for that New Deal now" maintains the optimistic tone of the song, the use of the second person singular, which appears for the first time, deliberately turns the attention to the listeners who are now in charge. Without their action, without their organizing, as the verse suggests, the New Deal will remain a hopeless endeavor doomed to fail.[33]

The song's last verse then serves to identify (with) the speaker:

> All I want is enough to eat;
> New Shoes on the Children's feet;
> I'm a Lookin' for that New Deal now;
> A little Work, and a little fun,
> A pocketbook with a little Money.
> I'm a Lookin' for that New Deal now.[34]

The enumeration of his wants and needs clearly identifies the speaker as a member of the working class.[35] He is one of the victims of the Great Depression, who suffers from unemployment, poverty and his inability to make his and his family's living. Yet, the last verse does not only allow the listener to identify the speaker, but also to identify himself *with* him: By outlining an almost prototypical image of a Depression victim, the song's last verse leaves the more abstract and far-away world of poker-playing politicians behind and portrays a situation its potential listeners are very likely to be familiar with.

To sum it up, Guthrie's song rehabilitates both Roosevelt and Olson and puts the blame for the malfunctioning of the New Deal on those who

33 That Guthrie was not entirely uncritical of the New Deal and, at the same time, convinced of the necessity of collective action, which, according to him, would even be more effective than the New Deal itself, is emphasized by his annotations to "I'm Looking for that New Deal now," in which he points out that "[t]he only New Deal that will ever amount to a dam thing will come from Trade Unions" (Lomax, Guthrie and Seeger 206).

34 WGA, Notebooks I, Notebook 5, 69.

35 Of course, the speaker's deviations from the grammatical standard reveal his working-class background right from the beginning of the song. Still, the last verse provides a more detailed picture of his fate.

represent the capitalist system of laisser-faire: the bankers, the Wall Street gang, the conservative politicians and, as regards California, the big landowners. They are depicted as cheats in a poker game, in which the honest and committed Roosevelt and Olson do not have a chance, unless there will be a "brand new deck," and unless the working people – including, to be sure, the speaker of the song, who clearly identifies himself as one of them – will unite and support the 'team' of the Roosevelt-Olson administration. Thus, by elaborating in detail on the metaphorical implications of the term 'New Deal,' which derives from the semantic field of gambling, Guthrie's song separates the good from the bad and thus adopts a distinct position in the discourse on the New Deal, which, at that time, was already on its downturn.

The prospect of a brighter future, which is emphasized by the almost stoic repetition of the speaker's "I'm a Lookin' for that New Deal now," is the central topic of another of Guthrie's songs on the New Deal, called "Roosevelt-Olson," the first two verses of the song read:

> Our good ship is sailing o'er the sea
> Our good ship is sailing o'er the sea
> It's a hard ocean trip through the rain and the storm
> Our good ship is sailing o'er the sea.
>
> Our good ship is sailing through the storm
> Our good ship is sailing through the storm
> With Olson at the sail, and Roosevelt at the wheel,
> Our good ship is sailing through the storm.[36]

As in the song discussed earlier, Guthrie uses a single metaphorical frame running through the entire song to render the political situation in the country and to take his discursive position towards it. This time, he draws upon nautical imagery, comparing Roosevelt and Olson to the captain and the first mate on a ship which allegorizes the American nation. The ship, as the verse tells us, has to be guided through a devastating storm, mapping the economic turmoil of the Great Depression. While "Roosevelt at the wheel" has to decide on the direction of the ship, Olson executes his captain's orders and speeds up the ship by making sail. This clear-cut division of labor on board the ship is emphasized in the next verse:

> Our good ship is sailing o'er the blue
> Our good ship is sailing o'er the blue
> Roosevelt at the compass, and Olson at the helm,
> Our good ship is sailing through the blue.[37]

36 WGA, Notebooks I, Notebook 5, 159.

Again, "Roosevelt at the compass" is responsible for the direction, whereas "Olson at the helm" executes the captain's orders. Just like Guthrie's comparison of the world to a poker game, in which Roosevelt and Olson are constantly cheated by corrupt and morally inferior bankers and land owners, the analogy between a political leader and the captain of a ship instantly identifies the two politicians as those who will safely guide the country out of the economic plight symbolized by the storm. Thus, similar to Guthrie's "I'm Looking for that New Deal Now," the song takes a decisive stand for Roosevelt and his political endeavors, which is underlined by the frequent use of the adjective "good" qualifying the ship which has to be steered through turbulent waters.

With the song's metaphorical frame, Guthrie takes up a tradition that goes back to Greek and Roman literature. Probably the most frequently cited and best-known source for the 'ship of state'-metaphor is Horace's poem "O navis," which allegorically elaborates on a ship of state, addressed by one who loves it. Storm-tossed, the ship has been severely damaged and, in order not to sink, it is urged by the speaker of the poem to come back to its harbor to avoid the worst.[38] This image of a tempest-tossed ship, which would soon evolve into a literary commonplace occurring in different genres throughout the various epochs, eventually became part of the rhetorical repertoire of politicians as well, who used it as a metaphor for crisis in situations of political or economic turmoil.

There are, basically, two reasons why the nautical metaphor has become so successful as a means to configure moments of crisis and chaos: First, it suggests itself as a metaphor of crisis, for it provides a whole bundle of correspondences between the state of a nation and the state of a ship at sea and is thus appropriate to map a variety of features at a

37 WGA, Notebooks I, Notebook 5, 159.

38 Cf. the English translation of Horace's poem quoted from Charles A. Miller, *Ship of State: The Nautical Metaphors of Thomas Jefferson, with Numerous Examples by Other Writers from Classical Antiquity to the Present* (Lanham, Maryland: UP of America, 2003) 138-39: "On such billows as these you will again be swept / Out to sea, O my ship! What are you doing! Make / Utmost effort to reach port! On your one side your oars are lost; / See, your mast has been split under the Southwind's gusts, / Yard-arms groan with the strain, and, with its cable burst, / Not for long will the keel stand/ This implacably hurtling sea's / Force. Your sails are in shreds, battered and broken off / Stand the after-deck gods heedless of cries for help. / Pontic pine though you are, still, / Famous daughter of forests green, / It will do you no good boasting your race and name; / Daunted sailors do not pluck up their courage from / Painted prows. Have a care your / Fate is not to be gale-winds' toy. / Once my anxious concern and my most heartsick care, / Now, the theme of my thoughts, O my beloved ship, / Shun the sea lanes where thick strewn / Lie the glittering Cyclades."

single time: As regards Guthrie's song, for example, it is used to map both the situation of the American economy and that of its most important politicians during the Great Depression. Second, and closely connected to this structural aspect of "systematic correspondences,"[39] one has to consider the metaphor's multiple functions in order to explain its popularity, especially in political discourse. Not only does it, as Nünning argues, "impose forms upon an untidy reality"[40] and thus helps to make sense of a world which seems to be out of joint; it also, in doing so, "provide[s] contemporaries with simplified, but more or less coherent frameworks for reinterpreting historical developments."[41] Of course, such interpretive frameworks are not neutral, but always ideologically charged. Thus, metaphors also serve a political purpose in that they may be employed to strengthen one's own position and to weaken oppositional forces, as done in Guthrie's song at hand.

For the United States, as Charles A. Miller observes, it was Thomas Jefferson who discovered the enormous potential of the nautical metaphor both *for* and *as* political argument. Well aware of the classical tradition, Jefferson popularized the image of the 'ship of state' by frequently resorting to it in his political speeches and addresses in multiple variations and rephrasings.[42] After Jefferson, various presidents and high-ranking politicians as well as economists carried the image of the storm-tossed ship forward in their accounts of the state of the nation. "Outside literature," as Miller has it, "a procession of nautical metaphors continue[d] to march through [...] public life."[43] It thus seems reasonable to believe that such nautical metaphors were also employed to describe the plight of the Great Depression, which, obviously, constituted a situation of major political and economic turmoil.

39 Philip Eubanks, quoted in Ansgar Nünning, "Metaphors the British Thought, Felt and Ruled By, or: Modest Proposals for Historicizing Cognitive Metaphor Theory and for Exploring Metaphors of Empire as a Cultural Phenomenon," *Literature and Linguistics: Approaches, Models, and Applications. Studies in Honour of Jon Erickson*, ed. Marion Gymnich, Ansgar Nünning and Vera Nünning (Trier: WVT, 2002) 110. The systematic correspondences can even be observed on a linguistic level – mind the etymology of the word 'governor,' which is derived from the word 'gubernator,' which is Latin for 'helmsman.'

40 Nünning, "Metaphors" 113.

41 Nünning, "Metaphors" 114. Though Nünning, as the title of his contribution reveals, is primarily concerned with metaphors of empire and does not refer to the 'ship of state'-metaphor, the functions of metaphors identified by him may still be applicable to nautical metaphors as well.

42 Cf. Miller 16.

43 Miller 76.

Yet, it was not only its association with a moment of utmost crisis that called forth such images. Once we consider Guthrie's song, we will immediately notice that the nautical image employed there centers not so much on the storm-tossed ship, but on the steering captain, who is out to save it from shipwreck. Thus, the nautical image employed not only allegorizes the critical economic situation in the country, but also points to the political and economic implications of the New Deal, whose strongly interventionist agenda indeed required political 'steering' and guidance. Only competent leadership, intellectual forces behind Roosevelt's political program believed, would be able to overcome the crisis of the 1930s. Consider, for example, the following statement by John Maynard Keynes, whose theory on political intervention formed the theoretical backbone of Roosevelt's New Deal. Reflecting possible means to handle "the unemployment of labour, or the disappointment of reasonable business expectations, and [...] the impairment of efficiency and production,"[44] he comes to the conclusion that

> the cure for these things is partly to be sought in the deliberate control of the currency and of credit by a central institution, and partly in the collection and the dissemination on a great scale of data relating to the business situation, including the full publicity, by law if necessary, of all business facts which it is useful to know. These measures would involve society in exercising directive intelligence through some appropriate organ of action of the inner intricacies of private business [...].[45]

Following Keynes's thesis, there had to be an "appropriate organ of action" which was supposed to centralize information and control it to a considerably high degree in order to revive the economy and to eventually overcome the great slump in the United States.

For Keynes, such a leading "organ of action" was necessary, as the self-regulating forces of the market had, most obviously, failed. In his opinion, the ideal businessman, who, by pursuing private profits, also took care of public needs, was no longer extant. Employing nautical imagery, Keynes describes this businessman, who has "becom[e] a tarnished idol,"[46] as the "great captain of industry, the master-individualist, who serves us in serving himself, just as any other artist does."[47] Quite pessimistically,

44 Keynes, "The End of Laisser-Faire" 291.
45 Keynes, "The End of Laisser-Faire" 292.
46 Keynes, "The End of Laisser-Faire" 287.
47 Keynes, "The End of Laisser-Faire" 287.

Keynes goes on stressing that "[w]e grow more doubtful whether it is he who will lead us into paradise by the hand."[48]

Guthrie does not grow doubtful at all. He clearly identifies a new captain of industry, who, after the Depression had shaken the belief in private business, will take matters in his (political) hands: It is Franklin D. Roosevelt, backed by his administration and his large-scale New Deal program, who is said to find a way out of the desperate situation. With the help of nautical images, which are "especially apt for the legitimization of hierarchical order and authoritarian leadership,"[49] Guthrie's song propagates the President's ability to overcome the economic recession and, in a way, legitimizes his political planning at a time when its success was long overdue. Thus, the song provides its listeners with what Philip Eubanks would call a 'licensing story.' Such stories, as Eubanks has it, "are narratively structured representations of an individual's ideologically inflected construal of the world"[50] which help to rationalize and to justify "how the world works and how the world should work."[51]

As a look at the contemporary textual archive reveals, this licensing narrative projected by nautical imagery had indeed a certain appeal and was frequently employed to grapple both with the Depression and the New Deal. Interestingly enough, it was Roosevelt himself who employed a nautical metaphor to describe the functioning of his New Deal in one of his so-called 'Fireside Chats,' i.e., his addresses to the nation which were, on a regular basis, delivered by radio from the White House. On April 28th, 1935, he began his chat with the contention that

> [t]he job of creating a program for the Nation's welfare is, in some respects, like the building of a ship. At different points on the coast where [sic] I often visit they build great seagoing ships. When one of these ships is under construction and the steel frames have been set in the keel, it is difficult for a person who does not know ships to tell how it will finally look when it is sailing high seas.[52]

Roosevelt employs the image of the ship in a way different from Guthrie's, as he compares the *construction* of a ship to the establishment of a comprehensive welfare program for his nation. As a regular shipyard visitor,

48 Keynes, "The End of Laisser-Faire" 287.

49 Hanne Birk, "Mediating Imperial Collective Memory: 'Metaphors of Empire,'" *Literature and Memory: Theoretical Paradigms – Genres – Functions*, ed. Ansgar Nünning, Marion Gymnich and Roy Sommer (Tübingen: Niemeyer, 2006) 275.

50 Quoted in Nünning, "Metaphors" 118.

51 Quoted in Nünning, "Metaphors" 118.

52 www.mhric.org/fdr/chat7.html. [16.09.2006].

he is qualified to survey and control the construction process, which, "for a person who does not know ships," is hard to oversee.[53]

As Roosevelt's 'Fireside Chats' were distributed via the radio, they reached a substantial part of the population, and thus one may well argue that the President's rhetorics contributed to shaping the people's perception and understanding of the New Deal.[54] Indeed, there were a number of reactions to Roosevelt's speeches directly referring to the metaphor he had introduced. Pastor Frederick E. Tilly from the St. Jacobus Evangelian Lutheran Church in Woodside, New York, for example, commented upon Roosevelt's addresses in a letter to the President and pointed out that his "encouraging Radio Talks have helped to let the people know about the arduous labor of piloting the Ship of State. The economic storms are being faithfully weathered."[55] Of course, one cannot be sure whether the nautical imagery Tilly employed was inspired by Roosevelt's words, or whether they belonged to the standard repertoire of a Lutheran pastor anyway; yet, what one can be sure of is the wide circulation of such images, which must have come down to Woody Guthrie as well, who utilized them in the song at hand.

What one can also be sure of is that both Roosevelt's 'building of a ship'-metaphor and Guthrie's image of a 'good captain' crucially differ in tone from the traditional metaphor of a storm-tossed ship as outlined in the classical pretexts. While Horace's timid picture of a severely damaged ship shows pessimistic tendencies, Roosevelt's and, first and foremost, Guthrie's rendering of the ship of state is characterized by a spirited and hopeful tone. Guthrie's song not only fashions Roosevelt and Olson as the captain and first mate of the ship of state; it also renders a utopian vision of what is to come when the "economic storms," to use Tilly's words again, have been left behind. Here is the next verse of the song:

> We are sailing to a land that is free
> We are sailing to a land that is free

53 His 'building of a ship'-metaphor has its origin in a poem by Henry Wadsworth Longfellow called "The Building of the Ship" from 1849. In 1941, Roosevelt wrote it out to Winston Churchill. That is why we might well assume that he already used the poem as an inspiration for his Fireside Chat.

54 The 'Fireside Chats' were a series of 30 radio talk given by Roosevelt between 1933 and 1944. Originally, they were supposed to advocate his New Deal, but Roosevelt continued with the 'chats' even after the Depression had gone.

55 <http://newdeal.feri.org/clergy/cl012.htm>, 16 Sept. 2006.

And great is the fate of the good ship of state
With Roosevelt & Olson at the wheel.[56]

With Roosevelt and Olson, as the verse implies, there will be a bright and prosperous future in a “land that is free” – free of capitalist oppression, free of maldistribution and of social misconditions, as one might be invited to add. Falling back on the American topos of the ‘land of the free,’ the verse calls forth a notion which has always been constituent for American collective identity. In times of social and economic disintegration, it therefore provides an integrating momentum and utters, to apply Robert McElvaine’s words, “hope in the midst of despair,”[57] which seems to be more than justified, as the verse’s third line promotes an idea of Manifest Destiny by heralding the “great [...] fate of the good ship of state.”

The vision of a prosperous future, which is, to be sure, strongly connected to that of a guiding captain, was part of a ‘rhetorics of hope’ New Deal advocates employed to herald the age to come and to lessen the general frustration among the people during the great slump.[58] As early as 1934, Henry A. Wallace, then secretary of agriculture in the Roosevelt administration, employed the image of a “new world” in his famous book *New Frontiers* to set something against the utter despair the economic recession had caused. Yet, quite in contrast to the traditional concept of the frontier as formulated by Turner in 1894,[59] Wallace describes this new world in terms of a change of mind rather than as a real geographical expansion. For Wallace, the keynote of the new land, or the ‘new frontier’ which has to be found

> is cooperation just as that of the old frontier was individualistic competition. The mechanism of progress of the new frontier is social invention, whereas that of the old frontier was mechanical invention and the competitive seizure of opportunities for wealth. Power and wealth were worshipped in the old days. Beauty and justice and joy of spirit must be worshipped in the new.[60]

56 WGA, Notebooks I, Notebook 5, 159.

57 This ‘integrating momentum’ of the song is also emphasized by the constant use of the first person plural “we” or “our” respectively, which matches the nautical imagery used in the song, as it underlines the notion that the speaker of the song, his audience and even the President and the Governor of California are ‘all in the same boat.’

58 Cf. Nate 57ff.

59 Cf. Frederick J. Turner, *The Significance of the Frontier in American History* (1894; Madison, Wisconsin: Silver Buckle Press, 1984).

60 Quoted in Nate 56.

The binary opposition of the old and the new frontier, which was once employed to describe the continuous westward movement of American settlers and entrepreneurs, is here applied to forebode a shift in economic politics from a Darwinian struggle for survival to a collective social responsibility, which has to be brought about in order to overcome the social misconditions in the country. And the means to bring about such a shift was, to be sure, Roosevelt's New Deal, which did not only mark a mental turn towards a radically different idea of economic guidance, but indeed initiated the physical movement of thousands of Americans through its policies of rebuilding and resettlement.

The rhetorics of hope which accompanied Roosevelt's New Deal did not only manifest themselves in the political writings and addresses of the representatives of his administration, but also found expression in contemporary literature and folklore, one example being Guthrie's song "Roosevelt-Olson," which epitomizes the belief in a new land and the great fate of a country which, in the past, had suffered from chaos and disorder. It employs the image of a ship sailing through a storm in order to highlight the need for a potent captain and a reliable mate taking responsibility for the passengers' well-being in a situation of chaos and disorder. Moreover, the song directly links this utopian future to those who are supposed to bring about the implied change and highlights the power and ability of the country's leading politicians: Roosevelt and Olson. Their interventionist politics are both legitimized and praised as the means to take care of the masses of unemployed and thus to overcome the economic recession. They will, as the song suggests, take care of "the good ship of state" and intervene, whenever necessary, to prevent it from going off course.[61]

In the course of the Great Depression, Roosevelt's and Olson's power and ability were, however, called into question by a number of New Deal opponents. Though a majority of the working people indeed believed that it was their task to find a way out of the Great Depression, the oppositional forces increased continuously, especially when the shortcomings of Roosevelt's interventionism became more and more obvious in the second half of the Great Depression. The New Deal critics, mostly from

[61] What seems worth highlighting here is the double entendre of the expression "good ship of state." On the one hand, and most likely, it could refer to the American society, which is led out of social and economic chaos by the Roosevelt administration "at the wheel." On the other hand, taking into account the interventionist character of the New Deal, the addition "of state" could also be understood in a more narrow sense, both denoting and underlining the responsibility of the government to tackle the economic problems in the country.

a conservative or rightwing background, were against any ideas of redistributing wealth by a government-run welfare system. Instead, they believed that everyone was responsible for his or her own fate; consequently, the poor and unemployed were regarded as deserving to be poor and unemployed, since they did not have the industriousness and the ambition needed to accumulate wealth in prosperous years, which could have helped them during the hard times of the Depression.

Here is the first part of a letter to Eleanor Roosevelt dated December 14th, 1937, which captures the conservative attitude towards New Deal politics:

> Mrs. Roosevelt: I suppose from your point of view the work relief, old age pensions, slum clearance and all the rest seems like a perfect remedy for all the ills of this country, but I would like for you [sic] to see the results, as the other half see them.
> We have always had a shiftless, never-do-well class of people whose one and only aim in life is to live without work. I have been rubbing elbows with this class for nearly sixty years and have tried to help some of the most promising and have seen others try to help them, but it can't be done. We cannot help those who will not try to help themselves and if they do try a square deal is all they need, and by the way that is all this country needs or ever has needed: a square deal for all and then, let each one paddle their own canoe, or sink.[62]

In the first paragraph of the letter, the writer clearly takes her position as being one of "the other half," opposing the politics of the Roosevelt administration. As she goes on to explain "the other half['s]" point of view and their attitude towards the New Deal, she employs the standard argument of the conservatives: Those at the bottom of society are there, because they do "not try to help themselves." The "never-do-well class of people" was not and will never be able to get out of its disastrous situation, as it is lacking the necessary motivation to do so. Her sixty years of vain attempts to help those people find a way out have turned her into a resigned, frustrated and angry woman, who cannot but conclude that "each one paddle[s] their own canoe, or sink[s]."

Interestingly enough, it is the canoe-metaphor the writer of the letter employs to sum up her point which brings us back to Guthrie's song, as it is reminiscent of his "good ship of state." To be sure, the metaphor is (part of) a colloquial idiom and was thus presumably not chosen as a deliberate response to the rhetorics of New Deal advocates. Nevertheless, it was employed to highlight the individualistic and competitive nature of economics, which does not need any administrative 'steering.' Thus, con-

62 Quoted in McElvaine 145-46.

sidering the contemporary dissemination of nautical imagery, the idiom, as one might well argue, was certainly recharged with social energy.

To conclude, the versatility of the nautical metaphor, both from a diachronic and, what is of a particular relevance here, from a synchronic perspective, has turned it into a viable means to give plausibility to or, to draw from Eubanks once again, to 'license' particular political views or decisions. It allowed New Deal advocates to develop "ideologically inflected narratives, short and long, individual and cultural"[63] and, in so doing, to take a distinct position in the contemporary political discourse on the President's political program. Both Guthrie's "I'm Looking for that New Deal Now" and his "Roosevelt-Olson" thus work with images and metaphors, which, as the analysis of a number of texts from the contemporary archive has revealed, were commonly employed to grapple with the New Deal. However, the songs are not only culturally produced, as they take up and modify widely circulating cultural forms of expression. By resorting to the rhetorical strategies of New Deal supporters, they are also culturally productive, as they take a distinct stand in the political discourse of the time by shaping their audience's perception and understanding of Roosevelt's New Deal. Both songs promote the President's interventionist plan of action and, at the same time, debunk and denounce laisser-faire capitalism and its representatives. In doing so, Guthrie's songs leave any kind of philosophical or ideological abstraction behind and draw rather upon clear-cut metaphorical frames which reduce the complexity of the political discourse and which helped thus to reach and, as one may add, to convince Guthrie's potential listeners to maintain their loyalty to Roosevelt and his New Deal.

The "metaphoric scenario[s]" Guthrie employs therefore function, as Musolff has it, as cognitive model[s] for the interpretation of socio-political reality. Not only [do they]," as Musolff goes on arguing, "provide [frames] for the 'ontological' categorisation of political experience, but [...] also suppl[y] the speakers [or the singers] – and the audience – with default evaluations by way of presupposing specific conclusions about likely/typical outcomes of the 'scenes' or 'story-lines' that are invoked":[64] While the imagery of gambling predominantly functions to separate the corrupt representatives of the capitalist elites from the morally superior Roosevelt and Olson, who are praised as prototypes of integrity, the nautical metaphor is mainly employed to set up the contrast between a disastrous past and a bright and prosperous future with the help of the Presi-

63 Philip Eubanks, quoted in Nünning 118.

64 Andreas Musolff, quoted in Birk 272-73, addition mine.

dent's New Deal.[65] Thus, both songs "establish argumentation patterns that are prima facie self-evident and apparently conclusive, due to their grounding in everyday experience, folk-theories and discourse traditions,"[66] or, as one may well add, part of the cultural knowledge of Guthrie's contemporaries.

65 To be sure, both implications are closely connected. Of course, there can only be a bright and prosperous future if there is a morally reliable leader who will guide his nation out of chaos and (moral) disorder. Nevertheless, I argue that each song highlights one of these implications.

66 Andreas Musolff, quoted in Birk 273.

4 Sung Negotiations: Processing Cultural Knowledge in Woody Guthrie's Songs about Dust and Depression

I did not really begin with the desire to sing with the dead.

Rather were my efforts to contextualize Woody Guthrie's sung renderings of the Dust Bowl migration and the Great Depression grounded in the endeavor to 'make sense' of his songs, that is to say, to understand and to elucidate their complex relationships with the cultural patterns they were both shaped by and contributed to shaping. With this study, I also attempted to react to Edwin Cohen's complaint that "[w]e often become embroiled in Woody's politics, his Union activities, and make moral judgements of his life, losing sight of the real issue in evaluating the artist: the contribution of his works."[1] Starting from the assumption that this 'contribution,' i.e., the cultural and social significance of Guthrie's songs, can indeed be made visible, I reconstructed the intertextual ties to other manifestations of the contemporary cultural archive, which, in turn, helped relocate the songs in the cultural environment in which they were composed and performed.

As the correlation of his songs to other textual artifacts of the contemporary archive has shown, the forms of intertextual ties in Guthrie's songs are manifold, ranging from marked references, e.g. those to John Steinbeck's novel *The Grapes of Wrath*, to references to larger cultural concepts such as the 'Californian Dream' or the American myth of the frontier. By exploring linguistic, formal and rhetorical similarities between Guthrie's songs and texts taken from the cultural archive, the close readings have revealed that the songs employ images, tropes and metaphors which were, during the 1930s, widely disseminated and belonged to the people's cultural knowledge. Being thus culturally produced, Guthrie's songs function as a kind of seismograph tracking the cultural and political developments and transformations that took place during the Great Depression. Moreover, besides being tied to the contemporary cultural contexts, Guthrie's songs employed various lyrical and musical traditions. His palimpsest-like rewritings of traditional religious hymns, for example, clearly appropriate Joe Hill's mode of songwriting, which has shaped the political song ever since the beginning of the 20th century.

1 Cohen 11.

However, the formal and rhetorical elements and patterns Guthrie's songs 'borrow' both from the cultural environment and from lyrical and musical traditions, are not simply given back to them in their original form. Rather do the songs transform, or 'negotiate,' these elements and patterns by putting them into new syntagmatic contexts, as is the case e.g. in Guthrie's "The Rancho Grande Vigilante," which appropriates the herding-metaphor so prominent in the racist discourse on the migrant or, to give another example, in his "Roosevelt-Olson," which employs the classical image of the 'ship of state' as a metaphorical framework to promote Roosevelt's New Deal. Moreover, the correlation of Guthrie's songs to the cultural archive made evident that a number of his songs also play on the ambivalent potential of certain culturally significant terms and expressions (e.g. in his "California California"), thereby critically commenting upon the underlying concepts these widely disseminated terms allude to or represent. A third variety of negotiating elements and patterns of cultural knowledge is the songs' rendering them along the lines of semantically charged compositional forms as the Talking Blues or the traditional ballad, e.g. in Guthrie's "Talking Dust Bowl Blues" or his "Pretty Boy Floyd" respectively.

Following from this, Guthrie's songs are both culturally produced and culturally productive in that they collect, transform and (re)assemble the 'borrowed' cultural elements and patterns, which are, in turn, charged with social energy. For this reason, his sung renderings of the Dust Bowl migration and the Great Depression are by no means merely documenting the economic and political turmoil of the 1930s. By referring to widely circulating images, they rather take distinct stands on larger cultural concepts, either enhancing or undermining them, thus shaping the people's cultural knowledge and taking part in contemporary discourses.

The cultural productivity of Woody Guthrie's songs also lies in their function to communicate certain patterns of cultural knowledge or discursive positions, "concentrated in manageable aesthetic form,"[2] to their listeners. As the analysis of the compositional strategies employed by Guthrie has shown, the reference to well-known tunes for a number of his songs about the social and economic plight of the 1930s enhanced their communicative function, as such tunes were easier to remember and to sing along to due to their popularity. Moreover, the appropriation of popular tunes provided Guthrie's listeners with a readymade framework of associations, which, at least in some cases, significantly contributed to the political potential of Guthrie's songs, e.g. in his "Do Re Mi," which was sung to the tune of the Blue Sky Boys' "Hang Out the Front

2 Greenblatt, *Shakespearean Negotiations* 5.

Door Key," or in his song about Jesus Christ, which deliberately appropriated both the tune and the storyline of the traditional ballad on Jesse James. Thus, the consideration of the musical dimension of the sung word turned out to be extremely helpful in order to examine the social energy of the songs of the Dust Bowl balladeer.

Apart from their communicative function, which is certainly enhanced by their musical dimension, Guthrie's songs also provided his listeners with a sense of shared identity. To achieve this effect, Guthrie, more often than not, creates a speaker who represents the typical farmer or the typical migrant. Moreover, he frequently makes use of the first person singular or plural, thus fashioning the speaker as a member of the community addressed by his songs. Avoiding markers of individuality, the songs portray archetypes and thus allow his listeners to identify with the respective speaker(s). The analysis of his "Dust Storm Disaster," to give an example, has shown that Guthrie replaced the regionally restricted scenario in the song's pretext, which is predominantly rendered in a third person singular narrative, with a description of a nationwide catastrophe from a first person plural perspective.

To enhance the songs' potential for identification, Guthrie also employed various performative strategies. Besides the reference to traditional or popular tunes mentioned already, he deliberately made use of a Southwestern accent, which helped his migrant audience to identify with him and contributed to creating a feeling of collective identity among them.[3] Moreover, he also appropriated both formal and rhetorical devices characteristic of traditional English and Scottish ballads to catch and hold his listeners' attention.

Even after exploring the potential functions of Guthrie's songs, which are mainly derived from their intertextual ties to their cultural environment, it remains difficult, if not impossible, to answer the question of how Guthrie's songs were actually perceived by his contemporary listeners. Texts which give insight into the response are hard to find. And even if we found them, a reading of them would at best allow some cautious speculations about what and how Guthrie's contemporaries thought of his songs. Nobody knows how many migrants actually listened to Guthrie while performing "on the air" or at the camps in the Californian fields. Gregory, to give one estimation, is convinced that Guthrie was "relatively unknown to the migrants themselves [and] just one of many hillbilly per-

3 Guthrie also employed typical Southwestern speech patterns to distinguish himself from other songwriters and, particularly during his time in New York, to contribute to his image as a 'true Okie' (cf. Morgan).

formers struggling to make names for themselves."[4] I would concede that Guthrie became a well-known folk artist only when his songs were reappropriated by the folk revival in the 1960s;[5] yet, I would also argue that the importance and impact of a songwriter and performer is not exclusively a question of their popularity, but also one of cultural significance. This assumption is backed by the observation of Guthrie's contemporary Dorothy Healey, who, in an interview, states that "Woody [...] was another Okie who had talent. But [when he was singing] you'd feel the impact."[6] Especially in situations of labor strikes, Healey feels, "he could identify more [with the strikers] than anyone else could."[7]

That Guthrie's songs reached the Southwesterners' ears before they were recorded might also be substantiated by Maxine Dempsey, who, under the pseudonym 'Lefty Lou,' accompanied Guthrie on his radio program on KFVD in Los Angeles starting in the summer of 1938. In an interview, she points out that their program had a "built-in audience [of] all those displaced persons [sic] from the Dust Bowl."[8] Though they played a lot of "back-home music,"[9] as she calls it, some of the songs about the migration and the Great Depression were among their regular setlist.

After his *Dust Bowl Ballads* were eventually recorded in 1940, public attention grew and even reached national dimensions. Yet, there are only a few reviews left, which, as highly conventionalized forms of evaluating music, only give sparse information about the actual reception of Guthrie's songs. What they do reveal, however, is that either Guthrie's formal and rhetorical strategies in his songwriting worked and convinced a number of listeners that he was indeed "one of those farmers blown about by dust storms and 'tractored' off their land,"[10] as one review put it, or that these reviews deliberately fashioned him as the archetypal Okie that he never was. Another review pushed it to the extreme and sketched Guthrie's biography as if it were the biography of one of his songs' speakers: "Guthrie was born in the Dust Bowl, lived for years in an abandoned oil boom shack that he bought for $25. After the fury of the worst storms in 1935 to 1937, he joined the hordes of others in the

4 Gregory 231-32.
5 Cf. Morgan.
6 Dorothy Healey, interview with Joe Klein, n.d. (WGA, Accessions 2004, 67,4, Box 1, Folder 12).
7 Dorothy Healey, interview with Joe Klein.
8 Maxine Dempsey, telephone interview, 1 Mar. 2005.
9 Maxine Dempsey, telephone interview, 1 Mar. 2005.
10 "New Phonograph Records," *Southbridge Evening News* 2 July 1940: n. pag.

migration to California, walking most of the way. There, with the others, he lived in 'jungle camps.'"[11]

Perhaps the most illuminating comment about Guthrie's songs in a review, at least regarding the focus of this study, was made by Guthrie himself, who pointed out that "I've tried to bring out that these songs, although written down by me and all that stuff, are songs that come out of the hearts and mouths of the Okies during their trips to California."[12] Leaving aside the questions of actual reception, which may never be satisfactorily answered, and following Guthrie's comment, the contextualizing analysis of a number of Guthrie's songs in this study has shown that they indeed came "out of the hearts and mouths" of the Southwestern migrants in that they both articulated and perpetuated contemporary cultural knowledge.

In the examination of how collective beliefs and experiences were taken up, shaped and distributed by Woody Guthrie's songs, the 'poetics of culture' provided a viable theoretical framework, which, though originally designed to examine literary texts, could be modified and extended and thus made applicable to an analysis of the sung word. Of course, nobody would ever deny that such a textual approach towards the investigation of cultural phenomena as pursued in this study does not do justice to those forms of cultural expression which do not become manifest in any kind of textual artifact. Yet, the correlation of Guthrie's songs with a selection of other contemporary texts from an albeit "bewildering mass of [textual traces]"[13] has allowed us to shed light on the songs' cultural significance and to glimpse at the "half-hidden cultural transactions,"[14] that is to say, at the collective exchanges and borrowings taking place in the intertextual network representing, in turn, patterns of the cultural knowledge of the 1930s: Guthrie's songs took part in the dynamics of cultural transformation and change, as they resorted to contemporary linguistic and rhetorical conventions, narrative structures and collective memories, processed them and thus contributed to fashioning contemporary attitudes and dispositions. They 'made sense' of the ecological and economic turmoil caused by the dust storms and the recession by providing interpretations and offering solutions to the problems of the 'down and out' in the times of the Dust Bowl migration and the Great Depression.

11 Christoph M. Oakley, "Strictly Off The Road," *Hartford Courant* 7 July 1940: n. pag.

12 Quoted in Oakley: n. pag.

13 Greenblatt, *Shakespearean Negotiations* 3.

14 Greenblatt, *Shakespearean Negotiations* 4.

After all, this study provided insight into a relatively small selection of Guthrie's extraordinarily voluminous oeuvre. Though I included songs which have not been recorded or published, a considerable number of the songs considered belong to a kind of 'Guthrie-canon,' which already took shape in the early 1940s, when Alan Lomax began to compile songs for the Library of Congress recordings, and which was further established when Guthrie's songs were rediscovered in the 1960s.

Thus, taking the vast amount of available material into account, further research could focus on songs or groups of songs which have not gained that much critical attention yet. A contextualizing analysis of Guthrie's sung renderings of the Second World War and the fascist threat of the Nazi regime, for instance, might give insight into the perception of and attitudes towards European war politics and the American intervention in the first half of the 1940s. Another group of songs, which has been recorded and reprinted, but not yet closely analyzed, are the songs he wrote particularly for children – an examination of the stylistic and rhetorical devices Guthrie employed in order to increase their didactic potential would certainly be a promising endeavor. Moreover, Guthrie's love songs, of which there are many among the files in the Woody Guthrie Archives, still lack scholarly attention.

Another interesting topic for research could also be the question of the identity-forming potential of Guthrie's songs (or of songs in general) which was also addressed in this study. The examination of the various formal and rhetorical features the sung word employs to evoke a sense of shared identity among the recipients is central to the analysis of songs and could be further pursued in Guthrie-scholarship and beyond.

As a number of Guthrie's songs have been covered by musicians or bands of various styles, further research could examine the forms and functions of these appropriations of Guthrie's songs in different historical and cultural contexts. Such an investigation could well provide answers to the question of why some of Guthrie's songs, first and foremost his "This Land is Your Land," have a seemingly timeless appeal.[15] Guthrie's best-known song, to give just a few examples which hint at the variety of reappropriations, was covered by the Canadian folk music group The Travellers, was and still is employed in the struggle for Northern Ireland's independence and was, more recently, used as a campaign song in George Bush's runs for Presidency. An in-depth study of the manifold reappropriations of Guthrie's songs could thus help explain the high popularity they have been enjoying ever since they were written, and, in a more

15 Some of these appropriations are examined in Jackson 19ff.

general sense, could also shed light on the role of songs in the dynamics of cultural transfer.

5 Bibliography

5.1 Primary Sources[1]

Woody Guthrie manuscripts & typescripts

Guthrie, Woody. "A Hard-Working Man Was Jesus." Woody Guthrie Archives (WGA), New York City, Notebooks I, Notebook 4, 180, 1940.

---. "Ain't A Gonna Grieve." WGA, Songs I, Box I, Folder 1.

---. "Ain't Got No Home." WGA, Songs I, Box I, Folder 1, 1940.

---. "The Ballad of Pretty Boy Floyd." Smithsonian Center for Folklife and Cultural Heritage, Ralph Rinzler Folklife Archives and Collections (RRFAC), Washington, D.C., *Woody Guthrie Papers*, Box 1, Folder 6.

---. "By The Valley So Green & The Ocean So Blue." WGA, Notebooks I, Notebook 5, 31, 1939.

---. "Can't Feel at Home in This World Anymore." WGA, Notebooks I, Notebook 4, 157.

---. "California California." WGA, Songs I, Box I, Folder 5.

---. "California! California!" Smithsonian, RRFAC, *Woody Guthrie Papers*, Box 2, Folder 4, 1937.

---. "Christ For President." WGA, Notebooks I, Notebook 5, 105.

---. "Dust Bowl Refugee." WGA, Songs I, Box 1, Folder 7.

---. "The Farmer-Labor Train." WGA, Songs I, Box 1, Folder 9.

---. "Garden of Eden". Cartoon. Smithsonian, RRFAC, *Woody Guthrie Papers*, Box 3, Folder 4.

---. "If you ain't got the Do Re Mi." WGA, Songs I, Box 1, Folder 7, 1938.

---. "I'm Looking for that New Deal Now." WGA, Notebooks I, Notebook 5, 69, 1939.

[1] The list of primary sources also includes those texts which I used as intertexts in my analyses.

---. Letter to Alan Lomax, 19 Sept. 1940. WGA, Correspondence I, Box 1, Folder 39.

---. Letter from Alan Lomax, 9 July 1942. WGA, Correspondence II, Box II, Folder 17.

---. "Life's Railroad to Heaven." WGA; Notebooks I, Notebook 5, 62.

---. Manuscript page (back of "Ain't A Gonna Do"). WGA; Songs I, Box 1, Folder 1, 1941.

---. Manuscript page from "A song of music". WGA, Notebooks I, Notebook 26, 24-25.

---. "No Disappointment in Heaven." WGA, Notebooks I, Notebook 4, 82.

---. Notes to "Jesus Christ". Manuscript page from "Woody Guthrie Album". WGA, Manuscripts II, Box 1, Folder 35.

---. "Pretty Boy Floyd." WGA, Notebooks I, Notebook 4, 101, 1939.

---. "Pretty Boy Floyd." WGA, Notebooks I, Notebook 5, 17.

---. "Pretty Boy Floyd No. One." WGA, Songs I, Box 3, Folder 21.

---. "The Rancho Grande Vigilante." WGA, Songs I, Box 3, Folder 23.

---. "Riding on that Salvation Train." WGA; Notebooks I, Notebook 4, 146, 1939.

---. "Roosevelt-Olson." WGA, Notebooks I, Notebook 5, 159, 1939.

---. "The Sherman Texas Cyclone." WGA, Notebooks I, Notebook 4, 10.

---. "Talking Dust Bowl Blues." WGA, Notebooks I, Notebook 78, 90.

---. "They Laid Jesus Christ In His Grave." WGA, Songs I, Box 2, Folder 14, 1940.

---. "Union's my Religion." WGA, Songs I, Box 4, Folder 28.

---. "Woody Guthrie by Woody Guthrie." Smithsonian, RRFAC, *Woody Guthrie Papers*, Box 3, Folder 6.

---. "Woody's Talking Dust Bowl Blues." WGA, Songs I, Box 1, Folder 5.

---. "You see, I lost the farm trying to finance the jallopie!" Cartoon. WGA, Notebooks I, Notebook 2, 32, 1938.

Woody Guthrie records

Guthrie, Woody. *Dust Bowl Ballads.* New York: Buddha Records, 2000.

---. *This Land is Your Land: The Asch Recordings*, Vol. 1. Washington, D.C.: Smithsonian Folkways Recordings, 1998.

---. *Muleskinner Blues: The Asch Recordings*, Vol. 2. Washington, D.C.: Smithsonian Folkways Recordings, 1998.

---. *Hard Travelin': The Asch Recordings*, Vol. 3. Washington, D.C.: Smithsonian Folkways Recordings, 1998.

---. *Buffalo Skinners: The Asch Recordings*, Vol. 4. Washington, D.C.: Smithsonian Folkways Recordings, 1998.

Song Anthologies

Belden, Henry M., and Arthur Palmer Hudson, eds. *The Frank C. Brown Collection of North Carolina Folklore, Vol. 2: Folk Ballads of North Carolina.* Durham, North Carolina: Duke UP, 1952.

Child, Francis J., ed. *The English and Scottish Popular Ballads,* Vol. 3. New York: The Folklore Press in association with Pageant Book Company, 1956.

Friedman, Albert B., ed. *The Viking Book of Folk Ballads of the English-Speaking World.* 1915. New York: Viking Press, 1976.

Guthrie, Woody, and Maxine Crissman. *Woody and Lefty Lou's Favorite Collection of Old Time Hill Country Songs.* Smithsonian, RRFAC, *Woody Guthrie Papers*, Box 2, Folder 4, 1937.

Industrial Workers of the World. *The Little Red Song Book: Songs to Fan the Flames of Discontent.* Columbia, South Carolina: Harbinger Publications, 1995.

Kleff, Michael, ed. *Hard Travelin': Das Woody Guthrie Buch.* Heidelberg: Palmyra, 2002.

Leventhal, Harold and Marjorie Guthrie, eds. *The Woody Guthrie Songbook.* New York: Grosset and Dunlap, 1976.

Lomax, Alan, ed. *The Penguin Book of American Folk Songs.* Baltimore: Penguin, 1964.

---, Woody Guthrie and Pete Seeger, eds. *Hard-Hitting Songs for Hard-Hit People.* New York: Oak Publications, 1967.

Lomax, John, ed. *Cowboy Songs and Other Frontier Ballads.* New York: Macmillan, 1922.

---, and Alan Lomax, eds. *American Ballads and Folk Songs*. New York: Macmillan, 1964.

Silber, Irwin, ed. *Songs of the Great American West*. New York/London: Macmillan, 1967.

Newspaper and magazine articles

"Apparent Decadence of the Salvation Army." *Literary Digest* 17 Feb. 1906: 761.

"Causes of Irreligion in the Proletariat." *Literary Digest* 17 Feb. 1906: 246.

"Indigents Barred At Arizona Line," *Los Angeles Herald Express* 4 Feb. 1936, <http: //newdeal.feri.org/tolan/tol09.htm>, 4 Sept. 2006.

Klein, Herbert, and Carey McWilliams. "Cold Terror in California." *The Nation* 24 July 1934: 97.

McGrath, Ellen. "State Patrol Chief Herds Last Scab." *People's World* 14 May 1939: 19.

"Michigan Press On The Copper War." *Literary Digest* 10 Jan. 1914: 47-48.

"More Deadly Than the Male." *Sunday News* 2 Dec. 1945: 2.

"New Phonograph Records." *Southbridge Evening News* 2 July 1940: n. pag.

Oakley, Christoph M. "Strictly Off The Record." *Hartfourd Courant* 7 July 1940: n. pag.

"Outline Map of California!" Cartoon. *Los Angeles Times* 5 Feb. 1936: 4.

"Pickett, Steinbeck, And Mr McWilliams." *People's World* 4 Aug. 1939: 77.

"Rule Guard At Border Legal." *Los Angeles Herald Express* 6 Feb. 1936, <http:// newdeal.feri.org/tolan/tol09. htm>, 4 Sept. 2006.

Stolberg, Benjamin. "Vigilantism, 1937." *The Nation* 14 Aug. 1937: 166-168.

Stone, I.F. "The Romans Would Understand." *The Nation* 2 Oct. 1937: 345-46.

Todd, Charles L. "Trampling Out The Vintage." *Common Sense* July issue 1939: 7-8+.

---. "The 'Okies' Search For A New Frontier." *New York Times Magazine* 27 Aug. 1939: 10-11+.

"Vagrants Rounded Up In City And County." *Los Angeles Times* 7 Feb. 1936: 1+.

"Vigilantes Tar 'Reds.' Three Okies Beaten By Night Raiders' Drive On Communists." *Los Angeles Times* 23 Aug. 1935: 15.

Welldon, J.E.C. "The Church and the Labour Party." *The Nineteenth Century And After. A Monthly Review*. London: Spottiswoode & Co, 1913: 943-959.

"Where Christianity Negatives Itself." *Literary Digest* 31 Dec. 1910: 1238.

Miscellaneous

Ainsworth, William H. *Rockwood. A Romance*. New York: 1873 Press, 1999.

Carroll, Robert, and Stephen Prickett, eds. *The Bible: Authorized King James Version. With Apocrypha*. New York/Oxford: Oxford UP, 1998.

Dempsey, Maxine. Interview. Telephone Interview. 1 Mar. 2005.

Dylan, Bob. *Eleven Outlined Epitaphs/Elf Entwürfe für meinen Grabspruch: Englisch/Deutsch mit Übersetzungen von Wolf Biermann.* Köln: Kiepenheuer und Witsch, 2003.

Gikas, John. Interview. Ed Cray. 14 Mar. 1999. WGA, Accessions 2004, 67.4, Box 1, Folder 11.

Guthrie, Woody. *Bound for Glory: The Hard-Driving, Turth-Telling Autobiography of America's Great Poet-Folk Singer*. 1943. New York: Penguin, 1983.

---. *Woody Sez*. Ed. Marjorie Guthrie, Harold Leventhal, Terry Sullivan and Sheldon Patinkin. New York: Grosset & Dunlap, 1975.

---. *Pastures of Plenty: A Self-Portrait*. Ed. Dave Marsh and Harold Leventhal. New York: Harper Perennial, 1992.

Healey, Dorothy. Interview. Joe Klein. N.d. WGA, Accessions 2004, 67.4, Box 1, Folder 12.

Henderson, Caroline. *Letters from the Dust Bowl*. Ed. Alvin O. Turner. Norman, Oklahoma: U of Oklahoma P, 2001.

Houston, Cisco. Interview. Lee Hays. 10 Jan. 1961. Smithsonian, RRFAC, *Woody Guthrie Papers*.

Keynes, John M. "The Consequences to the Banks of the Collapse of Money Values." *Collected Writings, Vol. IX: Essays in Persuasion*. By John M. Keynes. London/Basingstoke: Macmillan, 1972. 150-158.

---. "The End of Laisser-Faire." *Collected Writings, Vol. IX: Essays in Persuasion*. By John M. Keynes. London/Basingstoke: Macmillan, 1972. 272-294.

McElvaine, Robert, ed. *Down and Out in the Great Depression: Letters from the Forgotten Man*. Chapel Hill: U of North Carolina P, 1983.

McWilliams, Carey. *Factories in the Fields: The Story of Migratory Farm Labor in California*. 1939. Berkeley/Los Angeles: U of California P, 2000.

Nietzsche, Friedrich. *Zur Genealogie der Moral: Eine Streitschrift. Friedrich Nietzsche. Werke in drei Bänden*, Band II. Ed. Karl Schlechta. München: Carl Hanser Verlag, 1969. 761-900.

---. *Der Antichrist: Fluch auf das Christentum. Friedrich Nietzsche. Werke in drei Bänden*, Band II. Ed. Karl Schlechta. München: Carl Hanser Verlag, 1969. 1161-1235.

Riney-Kehrberg, Pamela, ed. *Waiting on the Bounty: The Dust Bowl Diary of Mary Knackstedt Dyck*. Iowa City: The U of Iowa P, 1999.

Robbin, Edward. *Woody Guthrie and Me: An Intimate Reminiscence*. Berkeley, California: Lancaster-Miller, 1979.

Sinclair, Upton. *An Upton Sinclair Anthology*. Ed. I.O. Evans. Newcastle-on-Tyne: Northumberland Press, 1934.

Steinbeck, John. *The Grapes of Wrath*. 1939. London: Penguin, 1992.

---. "Dubious Battle in California." *America and Americans (and Selected Nonfiction)*. Ed. Susan Shillinglaw and Jackson J. Benson. New York: Penguin, 2002. 71-77.

Terkel, Studs. Interview. Ed Cray. 8 Aug. 1998. WGA, Accessions 2004, 67.4, Box 1, Folder 13.

---, ed. *Hard Times: An Oral History of the Great Depression*. New York: The New Press, 2000.

United States Congress Senate, Comittee on Education and Labor, 77th Congress. *Violations of Free Speech and Rights of Labor*. Washington, D.C.

Online text collections and databases

<http://arnet.pair.com>

<http://ingeb.org>

<http://newdeal.feri.org>

<http://www.californiahistoricalsociety.org>

<http://www.cowboylyrics.com>

<http://www.dictionary.oed.com>

<http:// www.historycooperative.org>

<http://www.labelframes.com>

<http://www.livinghistoryfarm.org>

<http://www.marxists.org>

<http://www.memory.loc.gov>

<http://www.mudcat.org>

<http://www.netstate.com>

<http://www.spartacus.schoolnet.co.uk>

<http://www.sun-maid.com>

<http://www.traditionalmusic.co.uk>

5.2 Secondary Sources

Liner notes

Greenway, John. “The Talking Blues.” Liner notes to Folkways Records Album No. FH 5232. New York: Folkways, 1958.

Liner notes to V/A. *’Til We Outnumber ’Em: Live from Cleveland.* Buffalo, NY: Righteous Babe Records, 2001.

Place, Jeff. Liner notes to “Blowing Down that Old Dusty Road.” *Buffalo Skinners: The Asch Recordings*, Vol. 4. Washington, D.C.: Smithsonian Folkways Recordings, 1998.

---. Liner notes to “Going down the Road Feeling Bad.” *This Land is Your Land: The Asch Recordings*, Vol. 1. Washington, D.C: Smithsonian Folkways Recordings, 1998.

---. Liner notes to “Gypsy Davy.” *This Land is Your Land: The Asch Recordings*, Vol. 1. Washington, D.C.: Smithsonian Folkways Recordings, 1998.

---. Liner notes to “Mean Talking Blues.” *Hard Travelin’: The Asch Recordings*, Vol. 3. Washington, D.C.: Smithsonian Folkways Recordings, 1998.

Essays and monographs

Adorno, Theodor W., and Max Horkheimer. "Culture Industry: Enlightenment as Mass Deception." 1947. *Dialectic of Enlightenment*. By Theodor W. Adorno and Max Horkheimer. New York: Continuum, 1993.

Anderson, Robert M. *Vision of the Disinherited: The Making of American Pentecostalism*. New York/Oxford: Oxford UP, 1979.

Bachmann-Medick, Doris, ed. *Kultur als Text: Die anthropologische Wende in der Literaturwissenschaft*. Tübingen: A. Francke, UTB, 2004.

Barker, Chris. *Cultural Studies. Theory and Practice*. London/Thousand Oaks: SAGE, 2000.

Baßler, Moritz. *Die kulturpoetische Funktion und das Archiv: Eine literaturwissenschaftliche Text-Kontext-Theorie*. Tübingen: Francke, 2005.

Birk, Hanne. "Mediating Imperial Collective Memory: 'Metaphors of Empire.'" *Literature and Memory: Theoretical Paradigms – Genres – Functions*. Ed. Ansgar Nünning, Marion Gymnich and Roy Sommer. Tübingen: Niemeyer, 2006. 265-279.

Bode, Christoph. "Anglistische Literaturwissenschaft und/oder Cultural Studies?" *Anglia* 114.3 (1996): 396-424.

Burbank, Garin. *When Farmers Voted Red: The Gospel of Socialism in the Oklahoman Countryside*. Westport, Connecticut: Greenwood Press, 1977.

Burke, Peter. *Popular Culture in Early Modern Europe*. London. Temple Smith, 1978.

Burke, Robert E. *Olson's New Deal for California*. Berkeley, California: U of California P, 1953.

Butler, Martin. "The Power of the Sung Word: Reconstructing the Social and Cultural Significance of Songs." *Kulturelles Wissen und Intertextualität: Theoriekonzeptionen und Fallstudien zur Kontextualisierung von Literatur*. Ed. Marion Gymnich, Birgit Neumann and Ansgar Nünning. Trier: WVT, 2006. 165-181.

Carney, George O. "Music and Place." *The Sounds of People and Places: A Geography of American Folk and Popular Music*. Ed. George O. Carney. Lanham: Rowman & Littlefield, 1994. 203-216.

Cohen, Edwin. "Neither Hero nor Myth: Woody Guthrie's Contribution to Folk Art." *Folklore* (1980): 11-14.

Cray, Ed. *Ramblin' Man: The Life and Times of Woody Guthrie*. New York: W.W. Norton & Company, 2004.

Cross, F.L., and Elizabeth. A. Livingstone, eds. *Oxford Dictionary of the Christian Church*. Oxford/New York: Oxford UP, 1983.

Curtis, James R. "Woody Guthrie and the Dust Bowl." *The Sounds of People and Places: A Geography of American Folk and Popular Music*. Ed. George O. Carney. Lanham, Maryland: Rowman and Littlefield, 1994. 253-262.

Davidson, Emily, and Robert Santelli, eds. *Hard Travelin'. The Life and Legacy of Woody Guthrie*. Hanover, New Hampshire: UP of New England for Wesleyan UP, 1999.

Denisoff, R. Serge. *Sing a Song of Social Significance.* Bowling Green, Ohio: Bowling Green U Popular P, 1972.

DeTurk, David A., and A. Poulin, Jr., eds. *The American Folk Scene: Dimensions of the Folksong Revival*. New York: Dell Laurel, 1967.

Empson, William. *Seven Types of Ambiguity*. 1930. New York: New Directions, 1966.

Engler, Bernd, and Isabell Klaiber. "Kulturelle Leitfiguren: Prozesse und Strategien ihrer Funktionalisierung." *Kulturelle Leitfiguren – Figurationen und Refigurationen*. Ed. Bernd Engler and Isabell Klaiber. Duncker & Humblot: Berlin, 2007. 9-28.

Faulstich, Werner *Rock – Pop –Beat – Folk: Grundlagen der Textmusikanalyse*. Tübingen: Narr, 1978.

Fiske, John. *Television Culture*. London: Methuen, 1987.

Fox-Genovese, Elizabeth. "Literary Criticism and the Politics of the New Historicism." *The New Historicism*. Ed. H. Aram Veeser. New York/London: Routledge, 1989. 213-224.

Frith, Simon. *Performing Rites: Evaluating Popular Music*. 1996. Oxford: Oxford UP, 2002.

Gadamer, Hans-Georg. *Philosophical Hermeneutics*. Berkeley, California: U of California P, 1976.

Gallagher, Katherine, and Stephen Greenblatt. *Practising New Historicism*. Chicago: The U of Chicago P, 2000.

Garman, Bryan. "The Ghost of History: Bruce Springsteen, Woody Guthrie, and the Hurt Song." *Popular Music and Society* 20.2 (1996): 69-120.

---. *A Race of Singers: Whitman's Working-Class Hero from Guthrie to Springsteen*. Chapel Hill & London: The U of North Carolina P, 2000.

Geary, Daniel. "Carey McWilliams and Antifascism." *The Journal of American History* 90.3 (2003) <http://www.historycooperative.org/journals/jah/90.3/geary.html>, 7. Sept. 2006.

Geertz, Clifford. *The Interpretation of Cultures*. 1973. New York: Basic Books, 2000.

Goodwyn, Lawrence. *The Populist Movement in America.* New York: Oxford UP, 1978.

Gould, Peter, and Rodney White. *Mental Maps*. Boston, Massachusetts: Allen & Unwin, 1986.

Grabes, Herbert. "Canon-Making and Cultural Memory: The Creation of 'English Literature' through the Writing of Literary Histories." *Journal for the Study of British Cultures* 10.1 (2003): 11-26.

Greenblatt, Stephen. *Renaissance Self-Fashioning: From More to Shakespeare.* Chicago: The U of Chicago P, 1980.

---. *Shakespearean Negotiations: The Circulation of Social Energy in Renaissance England*. Berkeley: U of California P, 1988.

---. "Towards a Poetics of Culture." *The New Historicism*. Ed. H. Aram Veeser. New York/London: Routledge, 1989. 1-14.

Greenway, John. *American Folksongs of Protest*. Philadelphia. U of Pennsylvania P, 1953.

Gregory, James N. *American Exodus: The Dust Bowl Migration and Okie Culture in California*. New York/Oxford: Oxford UP, 1989.

Grossberg, Lawrence. *We Gotta Get Out of This Place: Popular Conservatism and Postmodern Culture*. London and New York: Routledge, 1992.

Hall, Stuart. "Encoding/decoding." *Culture, Media, Language: Working Papers in Cultural Studies 1972-79*. Ed. Centre for Contemporary Cultural Studies:. London: Hutchinson, 1980. 128-138.

Hampton, Wayne. *Guerilla Minstrels: John Lennon, Joe Hill, Woody Guthrie, Bob Dylan*. Knoxville: U of Tennessee P, 1986.

Handy, Robert T. *The American Religious Depression, 1925-1935*. Philadelphia: Fortress Press, 1968.

Hentoff, Nat. "Playboy Interview: Bob Dylan." *The Best of the Playboy Interviews 1962-1992*. Playboy Enterprises Inc., 1990: 53-58.

Hopkins, Charles Howard. *The Rise of the Social Gospel in American Protestantism, 1865-1915*. New Haven, Connecticut: Yale UP, 1940.

Hornung, Alfred. "Literary Conventions and the Political Unconscious in Upton Sinclair's Work." *Upton Sinclair: Literature and Social Reform*. Ed. Dieter Herms. Frankfurt: Peter Lang, 1990. 24-38.

Howard, Jean E. "The New Historicism in Renaissance Studies." *Renaissance Historicism: Selections from English Literary Renaissance*. Ed. Arthur F. Kinney and Dan S. Collins. Maherst: The U of Massachusetts P, 1987. 3-33.

Iser, Wolfgang. *The Act of Reading: A Theory of Aesthetic Response*. Baltimore: Johns Hopkins UP, 1978.

Jackson, Mark A. *Prophet Singer: The Voice and Vision of Woody Guthrie*. Jackson: UP of Mississippi, 2007.

Jameson, Fredric. *The Political Unconscious: Narrative as a Socially Symbolic Act*. Ithaca, New York: Cornell UP, 1981.

Kincheloe, Samuel C. *Research Memorandum on Religion in the Depression*. New York: Arno Press, 1972.

King, Jeffery S. *The Life and Death of Pretty Boy Floyd*. Kent, Ohio/London: The Kent State UP, 1998.

Klein, Joe. *Woody Guthrie: A Life*. New York: Delta Publishing, 1980.

Klier, Ron. "Walt Whitman, Woody Guthrie, Bob Dylan, and the Anxiety of Influence." *The Midwest Quarterly* 40 (1999): 334-350.

Kristeva, Julia. "Word, Dialogue and the Novel." *The Kristeva Reader*. Ed. Toril Moi. Oxford: Blackwell, 1980. 24-33.

Lanser, Susan S. *Fictions of Authority: Women Writers and Narrative Voice*. Ithaca: Cornell UP, 1992.

Lewis, George H. "Popular Music and Research Design: Methodological Alternatives." *Popular Music and Society* 1.2 (1972): 108-115.

Link, Jürgen. "Literaturanalyse als Interdiskursanalyse: Am Beispiel des Ursprungs literarischer Symbolik in der Kollektivsymbolik." *Diskurstheorien und Literaturwissenschaft*. Ed. Jürgen Fohrmann and Harro Müller. Frankfurt a.M.: Suhrkamp, 1988. 284-307.

Liu, Alan. "The Power of Formalism: The New Historicism." *ELH* 56 (1989): 721-71.

Logsdon, Guy. "Woody Guthrie and his Oklahoma Hills." *Mid-America Folklore* 19.1 (1991): 57-73.

Lookingbill, Brad D. "Dusty Apocalypse and Socialist Salvation: A Study of Woody Guthrie's Dust Bowl Imagery" *Chronicles of Oklahoma* 72.4 (1994): 396-414.

---. "'A God-Forsaken Place': Folk Eschatology and the Dust Bowl." *Great Plains Quarterly* 14.4 (1994): 273-86.

---. "'The Living and the Dead Land': The Great Plains Environment and the Literature of Depression America." *Heritage of the Great Plains* 29.3 (1996): 38-48.

---. *Dust Bowl, USA: Depression America and the Ecological Imagination, 1929-1941*. Ohio: Ohio UP, 2001.

Luccock, Halford E. *Contemporary American Literature and Religion*. Chicago: Willett, Clark & Company, 1934.

McGovern,Charles F. "Woody Guthrie's American Century." *Hard Travelin': The Life and Legacy of Woody Guthrie*. Ed. Emily Davidson and Robert Santelli. Hanover, New Hampshire: UP of New England for Wesleyan UP, 1999. 111-127.

Meyer, Friederike. "Literary History and the History of Mentalities: Reflections on the Problems and Possibilities of Interdisciplinary Cooperation." *Poetics* 18 (1989): 85-92.

Miller, Charles A. *Ship of State: The Nautical Metaphors of Thomas Jefferson, with Numerous Examples by Other Writers from Classical Antiquity to the Present*. Lanham, Maryland: UP of America, 2003.

Mittelstraß, Jürgen. *Wissen und Grenzen: Philosophische Studien*. Frankfurt a. M.: Suhrkamp, 2001.

Montrose, Louis A. "Professing the Renaissance: The Poetics and Politics of Culture." *The New Historicism*. Ed. H. Aram Veeser. New York/London: Routledge, 1989. 15-36.

Moore, Harry Thornton. *The Novels of John Steinbeck: A First Critical Study*. Port Washington, New York: Kennikat Press, 1968.

Morgan, Jeff. "Hard Travelin': The Construction of Woody Guthrie's Legacy." Unpublished article, 2004.

Morley, David. *The* Nationwide *Audience: Structure and Decoding*. London: BFI, 1980.

Nate, Richard. *Amerikanische Träume: Die Kultur der Vereinigten Staaten in der Zeit des New Deal*. Würzburg: Königshausen & Neumann, 2003.

Nehring, Neil. *Popular Music, Gender, and Postmodernism: Anger Is an Energy*. London/Thousand Oaks: SAGE, 1997.

Neumann, Birgit. "Kulturelles Wissen und Literatur." *Kulturelles Wissen und Intertextualität: Theoriekonzeptionen und Fallstudien zur Kontextualisierung von Literatur*. Ed. Marion Gymnich, Birgit Neumann and Ansgar Nünning. Trier: WVT, 2006. 29-51.

Nünning, Ansgar. "Literatur, Mentalitäten und kulturelles Gedächtnis: Grundriß, Leitbegriffe und Perspektiven einer anglistischen Kulturwissenschaft." *Literaturwissenschaftliche Theorien, Modelle und Methoden: Eine Einführung*. Ed. Ansgar Nünning. Trier: WVT, 1995. 173-198.

---. "Metaphors the British Thought, Felt and Ruled By, or: Modest Proposals for Historicizing Cognitive Metaphor Theory and for Exploring Metaphors of Empire as a Cultural Phenomenon." *Literature and Linguistics: Approaches, Models, and Applications. Studies in Honour of Jon Erickson*. Ed. Marion Gymnich, Ansgar Nünning and Vera Nünning. Trier: WVT, 2002. 101-127.

---, and Roy Sommer. "Kulturwissenschaftliche Literaturwissenschaft: Disziplinäre Ansätze, theoretische Positionen und transdisziplinäre Perspektiven." *Kulturwissenschaftliche Literaturwissenschaft*. Ed. Ansgar Nünning and Roy Sommer. Tübingen: Narr, 2004. 9-29.

Onions, C.T., ed. *The Shorter Oxford English Dictionary on Historical Principles, Vol. II*. Oxford: Clarendon Press, 1934.

Otto, Erwin. "Flucht aus der Trivialität – Intention und Wirkungsästhetik politischer Popsongs." *anglistik & englisch-unterricht. Trivialliteratur* (1977): 151-171.

Partridge, Elizabeth. *This Land Was Made For You And Me: The Life And Legacy of Woody Guthrie*. New York: Viking, 2002.

Pascal, Richard. "Walt Whitman and Woody Guthrie: American Prophet-Singers and Their People." *Journal of American Studies* 24 (1990): 41-59.

Pfister, Manfred. "Konzepte der Interetxtualität." *Intertextualität: Formen, Funktionen, anglistische Fallstudien*. Ed. Ulrich Broich and Manfred Pfister. Tübingen: Niemeyer, 1985. 1-30.

Posner, Roland. "Kultur als Zeichensystem: Zur semiotischen Explikation kulturwissenschaftlicher Grundbegriffe." *Kultur als Lebenswelt und Monument*. Ed. Aleida Assmann and Dietrich Harth. Frankfurt a. M.: Fischer, 1991. 37-74.

Raven, Charles E. *Christian Socialism 1848-1854*. London: Macmillan, 1920.

Richards, Ivor A. *Practical Criticism: A Study of Literary Judgement*. 1929. New York: Harvest Books, 1956.

Ricoeur, Paul. *The Rule of Metaphor: Multi-Disciplinary Studies in the Creation of Meaning in Language*. 1975. Trans. Robert Czerny with Kathleen McLaughlin and John Costello. London: Routledge, 1978.

---. *Time and Narrative*, 3 vols. 1983. Trans. Kathleen McLaughlin and David Pellauer. Chicago: U of Chicago P, 1984.

Schöffler, Herbert. *Protestantismus und Literatur*. 1922. Göttingen: Vandenhoeck, 1958.

Schücking, Levin L. *Soziologie der literarischen Geschmacksbildung*. 1923. Bern/München: Francke, 1961.

Shindo, Charles J. *Dust Bowl Migrants in the American Imagination*. Kansas: UP of Kansas, 1997.

Smith, Henry N. *Virgin Land: The American West as Symbol and Myth*. Cambridge, Massachusetts/London: Harvard UP, 1978.

Spekat, Susanne. *Politische Straßenballaden im Zeitalter der Englischen Revolution (1640-1660): Eine kulturwissenschaftliche Untersuchung ihrer historisch-politischen, literatur- und mentalitätsgeschichtlichen Bedeutung*. Trier: WVT, 2002.

Stallings Jr., Frank L. *Black Sunday: The Great Dust Storm of April 14, 1935*. Austin, Texas: Eakin Press, 2001.

Starr, Kevin. *Inventing the Dream: California Through the Progressive Era*. New York/Oxford: Oxford UP, 1985.

---. *Endangered Dreams: The Great Depression in California*. New York/Oxford: Oxford UP, 1996.

Stein, Walter J. *California and the Dust Bowl Migration*. Westport, Connecticut: Greenwood Press, 1973.

Stoneback, Harry R. "Woody Sez: Woody Guthrie and 'The Grapes of Wrath.'" *Steinbeck Newsletter* (Summer 1989): 8-9.

---. "Songs of 'Anger and Survival': John Steinbeck on Woody Guthrie." *Steinbeck Quarterly* 23.1-2 (1990): 34-42.

Titzmann, Michael. "Kulturelles Wissen – Diskurs – Denksystem: Zu einigen Begriffen der Literaturgeschichtsschreibung." *Zeitschrift für französische Sprache und Literatur* 99 (1989): 47–61.

Trudgill, Peter. *On Dialect: Social and Geographical Perspectives*. Oxford: Basil Blackwell, 1983.

Turner, Frederick J. *The Significance of the Frontier in American History*. 1894. Madison, Wisconsin: Silver Buckle Press, 1984.

Volkmann, Laurenz. "Reconstructing a Useable Past: The New Historicism and History." *Why Literature Matters: Theories and Functions of Literature*. Ed. Rüdiger Ahrens and Laurenz Volkmann. Heidelberg: Winter, 1996. 325-344.

Wallis, Michael. *Pretty Boy: The Life and Times of Charles Arthur Floyd.* New York: St. Martin's Press, 1992.

Werner, Craig. "Democratic Visions, Democratic Voices: Woody as Writer." *Hard Travelin': The Life and Legacy of Woody Guthrie.* Ed. Emily Davidson and Robert Santelli. Hanover, New Hampshire: UP of New England for Wesleyan UP, 1999. 69-82.

Whisenhunt, Donald W. "The Bard in the Depression: Texas Style." *Journal of Popular Culture* 2 (1968): 370–386.

White, Hayden. *Tropics of Discourse: Essays in Cultural Criticism.* 1978. Baltimore: Johns Hopkins UP, 1987.

Wimsatt, William K., and Monroe C. Beardsley. "The Intentional Fallacy." *The Verbal Icon: Studies in the Meaning of Poetry.* William K. Wimsatt and Monroe C. Beardsley. Lexington: U of Kentucky P, 1954. 3-18.

Winter, Rainer. *Der Produktive Zuschauer: Medienaneignung als kultureller Prozess.* München: Quintessenz, 1995.

---. *Die Kunst des Eigensinns: Cultural Studies als Kritik der Macht.* Weilerswist. Velbrück Wissenschaft, 2001.

Worster, Donald. *Dust Bowl: The Southern Plains in the 1930s.* 1979. New York/ Oxford: Oxford UP, 2004.

Würzbach, Natascha. "An Approach to a Context-Oriented Genre Theory in Application to the History of the Ballad: Traditional Ballad – Street Ballad – Literary Ballad." *Poetics* 12 (1983): 35-70.

Yates, Janelle. *Woody Guthrie: American Balladeer.* Staten Island, New York: Ward Hill Press, 1995.

Permissions

I am grateful to Woody Guthrie Publications and to Ludlow Music for granting their permission to reprint from the following material:

Woody Guthrie Publications

Ludlow Music

Permission to publish materials from the Ralph Rinzler Folklife Archives and Collections, Smithsonian Institution, was secured through the Woody Guthrie Archives.

Contact:

Woody Guthrie Archives
257 West 57th Street, Suite 1218
New York City, NY
www.woodyguthrie.org

Index of Woody Guthrie Songs